The Holocaust and the War of Ideas

Edward Alexander

The Holocaust and the War of Ideas

Transaction Publishers

New Brunswick (U.S.A.) and London (U.K.)

Library of Congress Catalog Number: 93-11119
ISBN: 1-56000-122-4
Printed in the United States of America

Library of Congress Cataloging-in-Publication Data
Alexander, Edward, 1936
  The Holocaust and the war of ideas / Edward Alexander.
    p. cm.
  Includes index.
  ISBN 1-56000-122-4
  1. Holocaust, Jewish (1939-1945)—Historiography. 2. Holocaust, Jewish (1939-1945), in literature. 3. Jewish literature—History and criticism. 4. Literature, Modern—20th century—History and criticism. I. Title.
D804.3.A425 1993
940.53'18'072—dc20

93-11119
CIP

FOR THREE WOMEN OF VALOR
Rael Jean Isaac
Cynthia Ozick
Ruth R. Wisse

Contents

Acknowledgments

Grateful acknowledgment is made to the following for permission to quote from works to which they hold the copyright.

To Shirley Kaufman for her translations of Abba Kovner's *My Little Sister* and *A Canopy in the Desert* (University of Pittsburgh Press) and ot the Field Translation Series (Oberlin College) and Shirley Kaufman for an excerpt from her translation of Kovner's "A Dialogue at Night."

To Ruth Whitman for her translations of the poems of Jacob Glatstein in *The Selected Poems of Jacob Glatstein* (October House).

To the Jewish Publication Society of America for excerpts from Stephen Mitchell's translations of Dan Pagis, *Points of Departure*.

Introduction

> *Oh, that? Oh, that again? Well, yes, in a way. Be-*
> *cause by now, after all the powerful, anguished*
> *novels of Elie Wiesel, Jerzy Kosinski, Primo Levi,*
> *Aharon Appelfeld, and others, after all the*
> *simple, heartrending documentary accounts, the*
> *stringent, haunting historians' texts, the pained*
> *and arduous movies—that shocking newsreel*
> *footage . . . after all the necessary, nightmare*
> *lists of involuntary martyrology, by now our*
> *response to the singular horrific barbarity of our*
> *time is—just the tiniest bit dutiful.*
>
> —Johanna Kaplan

Johanna Kaplan's wry complaint,[1] written in 1987, about the "dutiful" aspect of facing the Holocaust, of forcing oneself to enter, again and again, through memory and imagination, into that unsanctified inferno, would have seemed strange just three decades ago. Until 1962, when Adolf Eichmann was brought to trial in Jerusalem for his role in the murder of European Jewry, the Holocaust was a subject largely avoided, among Jews as well as Christians. At the trial, it became apparent that those few victims of the Nazis who were left alive had stories to tell that merited, indeed demanded hearing, not only in the courtroom in Jerusalem, but in the courtroom of the collective conscience of the world.

Five years later, in spring 1967, the events leading to the Six-Day War brought that seemingly buried life to the surface once more. Gamal Abdel Nasser, the Egyptian dictator, justified his intention of "driving the Jews into the sea" by declaring that "Israel's existence is itself an aggression." When Egypt precipitated the war by blockading the straits of Tiran, the American government "could not find" President Eisenhower's written commitment to David Ben-Gurion to secure free navigation in that waterway vital to Israel's existence. Arab rhetoric and actions, combined with the Western nations' abandonment of the Jewish state, reminded both Jewish victims and Gentile bystanders of how the Jews of Europe, in their hour of greatest need, had been abandoned to Hitler by the Allies.

Ever since that time, the "duty" of reentering that nightmare world, to keep it from being forgotten, to protect it from what Deborah Lipstadt

1

calls the assault on truth and memory, has been felt by an ever-growing number of people. Yet the resistance to shameful memory and unsettling truth has also grown. Duty may be, as Wordsworth once wrote (echoing Milton), "Stern Daughter of the Voice of God," but since it involves doing what we don't like, many people will resent it. Jesse Jackson, for example, used to complain that he was "sick and tired of hearing about the Holocaust"—even though this did not prevent him, in November 1988, from inviting himself onto the platform of a Washington commemoration of the anniversary of Kristallnacht[2] (any more than it prevented Franjo Tudjman, president of Croatia and frequent regurgitator of the lies of the Holocaust deniers, from turning up at the opening of the United States Holocaust Museum in Washington, D. C. in April 1993). The opening of the museum coincided with the release of a poll which found that 22 percent of adults and 20 percent of high school students surveyed thought it possible that the Holocaust never happened at all.

The impossibility of putting the spectre of the Holocaust behind us has, in this *fin de siècle* decade, become more apparent than ever before. In April of 1990 Saddam Hussein, Iraq's dictator, began issuing threats to "incinerate half of Israel" with poison gas, the weapon he had used two years earlier on his Iranian adversaries and his own Kurdish population. By August, when Hussein invaded Kuwait, Palestinian Arabs within Israel and the disputed territories of Judea and Samaria were enraptured by the prospect of the use of poison gas against their Jewish neighbors, and marched through the streets chanting "Saddam, you hero, attack Israel with chemical weapons." When the American-led coalition went to war against Iraq, Hussein made good on his threat to attack the civilian population of Israel, though it had no part in the coalition and was "guilty" solely of the crime of existing, the same crime for which European Jewry had been murdered.

In a nightmarish reminder of their European past, one no novelist would dare to have invented, the Jews of Israel found themselves spending night after night in sealed rooms, wearing gas masks to protect themselves against the threat of missiles carrying chemical weapons. When it became common knowledge that 70 percent of Iraq's nuclear, chemical, and biological capacity (a $50 billion enterprise) had been provided by the Germans[3], some Jews, in their bitterness, insisted that GAS was really an acronym, standing for the words "Germans Always the Same." (This view [mistaken, to be sure] was hardly assuaged by

Foreign Minister Hans-Dietrich Genscher's public apology to the Israeli people, since it was well known that his own party [the Free Democrats] had long controlled the Economics Ministry which had allowed the weapons of mass destruction to be sold to Hussein.)

Two years later, the campaign of "ethnic cleansing" in the former Yugoslavia provoked countless commentators to allege (mistakenly, once more) an equation between the Nazi Holocaust and the atrocities perpetrated by Serbs, Croats, and Bosnian Muslims upon each other in the civil war. It also brought a plague of bizarre speculation, salvos in that war of ideas which is the subject of this book, about the actual (as distinct from metaphorical) Jewish role in the Yugoslavian civil war. "World Jewry has a special responsibility." This hectoring trumpet call blared forth from the midst of a *New York Times* op-ed piece (November 9, 1992) by Flora Lewis entitled "Save Lives in Bosnia." Jews, she argued, had acquired this special responsibility to Bosnian survivors of Serbian camps because their own ancestors had experienced concentration camps; now they had the opportunity "to show that concentration camps provoke the solidarity of victims of persecution." For Lewis, the lesson of the Holocaust is that Jews now have a responsibility to behave particularly well because their ancestors suffered so much persecution. The unstated corollary of this argument (as Conor Cruise O'Brien pointed out in another context in January 1983) is that the descendants of people who have not been persecuted do not have a special responsibility to behave particularly well, and the descendants of the persecutors of Jews can be excused altogether for behavior that would be very hard to excuse in other people.

Imaginative writers—poets, novelists, essayists—were, like most other people, "late" in coming to the subject of the Holocaust. But this tardiness resulted less from inattentiveness or thoughtlessness than from grave doubts as to whether it was possible or, if possible, decent to assimilate the moral enormity of the century into literary art. "All art," wrote the eighteenth- century poet Friedrich Schiller, "is dedicated to Joy. . . . The right art is that alone, which creates the highest enjoyment."[4] This did not mean that art had to avoid tragic circumstances; on the contrary, the great writers understood that the feeling of enjoyment might arise even from the representation of the deepest anguish, the most utter calamity, in a work of art. The more tragic the situation, the deeper might the enjoyment become.

But the emergence of a primordial destructive impulse within the very center of European civilization, and the resulting obliteration of European Jewry seemed to mock literary art's pretension and even stifle its desire to transmute suffering into joy, incoherent chaos into order and beauty. In the early 1950s Theodore Adorno declared (in a potently influential outburst) that "After Auschwitz, to write a poem is barbaric," for it means to "squeeze aesthetic pleasure out of artistic representation of the naked bodily pain of those who have been knocked down by rifle butts. . . . Through aesthetic principles or stylization . . . the unimaginable ordeal still appears as if it had some ulterior purpose. It is transfigured and stripped of some of its horror, and with this, injustice is already done to the victims."[5] Adorno did not really expect to silence writers intent on confronting the Holocaust, much less writers like Cynthia Ozick for whom the subject rises unbidden, even when they have no plan to make fiction of the data, or to poeticize or mythologize it. Adorno did, however, hope to alert them to the absence of any precedent for interpreting the "scientific" murder of a whole people, to the contradiction between aesthetic convention and the foul, unwholesome swamp of the Holocaust, and to the extreme difficulty or impossibility of contriving images and symbols to represent crimes that no one had imagined possible. Beyond this, he was saying that the very art that "succeeded" in representing the unprecedented horror, in "domesticating" and transcending it, would be the greatest failure, for it would give us pleasure from other people's pain, and thus visit further "injustice" upon the victims.[6]

What do we mean when we refer to "writing of the Holocaust"? That little preposition conceals a large ambiguity. Some of the writings discussed in the chapters that follow are "of" the Holocaust in the ordinary sense of being "about" it, of taking it as a subject or theme like any other. Others are "of" the Holocaust in the sense of having emerged from it and having been distinctively shaped by it. This shaping may take different forms. It may express itself as awareness of the German destruction process as an historically unprecedented event; it may be manifested in consciousness of the way that the Nazi death camps were a crime against the human status itself; it may reveal itself in a metaphysical sense that the removal of a member of the family of nations is a wound constellated in the universe itself; it may even show itself, paradoxically, in a writer's reluctance to attempt direct representation of the Holocaust. In his excellent discussion of the "problematics" of Holocaust literature, Alvin Rosenfeld[7] quotes the Israeli poet Uri Zvi Greenberg to illustrate the view that the Holocaust was something new in the world, beyond likeness or analogy:

> The Gentiles did not handle their sheep as they handled
> our bodies:
> Before slaughter they did not pull out the teeth of
> their sheep:
> They did not strip the wool from their bodies as
> they did to us:
> They did not push the sheep into the fire to make
> ash of the living
> And to scatter the ashes over streams and sewers.
> Are there other analogies to this, our disaster
> that came to us at their hands?
> There are no other analogies (all words are shades
> of shadow)—
> Therein lies the horrifying phrase: No other
> analogies![8]

Although I have not rigidly adhered to this broad distinction between different kinds of writing of the Holocaust as an exclusive litmus test for differentiating between "authentic" and "inauthentic" responses to the event, it has often entered into my judgment of authors and works discussed. It is also the reason why I have treated some discursive writing, by critics, historians, political scientists, and even journalists, with the degree of respectful scrutiny generally reserved for the art of poets and novelists. Writing of the Holocaust that fathoms the calamity's uniqueness, whatever its genre, may have a power and immediacy lacking in poems or novels or plays (like several criticized, unsympathetically, in this book) that treat this subject as if it were no more than an unusually flagrant instance of man's inhumanity to man. Of course, the Holocaust can and should be compared with other acts of genocidal savagery; but to compare is not to equate.

After an analysis of antisemitism as the primary cause of the Holocaust, this book turns to a discussion of Yiddish poetry. In some sense it represents the condition towards which Holocaust literature might be thought to aspire—not only because it is the most coherent in its themes and ruling metaphors but also because it is the least exposed and susceptible to the historical and ideological disputes that impinge on nearly all the other writing discussed in this book. Despite Yiddish literature's long commitment to secularism, its poets, after the war ended, came to believe that religious language supplies the only metaphors capacious enough to grasp the Jewish catastrophe. When, in the late nineteenth century, nearly every established truth threatened to dissolve in controversy, Matthew Arnold recommended taking refuge in poetry: "Poetry," said Arnold, "attaches its emotion to the idea; the idea *is* the fact."[9] But Holocaust literature is so profoundly enmeshed in a historical event that only authors who confine their arguments to God will find the refuge from debate that Arnold believed poetry would afford.

The chapters subsequent to the discussion of Yiddish literature gradually descend, as the subject of the Holocaust itself has descended in the past quarter century, into the swirl of controversy. The discussion of American writers centers on literary attempts to Americanize the Holocaust (an effort given existential realization in the aforementioned United States Holocaust Museum) and on the "personalization" of the event by literary latecomers to the subject who knew little of the Jewish past *other* than the Holocaust (and therefore could not know even that). The chapter on Israeli writers pits those who devoted themselves to integrating the European tragedy of the Jewish people into Israeli imagination against those whose main interest has been to ingratiate themselves with the radical avant-garde of Europe and America who think of Israel as the devil's own experiment station.

The controversies that impinge upon discussions of Holocaust writing in the first half of this book are dealt with more directly in the last three chapters. "In the Shadow of the Vatican" evaluates accusations of Vatican indifference and scrutinizes Primo Levi's fierce criticisms of German national character and the war against memory conducted both by the Nazis and "the constructors of convenient truth" who are their heirs. In the penultimate chapter I have reevaluated the writings of Hannah Arendt, of the Nazi-hunter Simon Wiesenthal, and of the Marxist playwright Peter Weiss on the subject of crime and punishment, especially in the light of recent historical research that gives the lie to claims that soldiers in the Nazi armies could not refuse assignments to murder Jews without putting their lives at risk. In the concluding chapter I have tried to survey some of the major recent controversies about the Holocaust—the denial that it ever took place; the appropriation of it as a valuable piece of moral capital; the relativization of it; the flagrant scandals of President Reagan's visit to Bitburg Cemetery and the construction of the Carmelite convent at Auschwitz. Here I try to make explicit what has been implicit throughout the earlier sections of the book: namely, that the pervasive deformations of the Holocaust arise largely from the fact that the war of ideas over this event of fifty years ago is to be understood as part of the larger war that has been forced upon the Jews by the foes of Zionism as an idea and Israel as a nation.

In looking back over the book, I am left with the uneasy feeling that perhaps the Yiddish writers, convinced that it was useless to talk any longer with men, were right in turning their attention and arguments to God. To wade through some of the polemical exploitations of the Holocaust requires the mental equivalent of hip-boots; and to be a belligerent in this war of ideas, one needs to be well-wadded around with insensitivity. The experience makes one appreciate the consoling force of an elegy by one of the greatest of the Holocaust poets, the Yiddish-writing Israeli Abraham Sutzkever:

> Who will last? And what? The wind will stay,
> and the blind man's blindness when he's gone away,
> and a thread of foam—a sign of the sea—
> and a bit of cloud snarled in a tree.
>
> Who will last? and what? A word as green
> as Genesis, making grasses grow.
> And what the prideful rose might mean,
> seven of those grasses know.
>
> Of all that northflung starry stuff,
> the star descended in the tear will last.
> In its jar, a drop of wine stands fast.
> Who lasts? God abides—isn't that enough?[10]

(Translated by Cynthia Ozick)

Notes

1. Johanna Kaplan, "Bad Dreams With No Awakening," review of Ida Fink, *A Scrap of Time and other Stories*, *New York Times Book Review*, July 12, 1987, 7.
2. *New Republic*, December 19, 1988, 6.
3. Michael Ledeen, "Iraq's German Connection," *Commentary*, 91 (April 1991): 27–30.
4. Friedrich Schiller, preface to *The Bride of Messina* (1803).

5. T. W. Adorno, "Engagement," in *Noten zur Literatur III* (Frankfurt am Main: Suhrkamp Verlag, 1965), 109-35.
6. See Irving Howe, "Writing and the Holocaust," *New Republic*, October 27, 1986, 27-39.
7. *A Double Dying: Reflections on Holocaust Literature* (Bloomington and London: Indiana University Press, 1980).
8. *Modern Hebrew Poetry*, edited and translated by Ruth Finer Mintz (Berkeley and Los Angeles: University of California Press, 1968), 124-26.
9. Matthew Arnold, "The Study of Poetry" (1880).
10. "Poems from a Diary: 1974," translated by Cynthia Ozick, from *The Penguin Book of Modern Yiddish Verse*, edited by Irving Howe, Ruth R. Wisse, and Khone Shmeruk (New York: Viking Penguin, 1987), 696.

1

Antisemitism and the Holocaust

Antisemitism [is] a passing phase in the history of culture.
—*Encyclopedia Britannica*, 11th edition, 1910.

From 1933 to 1945 the National Socialist regime of Germany carried out policies of discrimination, oppression, and murder that resulted in the destruction of about 5.8 million Jews. The Jews held a unique position in the Nazi world because they alone, among all the peoples subject to German rule, had been marked out for total destruction—not for anything they had done or failed to do but because they had been born of three Jewish grandparents. Their guilt lay exclusively in having been born. Although only Jews could be guilty of being Jewish, the centrality of Jews in the mental and political universe of the Nazis established a universal principle that involved every single person in German-ruled Europe: in order to be granted the fundamental human "right"—the "right to live"—you had to be able to prove that you were *not* a Jew.

The anti-Jewish policies of the Nazis, which ultimately resulted in the loss to world Jewry of one-third of its population and the destruction of European Jewish civilization, were the direct result of the ideology of antisemitism. Just as the person who boasts of knowing only the Bible cannot really know the Bible, so the person who studies only the Holocaust, or examines it only as a series of events beginning in 1933 (the date of Germany's first anti-Jewish legislation) and ending in 1945 cannot really know the Holocaust, or reply to the persistent questions: Why the Jews? Why the Germans?

To what extent was antisemitism continuous with the religious Jew-hatred institutionalized in Christendom when Christianity became the religion of the Roman Empire in the fourth century, to what extent a

9

nineteenth-century political innovation of secular ideology? The term *antisemitism* itself is certainly a modern invention. In 1879 the German racist agitator Wilhelm Marr, feeling the need for a more secular, "scientific," and hygienic term than *Jew-hatred*, invented this euphemism, importing it from the realm of disputes in physical anthropology and philology. Every Central European, however, knew who was meant by the term Semite. When T. S. Eliot referred, derisively, in the poem "Burbank With a Baedeker: Bleistein With a Cigar," to Bleistein as "Chicago Semite Viennese," every literate reader understood Semite to refer to Jew. In 1941, when Haj Amin el- Husseini, the leader of the Palestinian Arabs, arrived in Berlin to collaborate with Hitler in the destruction of European Jewry, Hitler designated Arabs as "honorary Aryans."

All of this would hardly be worth mentioning if the modern continuators of Haj Amin el-Husseini's political ideology had not acquired the habit of saying that Arabs can hardly be deemed antisemitic when they are Semites themselves. Thus Marc Ellis, the Jewish "liberation theologian" whose febrile lucubrations about the Holocaust and Israel represent the mental condition to which all Israel-haters aspire, locates antisemitism exclusively in the *Jewish* community's alleged mistreatment of "the Palestinian and Arab peoples, who are, after all, Semitic people."[1] Antisemites, as all normally attentive sixth graders used to know, do not hate "semites," they hate Jews. (Now that antisemitism has resulted in crimes greater than anyone had thought possible, it has lost its usefulness as a euphemism and had to be replaced by "anti-Zionism," the label usually given to the ideological campaign to destroy the moral image of Israel and the Jewish people.)

In his massive study of the destruction of European Jewry,[2] Raul Hilberg argued that "most of what happened in those twelve years had already happened before," and that the Nazi destruction process was "the culmination of a cyclical trend." He described the relation between Christians and Jews in Europe as a continuum epitomized by an ever-shortening sentence: "The missionaries of Christianity had said in effect: You have no right to live among us as Jews. The secular rulers who followed had proclaimed: You have no right to live among us. The German Nazis at last decreed: You have no right to live" (3). Hilberg offered a table of equations between Canonical (Church) and Nazi Anti-Jewish Measures. A few examples follow:

Canonical Law	Nazi Measure
Prohibition of intermarriage and of sexual intercourse between Christians and Jews, Synod of Elvira, 306	Law for the Protection of German Blood and Honor, September 15, 1935
Jews and Christians not permitted to eat together, Synod of Elvira 306	Jews barred from dining cars, December 30, 1939
Jews not permitted to show themselves in the streets during Passion Week, 3d Synod of Orleans, 538	Decree authorizing local authorities to bar Jews from the streets on . . . Nazi holidays, December 3, 1938
Burning of the Talmud and other books, 12th Synod of Toledo, 681	Book burnings in Nazi Germany
Compulsory ghettos, Synod of Breslau, 1267	Order by Heydrich, September 21, 1939

(Hilberg, 5–6)

Such a series of parallels seems to indicate that Nazi antisemitism, although anti-Christian (partly because, like Voltaire, the Nazis considered Christianity tainted by its Judaic parentage), would have been inconceivable without centuries of Christian "antisemitism": blood libels, badges, ghettos, expulsions, autos-da-fé, pogroms.

Many of the greatest figures of Christianity encouraged the belief that the Jewish people, though physically alive, was spiritually dead. In the "fullness of time," claimed Origen, a Christian theologian of the third century, "Judaism had come to naught." The Jews, once God's elect, had, by denying that Jesus was the Messiah, shown themselves to be spiritually blind, morally deficient. Also in the third century, a father of the Church named St. Cyprian declared that "the peoplehood of the Jews has been cancelled; the destruction of Jerusalem was a judgment upon them; the gentiles rather than the Jews will inherit the Kingdom." The greatest of the Greek Fathers of the Church, Saint John Chrysostom ("Goldenmouth") [347–407], proclaimed it "the duty of all Christians to hate the Jews." The Jews, he alleged, "sacrifice their children to Satan," their synagogue is "a brothel, a den of scoundrels . . . a place of meeting for the assassins of Christ." The Jews may appear to be human, but in fact have "fallen into a condition lower than the vilest animals." John's African contemporary, St. Augustine, almost as if he were aware that such teachings were hardly conducive to toleration, urged that humiliation and persecution of the Jews, however desirable, not be carried to the extreme of murder. In a special sermon to the Jews ("Tractatus Adversus

Iudaeos") he said: "You do not forget the law of God, but carry it everywhere, a witness to the nations, a shame for you." St. Thomas Aquinas (1225-74) wrote in a similar vein: "It would be licit . . . to hold Jews, because of their crime, in perpetual servitude, and therefore the princes may regard the possessions of Jews as belonging to the state; however, they must use them with a certain moderation and not deprive Jews of things necessary to life."[3]

There is, then, much to be said in favor of the view that the Holocaust is the culminating eruption of primordial forces long at work in Christendom. But it is easily carried to excess. Thus, Hilberg's equation between the canonical law of 1267 establishing ghettos and the Nazi establishment of ghettos starting in 1939 disguises the fact that the medieval ghetto had begun as a strategy for Jewish existence and survival, a Jewish Quarter within whose walls Jews could better defend themselves against such predators as the Crusaders. Even when the church changed the voluntary character of the Jewish quarter into the obligatory ghetto guarded by gatekeepers who locked the inhabitants in at night, the Jews were not in a prison. It hardly needs to be said that the ghettos of Lodz or Warsaw, in which Jews were starved, terrorized, and murdered, were very different places.

At the opposite pole from Hilberg is Hannah Arendt. In the first volume of her *Origins of Totalitarianism* she insisted that antisemitism was born only in the nineteenth century, and was decisively different from traditional, religious Jew-hatred. She believed that a main reason for denying this difference was that the Jews, after the destruction of the temple and their expulsion from their homeland, had no territory, no state, no means of resisting violence—and therefore came to think that all outbursts of violence against them were repetitions of what had gone before, and not something perhaps entirely new. She locates an early instance of antisemitism in Prussia after its defeat by Napoleon in 1807, largely as a result of the aristocracy's bitter reaction to Jewish emancipation. But the real beginning of modern antisemitism did not come, she alleges, until the last third of the nineteenth century, in Germany, Austria, and France. In the first two countries, antisemitic parties were distinguished by their claim to be not just another party but the true representative of the whole nation and (somewhat contradictorily) by their *supranational* organization of all antisemitic groups in Europe, in defiance of nationalistic slogans. Since—so the antisemites argued—the

Jews were organized as a party beyond other parties and as an inter-European group, the antisemites could only combat the Jews by doing the same.[4]

Typical of the international element in antisemitism was the fact that its leading exponent in Austria in the eighties was the left-wing German Liberal Party led by Georg Schoenerer. The first loyalty of these an-tisemites was not to their own country, but to ethnic Germans wherever they might be. Although the party gained its first successes at the universities, its mass support came in those German-speaking provinces without any "Jewish bankers" or Jewish social competitors, or, in fact, any Jews at all. No wonder Schoenerer and his followers declared that they "regarded antisemitism as . . . the most essential expression of genuine popular conviction and thus as the major national achievement of the century" (Arendt, *OT*, I, 44). Nothing, it seemed, had such magical power to unite the disintegrating societies of Europe. That may explain why, a hundred years later, in 1991, the writer Ruth Wisse could conclude, dejectedly, that antisemitism, which arose as a desperate attempt to explain and rectify the problems of the nineteenth century, had proved to be "the 20th century's most successful ideology."[5]

In *Mein Kampf*, Adolf Hitler recalled that "When I came to Vienna, my sympathies were fully and wholly on the side of the Pan-German tendency." He is condescending towards Schoenerer, but concedes that the pan-Germanists' antisemitism "was based on a correct understanding of the importance of the racial problem, and not on religious ideas." This would seem to support Arendt's view that German-Austrian antisemitism was, by virtue of its internationalism and its racism, different from old-fashioned religious Jew-hatred. Hitler's contempt for the latter is evident in his dismissive remark that "if the worst came to the worst, a splash of baptismal water could always save the business and the Jew at the same time."[6]

Austria and Germany did not have a monopoly on antisemitism. France was rife with racial ideologies, and the Dreyfus Affair (1894–1906) has often been considered a dress rehearsal for the Nazi movement. Neither were the German and Austrian Jew-haters the only ones who carried their hatred to the extreme of advocating genocide. But between the actuality of what the Germans did in the Holocaust and the poten-tiality of what the French or any other people might have done, there stretches a huge gap, announcing a huge question: Why the Germans?

Was it the pervasiveness in Germany of the tradition of Martin Luther, who in his booklet *Of the Jews and their Lies* (published in 1543 and reissued by the Nazis in 1935) proposed the following "program":

> First, their synagogues or churches should be set on fire, and whatever does not burn up should be covered or spread over with dirt so that no one may ever be able to see a cinder or stone of it. . . . Secondly, their homes should likewise be broken down and destroyed. . . . They ought to be put under one roof or in a stable, like gypsies. . . . Their rabbis must be forbidden under threat of death to teach any more. . . . If, however, we are afraid that they might harm us personally . . . then let us settle with them for that which they have extorted. . . from us, and after having divided it up fairly let us drive them out of the country for all time.[7]

Recent historians like Gavin Langmuir[8] and Paul Lawrence Rose,[9] who argue against the strict distinction between medieval-Christian and modern-secular forms of Jew-hatred, and claim—especially Langmuir—that the anti-Judaism of early Christianity paved the way for modern antisemitism but was not a sufficient cause of it, assign a special importance to another passage in this work by Luther:

> We are at fault in not avenging all this innocent blood of our Lord and Churches and Christians which they shed for three hundred years after the destruction of Jerusalem, and the blood of the children they have shed since then (which still shines forth from their eyes and their skin). We are at fault in not slaying them. (Rose, 7)

Here Luther gave particularly violent expression to the fixation on blood in Christian speculation about the Jews. "Through the influence of Luther's language and tracts," Rose writes, "a hysterical and demonizing mentality entered the mainstream of German thought and discourse; Luther in fact legitimated hysteria and paranoia in a major European culture" (Rose, 7–8). France and England had a similar heritage of Jew-hatred, but they had no Martin Luther.

The centrality of blood in Christendom's myths and fantasies about the Jews supplies a link between "old-fashioned" religious Jew-hatred and Nazi racism. Langmuir asserts that "the fantasy of ritual cannibalism [the allegation that Jews not only murdered Christian children, but also drank their blood] . . . can be seen as a halfway stage between the original fantasy of ritual murder by crucifixion and the fantasy about Jews and the Eucharist that appeared later" (Langmuir, 299). In Luther's Germany, as Robert Alter has pointed out, both leftists and rightists took "naturally" to the metaphor of blood. Moses Hess and Marx stressed the allegedly intrinsic bond between capitalism and the Jews, and Hess spoke of money as "social coagulated blood" while calling capitalist "exploitation" a reenactment of the crucifixion in secular form. Hess's tract of 1843, *The Essence of Money*, is, Alter notes, "filled with images of cannibalism and bloodsucking." At the other end of the political spectrum, Richard Wagner, in his essay *Judaism and Music* (1850), nearly outdid the leftists in blood-money metaphor-making: "All is turned to money by the Jew. Who thinks of noticing that the guileless looking scrap of paper is slimy with the blood of countless generations? What the heroes of the arts . . . have invented . . . from the millennia of misery, today the Jew converts into an art-bazaar." By the 1870s Wagner, a full-blown racist in the modern sense, alluded not only to the actual blood in Jewish veins, but to the blood that Jews, literally as well as figuratively, imbibed. Wagner even preceded Hitler, his admirer, in joining his hatred of Jews with (bloodthirsty) vegetarianism, arguing that Aryan Christianity had been infected by the alien Jews with the desire for the consumption of living animals.[10]

Another feature of German culture that may help to explain why it was here that Jew-hatred turned into the crime of genocide was the unusually fruitful interaction between Christian haters of Jews and Jewish haters of themselves in Germany and Austria. Luther's seemingly innovative program, outlined above, was in fact derived from the proposals of Johannes (born Josef) Pfefferkorn, a Jewish convert to Christianity who had, years earlier, exhorted his German countrymen to "drive the old Jews out like dirty dogs, baptize their children, and take their goods and give them to those to whom they belong." In the nineteenth century, a German-Jewish convert to Lutheranism (at age six) named Karl Marx incited his countrymen against Jews by telling them that capitalism was nothing other than the Talmud (of which Marx knew not a single word) written in the "real" language of the Jews, which is neither Hebrew nor Yiddish, but "haggling." Jews certainly contributed more than their fair share to the torrential flow of antisemitic propaganda that greeted Hitler when he came first to Vienna, to which city he remained forever grateful for turning him into an antisemite (Dawidowicz, *WJ*, 8).

Antisemitism, for all its unspeakable vileness, might never have led to the Holocaust if not for the advent of a mad revolutionary named Adolf Hitler. But how could this maniac, with his poverty of mind and loathsomeness of character (and visage) have become Chancellor of Germany? The late Lucy Dawidowicz, preeminent historian of the Holocaust, could answer this question only with another series of questions:

> How was it possible that a state whose people and culture ranked high in the world's civilization should have entrusted its fate to this deluded man who believed that he had been chosen to lead a holy war against the Jews? . . . Was it because their moral sense . . . had become atrophied under the effect of generations of virulent anti-Semitism? Had the German people already become mithridatized by anti-Semitic poison, so that they had become immune even to Hitler's deadly brand? Was it because he spoke for them? (Dawidowicz, *WJ*, 12)

At just what point in his war against the Jews Hitler decided to murder them all, has long been an occasion of dispute. Dawidowicz argued that the plan of mass murder existed in embryo in *Mein Kampf* (1924–26). Others maintain that Hitler did not hit upon the plan of annihilation until he saw that the other countries of the world did not care what he did with the Jews so long as he did not send them across *their* borders. By January 30, 1939, at any rate, he made little attempt to conceal his intentions: "Today I will be a prophet again: If international finance Jewry . . . should succeed once more in plunging the peoples into a world war, then the consequence will not be the Bolshevization of the world and therewith a victory of Jewry, but on the contrary, the destruction of the Jewish race in Europe." (Dawidowicz, 106)*

Hitler kept his promise; indeed, he was the only European leader who kept his promise to the Jews: he had sworn to destroy them, and he did. Under cover of his conventional war for territory and resources, he conducted his unconventional racial war against the Jews.

> The Jews of Europe were rounded up at various convenient points, and were compelled to stand naked, whole families together, at the edges of pits, hills, ravines, or graves they had dug themselves; then they were shot, and tumbled dead into the waiting void. When this proved to be inefficient (mere thousands could be dispatched

---

* In subsequent years Hitler repeatedly referred to his Reichstag speech of September 1, 1939, in which he cryptically announced that "Whoever fights with poison will be fought back with poison gas," as the speech in which he warned the Jews that they would be destroyed in the event of war. "On September 1, 1939, I declared . . . that this war would not end as the Jews imagine, namely, that the European-Aryan peoples will be annihilated, but on the contrary that the consequences of this war will be the destruction of Jewry." (January 30, 1942) "On September 1, 1939, I stated . . . that if Jewry would plot an international world war for the annihilation of the Aryan peoples of Europe, then not the Aryan peoples would be annihilated, but on the contrary Jewry. . . . " (September 30, 1942) "You will recall still that meeting of the Reichstag in which I declared [that] the consequence [of war] will be . . . the annihilation of Jewry in Europe." (November 8, 1942)

by so technologically primitive a method), the remaining Jews of Europe—millions—were locked into freight cars, stacked standing together like cordwood, some dying as they stood, the rest awash in a muck of excrement, urine, menstrual blood, and the blood of violence. When the transport reached its destination, the Jews were herded into a nearby wood, stripped naked, and made to gallop into so-called shower chambers, where they were gassed by an effective insecticide. Then their corpses were burned in commodious and serviceable furnaces designed explicitly for this purpose. Specially selected properties of their corpses were transmuted into other matter: baled human hair for bolsters and pillows; gold teeth for the war effort; eyeglasses for recycling; artificial limbs for the value of their materials.[11]

This description, by an American novelist, of Hitler's destruction of European Jewry, should stand as a powerful antidote to the amnesia induced by the passage of time and the mental confusion spread by wilful deception.

Notes

1. Marc H. Ellis, *Toward a Jewish Theology of Liberation*, 3rd ed. (New York: Orbis Books, 1990), 114. Subsequent references to this work will be cited in text as *TJT*.
2. Raul Hilberg, *The Destruction of the European Jews* (Chicago: Quadrangle Books, 1961), 3-4. Subsequent references to this work will be cited in text.
3. Yehuda Bauer, *A History of the Holocaust* (New York: Franklin Watts, 1982), 8-9. Subsequent references to this work will be cited in text.
4. Hannah Arendt, *The Origins of Totalitarianism*, 3 vols. (New York: Harcourt, Brace, and World, 1951), I, ix, 29, 35-40. Subsequent references to this work will be cited in text.
5. Ruth Wisse, "The 20th Century's Most Successful Ideology," *Commentary*, 91 (February 1991): 31-35.
6. Lucy S. Dawidowicz, *The War Against the Jews: 1933-1945* (New York: Holt, Rinehart & Winston, 1975), 11. Subsequent references to this work will be cited in text as *WJ*.
7. Martin Gilbert, *Exile and Return: The Struggle for a Jewish Homeland* (Philadelphia and New York: J. B. Lippincott, 1978), 20-21.
8. Gavin I. Langmuir, *History, Religion, and Antisemitism* (Berkeley: University of California Press, 1990). Subsequent references to this work will be cited in text.
9. Paul Lawrence Rose, *Revolutionary Antisemitism in Germany from Kant to Wagner* (Princeton: Princeton University Press, 1990). Subsequent references to this work will be cited in text.
10. Robert Alter, "From Myth to Murder," *New Republic*, May 20, 1991, 34-42.
11. Cynthia Ozick, *Art & Ardor* (New York: Alfred A. Knopf, 1983), 234-35. Subsequent references to this work will be cited in text as *AA*.

2

The Yiddish Writers

> *And the language was lost, murdered. The language—a museum. Of what other language can it be said that it died a sudden and definite death, in a given decade, on a given piece of soil? Where are the speakers of ancient Etruscan? Who was the last man to write a poem in Linear B? Attrition, assimilation. Death by mystery not gas. The last Etruscan walks around inside some Sicilian. Western Civilization, that pod of muck, lingers on and on. The Sick Man of Europe with his big globe-head, rotting, but at home in bed. Yiddish, a littleness, a tiny light—oh little holy light!—dead, vanished. Perished. Sent into darkness.*
> —Cynthia Ozick, "Envy; or, Yiddish in America"[1]

Yiddish developed in the Rhine between the tenth and twelfth centuries. Like modern German it began as a dialect of medieval high German. Originally it consisted of German words transliterated into Hebrew characters, but over time the German (medieval German, that is) underwent changes in pronunciation, meaning, and syntax. Because the Jews were scattered over Europe and the world, yet wished to be in touch with each other, Yiddish introduced foreign words from Romance and Slavic sources. Eastward migration to Poland and Russia increased the stock of Slavic words in Yiddish. By the end of the thirteenth century Yiddish was well on its way to becoming a language in its own right. Never looked upon as the equal of the holy tongue, Hebrew, it nevertheless survived, indeed flourished; and its survival, as Irving Howe and Eliezer Greenberg have written, "reflects the miracle of Jewish survival itself."[2]

According to Maurice Samuel,[3] Yiddish was a kind of mirror of the European Jewish condition of the past 2000 years, the most important of the many exile languages used by Jews. It was spoken, prior to the Holocaust, by far larger numbers than any other Jewish language, probably about eleven million people, which is five or six times as many as ever spoke ancient Hebrew. But the Holocaust changed all this, forever. As a character in Cynthia Ozick's story "Envy; or, Yiddish in America" (1969) laments, "A little while ago there were twelve million people . . . who lived inside this tongue, and now what is left? A language that never had a territory except Jewish mouths, and half the Jewish mouths on earth already stopped up with German worms" ("Envy," 44). After the war, the Yiddish writers who survived found themselves deprived of their subject and of their audience, which had been murdered. For many of them, therefore, Yiddish itself, the language of the majority of the victims of the Holocaust, came to be the most meaningful form of Jewish survival. This was especially true of the poets, who are dealt with in the first part of this chapter, but also of the great storyteller, Isaac Bashevis Singer, to be discussed in the second.

Yiddish Holocaust Poetry

> A remnant shall return, even the remnant of Jacob,
> Unto God the Mighty.
> For though thy people, O Israel, be as the sand of the sea,
> Only a remnant of them shall return;
> an extermination is determined, overflowing with righteousness.
> For an extermination wholly determined
> Shall the LORD, the GOD of hosts, make in the midst of all the earth.
> —Isaiah, 10: 21–23

> You only have I known among all the families of the earth;
> Therefore I will visit upon you all your iniquities.
> —Amos, 3:2

In the mind of the believing Jew, the tragic paradox of the Holocaust lay not so much in its blasphemous denial as in its spurious fulfillment of the divine promise, as set forth in such elucidations of the Covenant as those quoted above. To the sceptic, the destruction of European Jewry made a mockery of the sentences in the Jewish daily prayer-book: "With abundant love hast Thou loved us, O Lord." "With everlasting love hast Thou loved the house of Israel." To those who viewed Jewish life from the outside, the contradiction between God's professions of love for His Chosen People and the way in which these people had been tortured and killed, was absolute. But the believing Jew has traditionally accepted a structure of relations between the Chosen People and God in which love and chastisement are inseparable from each other. He has acknowledged that the Covenant contained a curse as well as a blessing. The Jews were chosen to receive the Law, but if they lusted instead after idols and violated the Covenant, they would be cursed and exiled and destroyed. The destruction was never to be total, however, for that would constitute God's violation of His own Covenant. Despite the endless transgressions of the people of Israel, "when they are in the land of their enemies, I will not reject them, neither will I abhor them, to destroy them utterly, and to break My covenant with them." The Jews' destiny, moreover, is in their own control and not in that of the nations of the earth. The God of Israel is the God of all mankind, but the nations of the world are instruments of the Lord in His dramatic struggle with His refractory people. In the lawsuit against His people, God calls heaven and earth to witness against His beloved adversary that "I have set before thee life and death, the blessing and the curse."

The whole structure of Jewish religious life was predicated on acceptance of responsibility for the exile and its endless humiliations and oppressions. These had been brought upon the Jews not by Assyrians or Babylonians or Romans or Crusaders or Cossacks but, ultimately, by their own transgressions. Regularly, in his festival prayers, the Jew acknowledged his responsibility for his condition of exile and debasement: "Because of our sins we were exiled from our land and removed far away from our country." This very act, moreover, of blaming their fate on their own sins tended to reenforce the Jews' belief in their chosenness because it enabled them to survive when other peoples, who had also suffered expulsion from their homelands and oppression in the lands of strangers, were disappearing. These peoples came to the outwardly sensible and reasonable conclusion that their miserable fate proved the inefficacy of their national god, whom they abandoned in order to worship the gods of their new neighbors; thus were they assimilated, thus did they disappear. The Jews, persistently interpreting their misery as divine punishment for their sins, clung to their God and to the promise of the covenant, and so survived, albeit in ever diminishing numbers. "Except the LORD of hosts Had left unto us a very small remnant, / We should have been as Sodom, We should have been like unto Gomorrah" (Isaiah, 1:9).

The covenantal relation between God and the Jewish people was so pervasive in Jewish life and in the Jewish imagination that it could withstand and accommodate a considerable resistance and rebellion from within. What is the book of Job but an instance of such rebellion and accommodation? It takes the traditional form of the lawsuit between the two partners to the Covenant, with enumeration of curses, invocation of witnesses, professions of innocence and allegations of guilt. Job desires "to reason with God" (13:3), to justify himself. Yet even at the height of his rebellion, when he insists "I will argue my ways before Him," he submits to the inherited structure of faith: "Though He slay me, yet will I trust in Him." Death itself, though it appears to be undeserved and unjust, becomes an aspect of endurance if it is acknowledged as a chastisement from God. This covenantal structure took such hold of Jewish life that it can still today provide a framework for modern Jewish poets and novelists of a secular cast of mind whose instinctive reaction to the Holocaust is, not to reject God, but to accuse and curse Him.

Just how irresistible was the inherited myth of the covenant between God and his Chosen People may be seen in Yiddish Holocaust poetry, one of the most coherent and substantial bodies of writing on the subject. From its inception, in the nineteenth century, Yiddish poetry had been secular in idea and outlook. Although most writers of Yiddish literature considered themselves Jews, they were devoted to a secularization of Jewish culture. Moreover, many who came to prominence in the second and third decades of this century sought to reject the traditional subect of Yiddish literature, the fate of the Jewish people. For why could not Yiddish writers, like French or German or English, range freely through the world for their subjects instead of being limited to the concerns of the collective body from which they had sprung? Thus, Jacob Glatstein wrote in 1920 of himself and his fellow poets in the Inzikh group, "We are Yiddish poets by virtue of the fact that we are Jews and write in Yiddish. Whatever a Yiddish poet may write about is ipso facto Yiddish. One does not need specifically Jewish themes."[4] But the Holocaust proved that the Jewish poet could no more than the Jews themselves become "normal." After the Holocaust, as Irving Howe has written,

"Yiddish poetry . . . returns . . . to its original concern with the collective destiny of the Jewish people. . . . In the desolation of memory, Yiddish poets find themselves turning back to the old Jewish God, . . . a God inseparable from Jewish fate, a God with whom one pleads and quarrels."[5]

In the poetry of Jacob Glatstein, the Yiddish tradition of intimate quarrel and mutual reproach between the Jew and God is continued, but subjected to strains and storms which threaten to shatter the old framework. In the wake of the Holocaust, the poles of the ancient antithesis between suffering and faith, the terms of the paradox whereby the unending misery of the Jews is precisely a sign of the unending covenant with God, move so far apart that their link is almost ruptured. Glatstein cannot fathom the Holocaust without viewing it as part of the ongoing quarrel between God and His chosen people. The Jews cannot be themselves without God, for "without our God / we have a funny look." Nor can God exist without the Jews, in whose post-Holocaust absence He is "pursued, forsaken, / wandering around, / looking for a Jewish face, / a hand to give you shalom: / Shalom aleichem, Jewish God." But neither, finally, can Glatstein live with the horror of believing that the Holocaust *was* part of God's ongoing quarrel with the Jews:

> From the crematory flue
> A Jew aspires to the Holy One.
> And when the smoke of him is gone,
> His wife and children filter through.
>
> Above us, in the height of sky,
> Saintly billows weep and wait.
> God, wherever you may be,
> There all of us are also not.
>
> ("Smoke," Translated by Chana
> Faerstein, *TYP*, 331)

The Holocaust does *not* confirm God's existence. Any impulse towards locating the source of the unspeakable horror in God must mercilessly be squelched. If the God of history has indeed been involved in the Holocaust, then the Jews must sue for divorce from Him.

Glatstein's Holocaust poetry is not informed by a consistent theology. Rather he seeks imaginatively to assimilate the Holocaust by perceiving it through the inherited myths of Jewish religion. He looks upon this religion to some extent as an outsider, one who has become alienated from its language and beliefs, and who revisits it nostalgically.

> It's as hard to return to
> old-fashioned words
> as to sad synagogues,
> those thresholds of faith.
> You know exactly where they are.
> Troubled, you can still hear their undertones.
> Sometimes you come close and look longingly
> at them through the windowpanes.
>
> ("Without Gifts")[6]

The world of his youth provides not so much truth as warmth, familiarity, and shelter: "I love you, dead world of my youth, / I command you, rise up, let your joy revive, / come close, letter by letter, warm, pulsing, meaning nothing" ("The Joy of the Yiddish Word," *JG*, 118). The religious myths which once provided the shelter of a protective covering have now been hollowed out, by intellect and by history. Yet still they seem to the poet the only framework within which he can begin to make sense of what has happened. Having been disillusioned by Western culture, by its "Jesus-Marxes" and "weak-kneed democracy" ("Good Night, World," *JG*, 59–60), the poet returns in imagination to his very beginnings in the ghetto and implores help from those whose lives are still bound by the all-embracing myths of religion: "You who still take your ease in the shadow of biblical trees / O sing me the cool solace / of all you remember, all that you know" ("Without Gifts," *JG*, 109).

Glatstein conceived of his Holocaust poetry as a safeguarding and even a resurrection of the dead. In a poem called "Nightsong" he imagines the post- Holocaust imaginative life of the Yiddish poet as a nightly stroll among the graves, among the "valleys and hills and hidden twisted paths" that have become the landscape of his mind. Here he gathers to himself the whole vanished Jewish world, in a heroic attempt to "grasp and take in / these destroyed millions" (*JG*,73). If they are to be redeemed, it can henceforward— such is the implication of the poem—only be through literature. The appropriate language of the literature is Yiddish, but its structure can be provided only by the myths of religion, that is to say, by the worldview which Yiddish literature, at its inception, was intended to erode and supplant. Glatstein's work is pervaded by anger towards many, but most of all by anger towards himself for failing to perceive, until both Jewry and Yiddish were virtually destroyed, that neither Yiddish literature nor Jewish life could survive without in some way incorporating their religious heritage. Amidst the wreckage of European Jewry, one lesson was clear: Yiddish, once the language of militant secularists, had suddenly become a "dead" language whose only future was as the sacred tongue of martyrdom: "Poet, take the faintest Yiddish speech, / fill it with faith, make it holy again" ("In a Ghetto," *JG*, 110).

Although the Holocaust does not, for Glatstein, confirm religious belief, some of his poems suggest that the catastrophe can best be viewed within the framework of biblical narrative. The poem "My Father Isaac,"* for example, gains its power at once from the sense of timeless, inescapable repetition of a pattern, and from a striking departure from it. The Isaac to be sacrificed here by the Nazis is a father (the poet's own) rather than a son, an old man rather than a young one. He is thoroughly accustomed to the procedure, as if he were the descendant of untold Isaacs who have been chosen by God and know that, unlike the Isaac of the Bible, they will not be rescued by a good angel from the sharpened blade. "Isaac, old, was not deceived / as when he'd been that lad from Genesis; / he knew that there would be no lamb." Always he speaks in "a tired voice," as if wearied of the process of being chosen and offered for sacrifice, and knowing better than to expect rescue from a God who has done nothing to rescue his Isaacs since the original binding told in Genesis. Indeed, the poem implies that the Genesis story is an archetype of Jewish experience except for its ending, which is not to be believed. But this ancient Isaac, having long ago learned not to expect mercy and rescue from this God, submissively goes to the altar: "and as he smelled the searing fumes, / he spoke his mind thus: / 'God will not interrupt this slaughter!' / He called out in a tired voice: / 'Here I am—prepared to be your ram'" (*TYP*, 246).

Several of Glatstein's Holocaust poems take the form of a dialogue between the poet who presents the accusations of his people, and the Jewish God who tries to justify His action or inaction during the great destruction. In "My Brother Refugee" (*JG*, 71-72), Glatstein appears at first to be sacrificing God's power in order to rescue the belief in His goodness. In the first part of the poem, God is presented as just another

---

* Translated by Etta Blum.

powerless, persecuted Jew, in fact a "brother refugee." The poet discovers new fellowship with so miserable a character, and wonders how he could in olden times have expended so much energy in profaning the words and blaspheming the person of so helpless and pitiful a creature. But is this "human" and lovable God really the God of the Jews, of Abraham, Isaac, and Jacob? Glatstein's mixture of scepticism and belief, of aggression and reconciliation, is conveyed in the declaration that "The God of my unbelief is magnificent."

This God, when His turn comes to speak, is in no mood to make great claims for Himself. In fact, He acknowledges that the Jews have now become, by virtue of their unprecedented "wallowing in dust," "godlier than I am," and predicts (just how mistakenly we now know) that the nations "will yet bow / to their anguish." But here the poet's irony and bitterness overcome his newfound affection. Who needed, who requested such exaltation? "Why have you exalted my people like this, / constellating their misfortune / across the whole sky?" To this question God provides an extraordinary and desperate answer which says, in effect, that since the Christian version of the Messiah—"a childish fable with foolish words"—left the world just as it had always been, He decided to crucify the whole Jewish people, thus "constellating their misfortune across the whole sky." No sooner does Glatstein allow himself to imagine a God with the power to act in history, than he imagines a God implicated in monstrosity, who confirms the election of His people through eternity by tormenting them, and dreams that His people "will bloom / crucified forever on a shining tree." The poem ends, therefore, with Glatstein's retreat into the image of a very small, childlike, helpless God, entirely dependent on the few remaining Jews willing to dream Him into existence.

If, as both Jews and Christians believe, God's ultimate purposes for the universe required the creation and election of the Jewish people, how can God condone the extinction of that people? The removal of any member of the family of nations is a crime against humanity, against human diversity and the nature of mankind. The removal of this particular member, however, must constitute God's self-destruction. Without Jews,

> Who will dream you?
> Who will remember you?
> Who deny you?
> Who yearn for you?

> Who, on a lonely bridge,
> Will leave you—in order to return?
> ("Without Jews," Translated by Nathan Halper)

These lines are not only an expression of the peculiarly intimate relation between the Jews and their God, or a sceptic's suggestion that God's existence is merely subjective, but a recognition that God had made the Jews the special instrument for the achievement of His purposes and their life His chief interest. The death of the Jews thus portends the death of God: "The Jewish hour is guttering. / Jewish God! You are almost gone" (*TYP*, 332).

Is this then what the Holocaust "teaches" in the realm of religion? For Glatstein, the idea of the Covenant between God and the Jewish people is the locus for his paradoxical mixture of faith and denial, submission and outrage. "Dead Men Don't Praise God," one of his most ambitious poems, is based entirely on the idea that the Jews as a people have been called into existence to serve God's purpose in the world. It relies especially on the doctrine that Jews of all generations were potentially present at Sinai, and were as much recipients of the Torah as those physically there. But it treats the Holocaust too as an event of more than human significance, whose full implications for Jewish existence can be fathomed only if it is understood in precisely the way Jews have traditionally understood the Covenant, of which it is at once a validation and a denial:

> We received the Torah on Sinai
> and in Lublin we gave it back.
> Dead men don't praise God,
> the Torah was given to the living.
> And just as we all stood together
> at the giving of the Torah,
> so did we all die together at Lublin.

If the gift of life at Sinai was a collective one to every generation of Jews, then the plague of death at Lublin-Maidanek (and all the other death factories for which it stands) must also implicate every Jew; if all stood at Sinai, then all fell in the slaughter at Lublin: "The souls of those who had lived out their lives, of those who had died young, / of those who were tortured, tested in every fire, / of those who were not yet born, / and of all the dead Jews from great grandfather Abraham down." That Moses,

Aaron, King David, and the multitudes already dead, should come to die again at Lublin perversely confirms the logic of the Covenant. What they were given at Sinai was not physical but spiritual life; if they are indeed being required to return the Covenant, then their souls must be killed as well as their bodies. What better place for such a second death than Lublin?

That the Jews of all generations should congregate for death in the Holocaust in the same way that they had congregated for life in the Covenant shows the continuity between Sinai and Lublin and the unity of the Jewish people. In both cases arbitrary fate visited upon all individual Jews, whether they liked it or not, and whether they "deserved" it or not, the collective fate of the Chosen People. But this continuity of chosenness is threatened by the discontinuity between the old and the new covenants. The pain and suffering which devolve upon the Chosen People may themselves be a sign of their invisible destiny, but the Holocaust, far from bringing a voice of redemption, seems to drown out the redeeming voice of Sinai. "Above the gas chambers / and the holy dead souls, forsaken abandoned Mount Sinai veiled itself in smoke." The Sinai Covenant makes its presence felt above Lublin, but the smoke of the death factories blackens and conceals Sinai itself. The new Covenant obliterates the original one, for if all Jews assemble to be killed at Lublin, then the new Covenant is for death; and it logically follows that the Torah has been returned: "Dead men don't praise God, / The Torah was given to the living" (*JG*, 68–70).

Glatstein's anguish moved him, again and again, to resort to traditional structures of religious meaning only to fill those structures with a body of experience that seemed both to make sense only within them, and yet to defy all sense whatever. Aaron Zeitlin, by contrast, stood virtually alone among Yiddish poets in viewing the Holocaust of the Jewish people not only within the confines of, but as a terrifying testimony to, the assumptions of orthodox Jewish religion.[7] He was among the few who claimed to hear a redeeming voice from Auschwitz, and would not back away from the recognition that God, if He is indeed the traditional Jewish God who acts within history, must be the God of the Holocaust as well as the God of Sinai. He may also be the hidden God of Isaiah, but he cannot be the reduced, powerless God sometimes imagined by Glatstein.

Zeitlin was saved by an accident of fate from perishing in the Holocaust. He had written a play about German militarism called *In*

Keynems Land (In No Man's Land) which opened in Warsaw in 1938. In the spring of 1939 he was invited by Maurice Schwartz to New York for the Yiddish Art Theatre's premiere of his play. While he was in New York, the war broke out and prevented his return to his family, all of whom were murdered by the Nazis. The Holocaust came to occupy the center of his emotional, poetic, and religious life. Unlike Glatstein, he wrote from the compulsion of religious conscience, rather than from the impulse to memorialize and resurrect the dead through art. In fact, the Holocaust seemed to him to have rendered the whole literary enterprise frivolous: "Were Jeremiah to sit by the ashes of Israel today, he would not cry out a lamentation, nor would he drown the desolate places with his tears. The Almighty Himself would be powerless to open up his well of tears. He would maintain a deep silence. For even an outcry is now a lie, even tears are mere literature, even prayers are false" (*TYP*, 53). It was a religious, not a literary impulse which moved Zeitlin to the composition of his two-volume justification of the ways of God to men: "I Believe" (*TYP*, 321–25).

Belief pervades the poem, since for Zeitlin the beginning of inquiry is not, "If there be a God, how could the Holocaust have been permitted to happen?" but "Since there is a God, what does the Holocaust mean?" The aggression directed towards God in other Yiddish poems on this subject is here directed primarily towards competing religions which claim to derive from Judaism. "Should I believe in Spinoza's geometric god?" he asks. This is a god "without horror or miracle," to be sure, but also without relation to men in general or Jews in particular. There is an intentional ambiguity in Zeitlin's reference to this monistic and naturalistic god as "a distant relative / who won't acknowledge me as his relation." The "me" refers not only to humanity at large but to Zeitlin's Jewish identity; and Spinoza's god is a kind of snobbish relative because he was conceived by a Dutch Jew yet explicitly rejected the election of the Jews acknowledged by Christianity itself. Rather than believe in this utterly detached and indifferent god of nature, Zeitlin would "willingly believe in Satan and damnation."

Christianity too is objectionable both for its general inadequacy to the human condition—its location of human guilt and divine mystery in the wrong places—and for its need to affirm itself through the denial of Torah, to found its life on Jewish death. "Should I believe in the redeemer who never redeems, / the dreamed-up god who dangles on all the crosses,

/ . . . the god of cloister bells / whom the dark dreams / of sadists bleed and kill with the deliberate will / to torture my truth with his lie?" Zeitlin here vents his resentment against the centuries-old exploitation of alleged Jewish guilt for the death of Jesus as a license to kill Jesus (repeatedly) and the Jews at once. How trivial, in any case, is the Christian mystery of a god become a man when viewed by a generation which has experienced the reality, and the mystery, of Hitler, "a devil who became a man, / who lived with us here upon earth/ lived and was seen, lived and was heard /and — incinerating, gassing—crucified / a people." Here are transformations enough to satisfy the most voracious appetite for mysteries.

Yet it is clear that the Christian myth evokes something more than vituperation from Zeitlin. Like Glatstein, Zeitlin is ensnared by a morbid fascination for the very Christian image which he excoriates into imagining the whole Jewish nation as a crucified people. By so doing, he claims (again like Glatstein) to be giving to a literary fable the moral significance which always inhered in it, but which was never fully realized until the Holocaust. Neither of these Yiddish poets seems aware of the fact that by insisting that the murder of six million Jews is the true crucifixion, he is endorsing the very Christian scheme which he derogates, since Christianity claims that the conformity between the Cross and the suffering of all mankind is precisely what makes innocent suffering bearable.

Having disposed of the claims of the Spinozistic and Christian rivals to Judaism as untenable in the aftermath of the Holocaust, Zeitlin dismisses modern secular ideologies and man-made religions with a mere wave of the hand as "More hollow than ever . . . / After the all-destroying flames." Whatever cries of rebellion emerge from the Holocaust should be flung only at the one God who could have ordained the Holocaust. What but an orthodox structure can make gestures of rebellion meaningful? "Who would rebel against pale Jesuses? / And who would rage / against a Spinozan god, / a nonbeing being?" Zeitlin feels himself and his God to be locked into a pattern from which there can be no escape except at the price of denying one's principle of being. "One is — what one is. / I am Jew as He is God." Zeitlin's must be a living God; and since He is living, He is of necessity and unavoidably the God of cataclysm and Holocaust.

Zeitlin's voice is generally far more personal, far less representative and collective than that of other Yiddish Holocaust poets. He typically uses "I" rather than "we." Yet in his most deeply felt expressions of the irrevocability of the covenantal relationship between the Divine Father and the favored but chastised child, Zeitlin is forced to link himself with all the others who are no more, and without whose tacit consent he could not decently accept justification or consolation for their suffering.

> Can I then choose not to believe
> in that living God whose purposes
> when He destroys, seeming to forsake me,
> I cannot conceive;
> choose not to believe in Him
> Who having turned my body to fine ash
> begins once more to wake me?

The pressure of emotion obliges Zeitlin, without ever forsaking the singular pronoun, to join himself with the body of the Jewish people whom God has burned in order to re-awaken. That "aspiration" to the Holy One through the crematory flue which provoked bitter irony in Glatstein becomes a declaration of faith —albeit tragic and paradoxical faith—in Zeitlin. Although he uses the Yiddish word, *Khurbn*, for Zeitlin the idea behind the English word *Holocaust* retains its full, original meaning, derived through the Greek *holokauston* from the Hebrew *olah*, "an offering made by fire unto the Lord" (Dawidowicz, *WJ*, xv).

Although Zeitlin does not hesitate to involve God totally in the Holocaust and to profess faith that the burning and the awakening are part of a single process, he gives no indication of where the signs of new life are to be found in this world. That so much suffering is even more difficult to conceive without God than with Him, that "even my pain confirms Him," that without God our cries are like dead letters reaching nowhere: all this is convincingly expressed. But that there is in truth a divine rationale for what the poet has himself labelled the devil's destructiveness remains an article of faith, a willed belief sustained by no evidence: "I believe God gives / His inconceivable hells / because somewhere else / His eye surmises / Inconceivable paradises / for his slaughtered fugitives." That "somewhere" has, to the mind of anyone but an unflinching believer, a fatal vagueness; for Zeitlin, however, it is the next world, whose standards are simply incommensurable with our own and which can therefore hardly be conveyed through human language.

Whereas Glatstein thought that the Covenant granted at Sinai was dissolved by the great slaughter at Lublin-Maidanek, Zeitlin insists that

God's presence manifested itself in both places: "Who so volcanic as my God? / If He is Sinai to me, / He is Maidanek as well." Maidanek too confirms the covenantal relationship between God and the Jews, who are depicted by Zeitlin as locked into a fatal embrace from which there is no escape but through death. "We cannot let go / of each other, / not He of me, nor I of Him." A secular poet like the Israeli Yehuda Amichai can respond to such a recognition with the ironic "My God, my God, / Why have you not forsaken me!?" But for Zeitlin the death which is the price of the Covenant breaks through the limits of this world to a new life. The Holocaust is for him nothing less than the Biblically promised destruction of the world by fire, as well as the catastrophe which according to Jewish tradition must precede the messianic deliverance. So far is Zeitlin from the view that Auschwitz and Maidanek represented a radical evil, wholly divorced from God's purposes, that he repeatedly, even compulsively, refers to God's "experiments" in the Holocaust, "experiments on me, / experiments in fire." He knows that no other word so effectively calls up the obscene, cold cruelty of the Nazis' treatment of people they had relegated to the status of laboratory rats. No other word could serve to involve God so totally in the depredations visited upon His people.

Few readers, whatever their religious convictions, are likely to give intellectual assent to Zeitlin's defiant affirmations. But they can hardly fail to be awed by so passionate a commitment to the Biblical promise of consolation, and so complete an expression of the experience of loss and gain, curse and blessing. Far from being suppressed, the pattern of violent oscillation between love and chastisement in God's tragic relationship with the Jews is the cornerstone of Zeitlin's faith:

> He lets no one go under,
> as He lets me go under,
> lets no one be
> so utterly
> a paradigm in fire.
> There is no one He will equally desire
> to find, to lose.
> And I for my part find and lose Him, too,
> lose Him and find Him,
> an interchange of beatitude and law,
> lamentations and the Song of Songs.

Isaac Bashevis Singer (1904–1991)

The best-known utterance about the Holocaust in the writings of Isaac Bashevis Singer is the concluding statement of the English version of *The Family Moskat*: "Death is the Messiah. That's the real truth."[8] The setting is Warsaw at the time of the Nazi bombardment and invasion in 1939. The statement gains its tremendous force less from the events within the novel than from the reader's knowledge of what will befall the Jews after the novel ends. But it is also intended to pass adverse judgment upon the Jewish impatience for redemption, an impatience that expresses itself still to some extent in the religious longing of the traditional Jew but primarily in the progressive superstitions of the modern secular Jew. The novel shows how the Russian Revolution of 1905, which had accelerated the break-up of the Jewish world, had, paradoxically, quickened the messianic expectations both of the Chassidim who deplored this disintegration and of the *maskilim* (enlighteners) and leftists who welcomed it.

The Family Moskat is a study of the prospective victims of the Holocaust and of the reasons for their victimization. That Singer should assume that the Holocaust is to be understood primarily as an event in Jewish history represents both an advantage and a shortcoming of his method. Singer never accepts the implications of the old joke told by liberals about the antisemite who claims that the Jews had caused World War I and gets the reply: Yes, the Jews and the bicyclists. Why the bicyclists? asks the antisemite. Why the Jews? asks the other. On the contrary, Singer sees the major catastrophes of Jewish history in the Diaspora as so many announcements of the Holocaust, of which they are prototypes. Nowhere does he assume that the Jews were the accidental victims of the Holocaust, or that the disaster might just as easily have befallen another people. When Reb Dan Katzenellenbogen ponders the relationship between the pacific ethos of the Jews and the orgiastic violence of the gentiles, about whom he asks "What were they seeking? What would be the outcome of their endless wars?" (*FM*, 287), we know what the answer is: the destruction of the Jews. A Europe for which the prospect of murdering Jews had become, in the late nineteenth century, a primary principle of social cohesion, cannot be said to have stumbled accidentally upon the Jews as victims. But if Singer avoids the pitfalls of assuming the perfect innocence of the Jews and the accidental nature of their victimization, he may be said to go to the other extreme in viewing the Nazis as only the latest in the long succession of murderous outsiders who have obtruded themselves upon Jewish history. "Yes," sighs the narrator of *Family Moskat*, "every generation had its Pharaohs and Hamans and Chmielnickis. Now it was Hitler" (*FM*,578).

In *The Slave*, a novel ostensibly dealing with the plight of Jews in seventeenth-century Poland in the aftermath of the fearful massacres perpetrated upon the body of the Jewish people by the Ukrainian peasant-revolutionary Chmielnicki, Singer is clearly writing about the Holocaust. Virtually all the questions that Singer's explicit Holocaust literature characteristically asks are posed in this novel: "Why did this happen to us?" one of the men asked. "Josefov was a home of Torah." "It was God's will," a second answered. "But why? What sins did the small children commit? They were buried alive." How, the novel's hero wonders, can the mind grasp such a quantity of horrors? "There was a limit to what the human mind could accept. It was beyond the power of any man to contemplate all these atrocities and mourn them adequately." What was the role of God in all this? Could so much evil really be explained as a test of man's faith, or his free will? "Did the Creator require the assistance of Cossacks to reveal His nature?" Could Chmielnicki really be a part of the godhead or was it perhaps true that this massacre of the Jews revealed the existence of a radical evil in the universe, a devil who had no celestial origins? *The Slave* also shows us Jews who are forced to dig their own graves before they are executed, berates the Jewish community for its shameful failure to offer forceful resistance to the murders, and preaches the sacred duty of remembering forever those who were slaughtered. "Through forgetfulness," Jacob says of himself, "he had also been guilty of murder."[9] In its dwelling upon the physical obscenities of the mass murders, *The Slave* may even be said to deal more concretely with the Holocaust than Singer novels and stories that approach it frontally.

Our reaction to Singer's tendency to generalize the Holocaust in this way will depend in part on how we answer the question raised in the previous chapter as to whether antisemitism is a phenomenon deeply embedded in Western culture or is a movement, quite distinct from religious Jew hatred, that originated in the nineteenth century. Since a novelist ordinarily writes about what he knows, which in Singer's case is the Jews and the Christians of Poland, we can hardly expect him to give us a portrayal of the German murderers of Polish Jewry. Yet we might reasonably expect that a writer who in treating the Holocaust recognizes the centrality of the question "Why the Jews?" should at least not preclude us from asking the question, even if he cannot ask it himself, "Why the Germans?" That Singer should implicitly short- circuit this question is the more disturbing in view of the fact that he cannot finally convince us or himself that the Holocaust is no different in kind from the long series of disasters that have befallen the Jews since the seventeenth century. *The Slave*, after all, celebrates survival and recovery; the characters of a modern story like *Enemies*[10] who have survived the camps never recover and cannot return to life.

Singer is not only not discriminating in his treatment of the murderers of the Jews; he at times comes close to viewing them as merely a function of the Jews' failure to be true to themselves and to their best traditions. The difficult and painful question of the Jews' alleged "co-responsibility" for the disaster that was to engulf them is raised often in *The Family Moskat*, both by Jews and gentiles. At a political discussion early in the book, one of those overheated conspiratorial gatherings of Jews that Singer loves to recall, a man named Lapidus upbraids his leftist friends with this classic utterance: "We dance at everybody's wedding but our own" (*FM*, 61). Leftist Jews, ready to spill their ink and their blood lavishly for the liberation of every other oppressed group, have called into question the very existence of the Jews as a people. The Bialodrevna rabbi, for his part, charges that the enlightened Jews are "lead[ing] their own children to the slaughterhouse" (*FM*, 82), a remark that gains in impact from the later description, filled with Singer's vegetarian passion, of the actual slaughterhouse that Asa Heshel and Hadassah visit.

If we suspect Singer of stacking the evidence against his left-leaning Jewish characters, we should remember that his accusation of self-destructive zealousness can be amply confirmed by external sources, and particularly by the testimony of two of the most astute Jewish leaders of the early part of this century. Chaim Weizmann said that hundreds of thousands of young Jews in early twentieth-century Russia were convinced revolutionaries "offering themselves for sacrifice as though seized by a fever."[11] Yitzchok Leibush Peretz wrote of the 1905 Revolution, which roused the hopes of so many leftist Jews, that the pogroms accompanying it demonstrated a painful truth that Jews would ignore at their peril: "In the hands of the Jew, the reddest of all flags has been placed forcibly and he has been told: Go, go on and on, with all liberators, with all fighters for a better tomorrow, with all destroyers of Sodoms. But never may you rest with them. The earth will burn under your feet. Pay everywhere the bloodiest costs of the process of liberation, but be unnamed in all emancipation proclamations. . . . You are the weakest and the least of the nations and you will be the last for redemption."[12]

Although it was frequently observed, sometimes by Singer himself,[13] that his literary roots lay outside the Yiddish tradition, although within the Jewish tradition, there is one important respect in which he is a continuator of the older, classic Yiddish writers, Abramovitch, Sholom Aleichem, and Peretz. Like them, he looks upon the Jews, with a rare, usually Zionist, exception as political imbeciles, incapable of recognizing either political actualities or the most fundamental human necessity—that of self- preservation. It is therefore hardly surprising that the verdict of his fiction should go clearly against those Jews who undermined first their right to exist as a people and then their right to exist at all by embracing the Socialist distinction between the Jews as a people— a reactionary and obscurantist people—and individual Jews who advertised their goodness by enlisting in the "party of humanity." The running argument in Singer's novels of modern life, over whether the hatred of Jews is increased by those Jews who retain their Yiddish and their caftan and their sidelocks or by those who assimilate themselves to the host culture by speaking Polish and shortening their jackets and their hair and their memory, was settled by history itself. The plan to eliminate Jews from the face of the earth originated in a country where Jews aped the manners and the culture and often the religion of their prospective murderers.

Singer's most ambitious Holocaust novel, *The Family Moskat*, is also his most Zionist one. The book offers a series of parallel scenes to demonstrate that neither believers nor skeptics are capable of fathoming the enormity of Jewish suffering. When, at the outbreak of World War I, the Jews are expelled from Tereshpol Minor, Rabbi Dan Katzenellenbogen, as he guides the exodus of his people, is assailed by the town freethinker and apostle of Western enlightenment, Jekuthiel the watchmaker:

> "Nu, rabbi?" he said.
> It was clear that what he meant was: Where is your Lord of the Universe now? Where are His miracles? Where is your faith in Torah and prayer?
> "Nu, Jekuthiel," the rabbi answered. What he was saying was: Where are your worldly

remedies? Where is your trust in the gentiles? What have you accomplished by aping Esau? (*FM*, 259–60)

To Jekuthiel it is inescapably clear that the Jewish God has been far less faithful to His people than they to Him; and to Rabbi Dan it is just as clear that if God cannot help the Jews, nothing can, for what salvation can come from imitating the ways of the oppressor? Both are right in what they deny, but unsupported in what they affirm. In either case, as Rabbi Dan says to himself: "The old riddle remained: the pure in heart suffered and the wicked flourished; the people chosen of God were still ground in the dust" (*FM*, 229).

If the mystery of Jewish suffering cannot be fathomed by the intellectual efforts of either the believers or the skeptics, perhaps the best response would be an existential one, in which action would cut through the knot that intellect has not been able to untie. "Get thee out of thy country" is an injunction with deep roots in Jewish consciousness, and one that sounds in the ears of several characters in *The Family Moskat*, including Asa Heshel himself, who after his first brush with antisemitism in Warsaw says to himself: "Yes, Abram is right. I've got to get out of Poland. If not to Palestine, then to some other country where there's no law against Jews going to college" (*FM*, 147).

Since Abram Shapiro, who is something of a Chassid but more of a lecher, is the most prominent spokesman for Zionism among the novel's major characters, the book can hardly be said to be a Zionist tract. Nevertheless, Zionism is distinctly set apart from socialism, communism, and other left-wing movements that arouse the wrath of the orthodox, for the very good reason that only Zionism grasped the dimensions of modern antisemitism and understood its implications for the future of the Jewish people.

Abram rails against the Jewish intellectuals who gain their university credentials by loudly proclaiming that Jews are a religion, not a nation, and that the backward, dirty Jews from the east pollute the Western European atmosphere. He insists that the Exile alone has made of the Jews the "cripples, *schlemiels*, lunatics" (*FM*, 140) who inhabit Warsaw: "Just let us be a nation in our own land and we'll show what we can do. Ah, the geniuses'll tumble out of their mothers' bellies six at a time—like in Egypt" (*FM*, 44). Abram's claim for Zionism are expressed with the hyperbole that characterizes all his utterances. Yet he sees with lucidity what is concealed, by vanity or self-interest or even good will, from the eyes of the modernizing, worldly assimilationists, who seek to become indistinguishable from the gentiles: "And I suppose if we all put on Polish hats and twist our mustaches into points, then they'll love us? . . . Read the newspapers here. They squeal that the modern Jew is worse than the caftaned kind. Who do you think the Jew-haters are aiming for? The modern Jew, that's who" (*FM*,46). All the subsequent events of the novel will bear out what Abram says.

Apart from the Orthodox Jews, the most active opponents of Zionism in the novel are the socialist and communist revolutionaries, whose devotion to "humanity" slackens only when the Jews come into view. *The Family Moskat* was the first major work by Singer in which the intensity of his dislike of leftist political movements made itself felt. It is significant that he endows an anti-leftist character named Lapidus with some of the memorable utterances of the novel even though he appears in but a single scene and has no role whatever in the action. Lapidus disturbs the smug humanitarianism of a circle of Jewish leftists by pointing out that they weep bitter tears over every oppressed nation of the world, except the Jews. He recounts an experience he had in Siberia that epitomized the self-deceptive masquerade of Jews seeking a secular substitute for the religion they had deserted: "I saw a bunch of Jews, with scrawny beards, black eyes—just like mine. At first I thought it was a minyan for prayers. But when I heard them babbling in Russian and spouting about the revolution—the S. R.'s, the S. D.'s, Plekhanov, Bogdanov, bombs, assassinations—I started to howl" (*FM*, 62).

Lapidus lashes these Jews who, in strict accordance with socialist doctrine, deny the existence of the Jews as a people. Some deep-seated impulse of treachery leads worldly Jews to deny only to the people from whom they have sprung those human rights that are indivisible from national rights. Bernard Lazare once wrote of emancipated French Jews: "It isn't enough for them to reject any solidarity with their foreign-born brethren; they have also to go charging them with all the evils which their own cowardice engenders. . . . Like all emancipated Jews everywhere, they have also of their own volition broken all ties of solidarity." Lapidus, for his part, is, like Abram, a Zionist who sees no solution to the anomaly of Jewish existence in an increasingly antisemitic Europe except "a corner of the world for our own" (*FM*, 62).

For the mature characters in *The Family Moskat*, Zionism is, as Theodor Herzl once said, "a return to the Jewish people even before it is a return to the Jewish homeland."[14] It is not accidental that Asa's first Zionist utterances in the novel come on the occasion of his return from Switzerland to Tereshpol Minor. Upon entering the synagogue, Asa is overcome by "a heavy odor that seemed . . . to be compounded of candle wax, fast days, and eternity. He stood silent. Here in the dimness everything he had experienced in alien places seemed to be without meaning. Time had flown like an illusion. This was his true home, this was where he belonged. Here was where he would come for refuge when everything else failed" (*FM*, 237). This joy in homecoming seems to depend on religion, yet when Asa tries to explain his feelings to his grandfather, what he says is that Jews are a people like every other people, and are now "demanding that the nations of the world return the Holy Land to them" (FM, 238). The conjunction of the two passages is striking. Very soon there will be no Tereshpol Minor synagogue in which to seek refuge and home when all else fails—as it does—and the Zionist contention that the Jews of Europe are building on sand will be borne out.

The entire novel is animated by a tremendous pressure toward some kind of apocalyptic resolution of the worsening condition of the Jews of Europe. Early in the book, before either of the World Wars has taken place, it seems to the orthodox that things cannot get worse than they are:

> Speakers were thundering that Jews should not wait for Messiah to come, but build the Jewish homeland with their own hands. . . . The truth was that the Jews were being persecuted more and more. Day by day it became harder to earn a living. What would be the end of it all? There was only one hope left—for Messiah to come, to come quickly while there were still a few pious Jews left. (*FM*, 166)

During World War I it seems even more certain to the orthodox that the cup must at last be full. What can be the meaning of the endless suffering of the Jews but that redemption is at hand? "Enough! It is time! High time for the Messiah!" Even the fabric of daily life is interwoven with messianic expectation, so that a woman's delivery pains provoke the remark: "Everything is attended by suffering . . . birth . . . Messiah . . . " With the approach of Hitler, even many of the pious go off to Palestine, complaining about their elders and their God: "The old generation knows only one thing: Messiah will come. God knows, he's taking his time" (*FM*, 530).

The culminating event of the novel would seem to be precisely the occasion on which Singer, if he wished, could demonstrate the convergence of catastrophe with redemption, Holocaust with rebirth in the homeland. It is the last Passover to be celebrated by the Jews of Warsaw and so recalls the great holiday occasions earlier in the novel, when the spiritually dispersed members of what had once been the community of Israel are briefly united with their people and with their best selves; but it also looks forward to the yawning emptiness of the Jewish future in Europe. So insistent is Singer on the irresistibility of Jewish fate that for this Passover celebration he goes to the trouble of recalling, from Palestine as well as America, those characters who have already emigrated, despite the fact that all the Jews still resident in Poland "were possessed of the same thought: to be helped to get out of Poland while there was still time" (*FM*, 566).

The Passover, described in great, loving detail by Singer, is the novel's most beautiful yet most terrible occasion. Not only does it summon up and reinforce the memory of past holidays; it is a holiday on which the original redemption of the Jews from bondage and deliverance to their promised land is commemorated and the hope of their imminent salvation and return to the ancestral homeland is more immediate than at any other time of the year. In a voice broken with weeping, Pinnie Moskat recites: "And it is this same promise which has been the support of our ancestors and of us, for in every generation our enemies have arisen to annihilate us, but the Most Holy, blessed be He, has delivered us out of their hands." From the point of view of Jewish religion, Hitler is only the latest repetition of the Amaleks who have plagued the Jews throughout their existence. Yet many at the seder table wonder to themselves: "Would a miracle happen this time too? In a year from now would Jews be able again to sit down and observe the Passover? Or, God forbid, would the new Haman finish them off?" (*FM*, 578).

The Passover service traditionally concludes with the exclamation "Next Year in Jerusalem!" If Singer wished to see in the qualified triumph of Zionism a kind of redemption for which the Holocaust had been a horrible price, or in the State of Israel a realization of the messianic expectations of so many of his Holocaust victims, here exactly would be the point for him to reveal his conviction. But he does nothing of the kind. Instead, he pointedly omits any mention of "Next Year in Jerusalem!" in his description of the seder and concludes with Pinnie's question: "These unleavened cakes, why do we eat them?" Even though the novel treats Zionism sympathetically, Singer will not endorse historicist views of the Holocaust as the labor pains of national rebirth or religious views of it as the price of redemption. Rather, he wants above all to convey the sense that for the Jews of Europe the end was at hand, and in a more absolute sense than any that could have been conceived by either orthodox or nationalist Jews. When Abram the Zionist tries to console the gloomy Asa by remarking that "the end of the world hasn't come yet," Asa replies that "the end of our world *has* come" (*FM*, 535). The final scene of the English version of the novel[15] allows no hint of apocalypse in this disaster, no glimpse of a redemption beyond the catastrophe.

In the deepest sense, then, the Zionists of *The Family Moskat* who flee to Palestine are as homeless, as desperate for refuge, as Herman Broder of *Enemies* in the United States. For Singer, the ultimate refuge is in the instruments of Jewish spirituality. For him, "the two thousand years of exile have not been a dark passage into nowhere but a grand experiment in upholding a people only on spiritual values. Even though we have attained the land we longed for . . . this experiment is far from being concluded."[16] At the end of *The Manor*, Calman Jacoby finds a refuge from the acrid dissolvents of Polish Jewry not in the land but in the spirit of his ancestors, as embodied in the shelves of sacred books that reunite him with past generations. "The Hebrew letters were steeped in holiness, in eternity. They seemed to unite him with the patriarchs, with Joshua, Gamaliel, Eliezer, and with Hillel the Ancient. . . . Among these shelves of sacred books, Calman felt protected."

For survivors of the Holocaust, Jewish books become not only the means of remaining human by returning into the buried life of one's ancestors; they become the instrument for the resurrection of the dead. As another character, Herman Gombiner in the story called "The Letter Writer," says: "The spirit cannot be burned, gassed, hanged, shot. Six million souls must exist somewhere." Gombiner, during an illness, goes in search of his lost relatives, and his quest leads him, via Canal Street in New York City, into an underworld charnel-house, where he meets a gravedigger tending the bones. "How," asks Herman, "can anyone live here?" "Who would want such a livelihood?" The answer, of course, is that this is where Singer chose to live.

We can see this very clearly in one of his supernatural tales called "The Last Demon." Of the many stories in which Singer uses a first-person narrator who bears marked resemblances to the author, none comes so close to representing the author's inner relationship to his own work as this one. The narrator of the tale tells of his plight as the last remaining demon, whose occupation is gone because man himself has become a demon: to proselytize for evil in these times would be carrying coals to Newcastle. Like Singer himself, the last demon has been deprived of his subject, the Jews of Eastern Europe. "I've seen it all," he says, "the destruction of Tishevitz, the destruction of Poland. There are no more Jews, no more demons. . . . The community was slaughtered, the holy books burned, the cemetery desecrated." Like Singer. the last demon attempts to speak as if history had not destroyed his subject and as if he could defy time: "I speak in the present tense as for me time stands still."[17] Like Singer, the last demon knows, or thinks he knows, that there is no judge and no judgment, and that to the generation that has indeed succeeded in becoming wholly guilty the only Messiah that will come is death: "The generation is already guilty seven times over, but Messiah does not come. To whom should he come? Messiah did not come for the Jews, so the Jews went to Messiah" (SF, 129). Like Singer, finally, the demon must sustain himself on dust and ashes and Yiddish books. "I found a Yiddish storybook between two broken barrels in the house which once belonged to Velvel the Barrelmaker. I sit there, the last of the demons. I eat dust. . . . The style of the book is . . . Sabbath pudding cooked in pig's fat: blasphemy rolled in piety. The moral of the book is: neither judge, nor judgment. But nevertheless the letters are Jewish. . . . I suck on the letters and feed myself. . . . Yes, as long as a single volume remains, I have something to sustain me" (SF, 130).

The attempt to resurrect, in Israel, the shattered remnant of Jewish life, one of the most extraordinary instances of national rebirth in history, one of the outstanding examples of Jewish defiance of history, ultimately plays but a minor part in the great body of Singer's fiction. Rather, he chooses to make of literature itself the instrument for preserving the memory, and resurrecting the souls, of the dead. The literature upon which this massive responsibility devolves is no longer a sacred one. Neither is it written in Hebrew, the traditional sacred tongue but also a tongue that, precisely because of the success of Zionism, is now "becoming more and more worldly" (Y, 27). Yet, through an ironic reversal of the traditional relationship between Hebrew and Yiddish, the language of the majority of the victims of the Holocaust becomes for Singer the loshen khoydesh, the holy tongue of the Jewish people. "The deader the language," Singer has said, "the more alive is the ghost. Ghosts love Yiddish, and, as far as I know, they all speak it. . . . I not only believe in ghosts, but also in resurrection. I am sure that millions of Yiddish-speaking corpses will rise from their graves one day, and their first question will be: Is there any new book in Yiddish read? For them Yiddish will not be dead."[18] In his literary character, which is to say in his subject and language, Singer made himself into a splendid anachronism whose spectacular literary career attempted to defy the death sentence imposed upon the Jewish people in the nineteenth century and nearly carried out in the twentieth. Nevertheless, his death in 1991 was as extraordinary an event as his life, for it marked the first time in literary history that the death of a single man brought to an end the prose fiction of a language.[19]

Notes

1. Cynthia Ozick, "Envy; or, Yiddish in America," *Commentary*, 48 (November 1969), 33. Subsequent references to this work will be cited in text as "Envy."
2. *A Treasury of Yiddish Stories*, edited by Irving Howe and Eliezer Greenberg (New York: Viking Press, 1953), 21. Subsequent references to this work will be cited in text as *TYS*.
3. Maurice Samuel, *In Praise of Yiddish* (New York: Cowles, 1971), 6. Subsequent references to this work will be cited in text.
4. Quoted by Irving Howe in "Journey of a Poet," *Commentary*, 53 (January 1972), 76.
5. *A Treasury of Yiddish Poetry*, edited by Irving Howe and Eliezer Greenberg (New York: Holt, Rinehart & Winston, 1969), 52-53. Subsequent references to this work will be cited in text as *TYP*.
6. *The Selected Poems of Jacob Glatstein*, translated by Ruth Whitman (New York: October House, 1972), 109. Subsequent references to this work will be cited in text as *JG*. Unless otherwise indicated, all translations of Glatstein are by Ruth Whitman.
7. All Zeitlin translations are by Robert Friend.
8. *The Family Moskat*, translated by A. H. Gross (New York: Farrar, Straus & Giroux, 1950), 6ll. Subsequent references to this work will be cited in text as *FM*.
9. *The Slave*, translated by I. B. Singer and Cecil Hemley (New York: Farrar, Straus & Giroux, 1962), 102-3. Subsequent references to this work will be cited in text as *Slave*.
10. *Enemies, A Love Story*, translated by Aliza Shevrin and Elizabeth Shub (New York: Farrar, Straus & Giroux, 1972). Subsequent references to this work will be cited in text as *Enemies*.
11. *Letters and Papers of Chaim Weizmann*, 2 vols., edited by Meyer Weisgal (London: Oxford University Press, 1971), II, 307.
12. *Peretz*, edited and translated by Sol Liptzin (New York: YIVO, 1947), 18.
13. Irving Howe and I. B. Singer, "Yiddish Tradition vs. Jewish Tradition: A Dialogue," *Midstream*, 19 (June/July 1973), 33-38.
14. Lucy S. Dawidowicz, *The Golden Tradition: Jewish Life and Thought in Eastern Europe* (Boston: Beacon Press, 1967), 50. Subsequent references to this work will be cited in text.

15. See Irving Saposnik, "Translating *The Family Moskat*," *Yiddish*, 1 (Fall 1973), 26–37, for a comparison between the Yiddish and English endings of the novel.
16. "Yiddish, the Language of Exile," *Judaica Book News*, (Spring/Summer 1976), 27. Subsequent references to this work will be cited in text as *Y*.
17. *Short Friday and other Stories* (New York: Farrar, Straus & Giroux, 1964), 120. Subsequent references to this work will be cited in text as *SF*.
18. See flap of paperback edition of *The Spinoza of Market Street*.
19. See Hillel Halkin, "The Last of the Great Yiddish Writers," *Jerusalem Report*, August 8, 1991, 38–39.

3

With Ancient History Why Bother?
American Jewish Writers and the Holocaust

"Your father, at the turn of the century, had three choices. One, he could have stayed in Jewish Galicia with Grandma. . . . Okay, that's number one: ashes, all of us. Number two. He could have gone to Palestine. You and Sandy would have fought the Arabs in 1948 and even if one or the other of you didn't actually get killed, somebody would have lost a finger, an arm, a foot, for sure. In 1967, I would have fought in the Six Day War, and at the least have caught a little shrapnel. Let's say in the head, losing the sight in one eye. In Lebanon your two grandchildren would have fought and, well, to be conservative, let's assume only one of them got killed. That's Palestine. The third choice he had was to come to America. Which he did. And the worst thing that can happen in America? Your grandson marries a Puerto Rican. "

—Philip Roth, *Deception*[1]

Three Choices: Europe, Palestine, America.

This "history lesson" is addressed to an American Jewish father dismayed by the prospect that his family's Jewishness, having survived the cataclysms of twentieth century history, will be finished off by intermarriage and assimilation, which in America pose a far greater threat to Jewish survival than antisemitism does. Despite its characteristically Rothian flamboyance and simplification, the scolding is essentially accurate in its vision of Jewish fate in relation to the three central, cataclysmic events of modern Jewish history: mass migrations of unprecedented magnitude from Europe to America; the violent destruction of European Jewish civilization; the reestablishment of Jewish sovereignty in the Land of Israel.

What the passage implies but does not say is that the Jews who stayed in "Jewish" Galicia (and scores of places like it) still had a culture and an inner world of their own, eventually to be erased by Nazi barbarism. The idealistic minority of European Jewry that went to Palestine in the hope of continuing Jewish culture in a new and secularized form but in the ancient land and the sacred language, found itself in perpetual struggle for survival against the onslaughts of Arab imperialism and racism, which could not accept a Jewish homeland in the midst of the Arab empire. The far larger, and far less idealistic segment of European Jewry that came to America—the golden land where millionaires were supposed to sprout like mushrooms—found a comfort and safety undreamt of by their Palestinian (later Israeli) cousins, but purchased at the heavy price of erosion of Jewish life. (Golda Meir, the transplanted Milwaukeean who became Israel's prime minister, used to say to her American friends who commiserated with her in time of war that she might worry about whether her grandson would be safe but not about whether he would be Jewish.)

Postwar Jewish Satirists

Prior to the Holocaust, the immigrant experience was central in American Jewish wrting, providing both the emotional and linguistic conflicts that excited the imagination of such writers as Delmore Schwartz, Henry Roth, Tillie Olsen. Irving Howe has argued that even in writers who deal with the experience of second-generation Jews, "what comes through . . . is the continued power of origins, the ineradicable stamp of New York or Chicago slums, even upon grandsons and granddaughters who may never have lived in or seen them."[2] The bountifulness of the immigrant material might have been one reason (among many) why American Jewish writers were very slow in turning to the subject of the Holocaust.

As late as 1974 the novelist Norma Rosen could report that she had been invited to a conference on Holocaust writing because—so she was told by its organizers—"I was one of the very few American fiction writers to have treated the subject." Most Jewish writers after the war were either still "drawing interest on money that an earlier time had put into our cultural bank" or else satirizing the smug prosperity of the suburban Jew, "very much at home out of Zion, having abandoned Jewish learning for himself and his children."[3]

But if the Holocaust is, as she says, "the central occurrence of the Twentieth century" (Rosen, 57), why had the American Jewish writers, by and large, omitted it from their work? They had neither treated it directly nor allowed it to impinge on their treatment of Jews. Rosen, far from chastising her colleagues for this great avoidance, held out the possibility of "authentic" reasons for it. Perhaps their lives really were shaken by the Holocaust, but they did not know how "the virtues of fiction—indirection, irony, ambivalence—[could] be used to make art out of the unspeakable occurrence." They also—so she charitably speculated—feared making bad art out of the Holocaust and even more making good art, because "it was not yet the right time for transcendence" (Rosen, 57). Perhaps Norma Rosen was too generous in proffering this *apologia*. The fear of American Jewish writers that, should it prove impossible to merge the Holocaust indiscriminately with "man's inhumanity to man," they would shut themselves out from Melville's ideal of "genius that all around the world stands hand in hand" (Rosen, 58) may have been the literary analogue of the fear of the American Jewish community, during the Second World War, to make itself heard demanding the rescue of European Jewry. The official slogan of the American government had been "Rescue through Victory," even though almost everybody knew (certainly by late 1942) that when Allied victory came, very few Jews would remain to be rescued. The official policy was even worse than the official slogan. As David Wyman puts it, in his authoritative book *The Abandonment of the Jews: America and the Holocaust, 1941–45*, "the basic policy was not rescue but avoidance of rescue."[4] By refusing to admit Jewish refugees to America or to oppose Britain's bar upon their entry to Palestine, and then by refusing to bomb Auschwitz or the rail lines leading to it, Roosevelt seemed to be largely indifferent to the Jewish catastrophe. Yet at the very time that he was abandoning hundreds of thousands of European Jews to their terrible fate, Roosevelt could rely on American Jews as his most fervent, uncritical, and reliable supporters. Was not his New Deal the next best thing to socialism, after all?

The postwar Jewish satirists who pilloried nearly every American Jewish malady—suffocating maternal affection, suburban vulgarity, materialism, religious illiteracy—studiously refrained from moral satire of the American Jews' abrogation of responsibility for their helpless European brethren during their hour of utmost need. "Satirist, heal thyself!" often rises to one's lips in reading these satirists.

An exception that, it might be argued, tests the rule is Saul Bellow's 1944 novel *Dangling Man*. Its hero Joseph, awaiting induction into the army, dreams that he is in a low chamber surrounded by rows of murdered people, one of whom he has been charged with identifying and reclaiming. His charnel house guide reads from an identity tag a place name which reminds Joseph that "in Bucharest . . . those slain by the Iron Guard were slung from hooks in a slaughterhouse. I have seen the pictures." In horror, he jumps back "in the clear," and claims that "I was not personally acquainted with the deceased. I had merely been asked, as an outsider." Why, he wonders, have he and his friends so easily accustomed themselves to the slaughter in Europe? Why have they so little pity for the victims? Even as he ventures a reply, he sees that it is rather too kind to himself: "I do not like to think what we are governed by. . . . It is not easy work, and it is not safe. Its *kindest* revelation is that our senses and our imaginations are somehow incompetent."[5]

It is not until the late 1950s that we find Jewish satirists turning their special talents to the subject of how the Holocaust influenced (or failed to influence) the lives of American Jews. The protagonist of Bernard Malamud's 1958 story, "The Lady of the Lake," comes into a small inheritance and decides to go abroad "seeking romance."[6] In the States, where "a man's past was . . . expendable" (*MB*,126), he was Henry Levin, but once in Europe Levin takes to calling himself Henry Freeman, thereby symbolically severing his Jewish ties. Meeting an attractive Italian girl named Isabella, he identifies himself as an American but conceals his Jewish identity. He wonders, since "he absolutely did not look Jewish," why she should ask the question of him, but quickly dismisses it as a quirk. "With ancient history why bother?" (*MB*, 115). One of her attractions, to be sure, is precisely a face that carries "the mark of history," that is, of "civilized," Italian history (*MB*, 113). But at the crucial moment, when he comes to propose marriage to Isabella, she reveals her breasts, on whose "softened tender flesh" he recognizes the tattooed blue numbers of the concentration-camp inmate that show her

Jewish identity. "I can't marry you. We are Jews. My past is meaningful to me. I treasure what I suffered for" (*MB*,132). Levin-Freeman discovers the emptiness of his freedom and, having deprived himself by his deception of what he most desired, can only stammer, "Listen, I-I am—" (*MB*,133). Before he can supply the missing label, however, Isabella disappears into the night. The implied verdict of the tale is that, in the aftermath of the Holocaust, the Diaspora of freedom proves empty. Neither being an American nor just "being" will give the American Jew what he desires; happiness unalloyed with suffering is now out of reach.

In 1959 Philip Roth placed "Eli, the Fanatic" as the final story in the collection called *Goodbye, Columbus*. Here we can already see Roth adumbrating the three paths of Jewish destiny defined in the epigraph to this chapter: Europe, Israel, America. The story also shows Roth beginning to use the motif of clothing to suggest his favorite themes of the double, the counterlife, impersonation, the path that might have been, but was not, taken: "there but for the grace of my grandparents," so to speak.

Although Israel is not mentioned in the story, Alan Berger's sharp eye[7] has noticed that the hero's son is born on May 15, 1948, the date of Israel's proclamation of statehood, obliquely referred to as "scribblings on bits of paper [that] had made history this past week."[8] Neither is the Holocaust dealt with directly, or even placed at the center of the story. Nevertheless Roth gives it sufficient symbolic weight to imply a standard by which to measure the debasement of Jewish life in America (a standard Roth rarely supplied in his early work).

The tale turns on the effort of a group of assimilated Jews in Woodenton to evict from their happily integrated, "progressive suburban community" (*GC*,261) a newly established yeshiva composed of Holocaust survivors, two adults (the headmaster and a black-coated Chassid) and eighteen children. (In Hebrew, eighteen is rendered as *Chai*, which is also the word for life.) In showing how fearful are the Jews that their Protestant neighbors will associate them with Jews who have failed to shorten their hair and their coats and their ancestral memories, Roth draws upon the immigrant material that had long nourished American Jewish writing. The nervousness of "old" German-Jewish immigrants about the uncouth manners and progressive politics of their recently arrived cousins from the east was an old theme. Roth gives it a new twist by adding to the taints of odd clothing, alien tongue, and genuine religious beliefs something yet more scandalous and disturbing.

The Jewish community's lawyer and the story's protagonist, Eli Peck, thinks that he can work out a compromise that will allow the yeshiva to remain because he believes that "what most disturbs my neighbors are the visits to town [the yeshiva is on a hill overlooking it] by the gentleman in the black hat, suit, etc." The long black coat and wide-brimmed hat strike Eli as precisely the "extreme practices" that led to the "persecution of the Jewish people" (*GC*, 262) in Europe. That is to say, antisemitism is caused by Jews, not antisemites—an argument of wide and enduring popularity.*

Eli pleads for sympathetic understanding of young Jews who might suffer shame if their gentile neighbors linked them with troglodyte ancestors who had stumbled from the Middle Ages into the twentieth century. But for the headmaster Leo Tzuref, as for all observant Jews, this is not the twentieth century at all: "For me the Fifty-eighth. . . . That is too old for shame." (*GC*, 266) In any case, "the suit the gentleman wears is all he's got" (*GC*, 263). It is with difficulty that he tries to convey the totality of loss to an American Jew cut off from history:

> *Nothing.* You have that word in English. *Nicht. Gornisht?*. . . A mother and a father? . . . No. A wife? No. A baby? A little ten-month-old baby? No! A village full of friends? A synagogue where you knew the feel of every seat under your pants? Where with your eyes closed you could smell the cloth of the torah? . . . And a medical experiment they performed on him yet! That leaves nothing, Mr. Peck. Absolutely nothing! (*GC*, 264)

The erasure of European Jewish civilization really *is* a revelation to these American Jewish believers in life, liberty, and—this above all—the pursuit of happiness. "No news reached Woodenton?" Tzuref asks; and he gets no reply.

When the frustrated Peck invokes the majesty of the law—not, of course, the law given at Sinai, but Woodenton's zoning ordinances, Tzuref angrily responds, "Stop with the law! You have the word suffer. Then try it. It's a little thing" (*GC*, 265). Into the midst of satire, Roth injects the idea that it is not the pursuit of happiness (a Woodentonian obsession) but a community of suffering that is the basis of ethical values. It is to this community of suffering that Eli is drawn as he exchanges clothes with the chassid and then goes out of his way to parade his

---

* One of its notable recent resurrections was in 1991 in the Crown Heights section of Brooklyn in the wake of what Mayor David Dinkins called "a lynching" and others a "pogrom" by blacks against these same black-coated Chassidim.

retailored (and perhaps reborn) second self on the streets of Woodenton, partly in order (to) *épater les Juifs.*

Since he has a history of nervous breakdowns, and since his friend Heller is convinced that all religious Jews are Abrahams keen to sacrifice any available Isaac, Eli is dragged away from his newborn child by hospital attendants armed with tranquilizers: "The drug calmed his soul, but did not touch it down where the blackness had reached" (*GC*, 298). Eli's "revelation" does in a way drive him mad, but he is so convinced of the authenticity of suffering that he will pass it on to his child. Not only does he refuse pleas to remove his black outfit, "He'd make the kid wear it! Sure! Cut it down when the time came. A smelly hand-me down, whether the kid liked it or not!" It is almost as though, in the very moment that he extends his sympathy to the American Jew who rejects the false community of hedonists for the true community of sufferers, Roth mischievously plants the seeds of future material for satire—satire, that is, of Jews who live on borrowed experience, who place at the center of their lives a Holocaust suffering and death they did not share. Even within the boundaries of the story, it is clear that Eli can hardly, at the very moment that he revels in fatherhood, be the double of a man deprived of the child he had and of the capacity to create another.

The Americanization of Anne Frank

If the residents of Woodenton had not been made aware of the Holocaust by the invasion of the yeshiva or the spectacular "conversion" of their own representative into a "fanatic" in 1948, they would probably not have received any immediate impressions of it until 1955, a full thirteen years after information about the "final solution" had become widely available in the press[9] and a decade after the end of the war. In that year, *The Diary of Anne Frank*, first published in Dutch in 1946 and then in English translation in 1952, reached a mass audience when it was brought to the stage, Americanized, in the Frances Goodrich-Albert Hackett "adaptation" of the book.

When the diary appeared as *Het Achterhuis* in Holland, its first reviewer, Jan Romein, professor of Dutch history at the University of Amsterdam, praised the book for its qualities of mind, spirit, and courage, but not for enabling readers to "transcend" the suffering of Anne Frank and of millions like her.

> The way she died is unimportant. More important is that this young life was willfully cut off by a system of irrational cruelty. We had sworn to each other never to forget or forgive this system as long as it was still raging, but now that it is gone, we too easily forgive, or at least forget, which ultimately means the same thing.

But, as Alvin Rosenfeld has demonstrated in a stunning essay on the popularization of Anne Frank,[10] American literary culture overlooked any such sombre suggestions arising from the text of the diary, and then obliterated them in the stage and movie versions. Meyer Levin (later to wage a strident campaign against "universalizing" distorters of the diary) not only said little of the book's Jewish character in his front page review in the *New York Times Book Review* but praised it as a "virtually perfect drama of puberty," to be read "over and over for insight and enjoyment" because it "simply bubbles with amusement, love, and discovery."[11] A still more treacly description of the book was peddled by Alfred Kazin and Anne Birstein in their introductory essay to *The Works of Anne Frank* (1959). On the basis of exactly nothing, they blithely speculated that "Perhaps when she went to bed on the night of August 3, 1944 [the night before the Frank family was arrested and deported] her last thought was of her own blessedness: her youth, her strength, her love for all the people and the growing things around her, her closeness to God, who had provided them."[12] (This is the same Alfred Kazin who scorned Lionel Trilling for failing to connect the life of the mind with "the gas.")

Even today, one wonders: can this be the Anne Frank who wrote the following diary entries? "In the evenings when it's dark, I often see rows of good, innocent people accompanied by crying children, walking on and on, in charge of a couple of these chaps, bullied and knocked about until they almost drop. No one is spared—old people, babies, expectant mothers, the sick—each and all join in the march of death" (November 19, 1942).[13] "If it is as bad as this in Holland whatever will it be like in the distant and barbarous regions [the Jews] are sent to? We assume that most of them are murdered. The English radio speaks of their being gassed" (October 9, 1942 [*AF*, 50]). "All civilized languages are permitted [in their "secret annexe"], therefore no German!" (November 17, 1942 [*AF*, 63]). "Nice people, the Germans! To think that I was once one of them too! No, Hitler took away our nationality long ago. In fact, Germans and Jews are the greatest enemies in the world" (October 9, 1942 [*AF*, 51]).

If Levin, Kazin (and many others) somehow interpreted this as "[bubbling] with amusement" and expressing "love for all the people . . .

around her," Goodman and Hackett simply edited out all of Anne's nasty talk about hatred, enmity, suffering, and murder—to say nothing of less than friendly feelings between Germans and Jews. "In essence," writes Rosenfeld, "the two authors recreated Anne Frank as a triumphant figure, one characterized by such irrepressible hope and tenacious optimism as to overcome any final sense of a cruel end" (Rosenfeld, 251–52). They lifted Anne's assertion that "in spite of everything I still believe that people are really good at heart" from its relative obscurity in the diary to make it the keynote of the play, a climactic benediction allowing the audience to leave the theater with a warm inner glow of happiness. They too knew what the Woodentonians traveling in from the suburbs for an evening's entertainment wanted. Walter Kerr, reviewing the play for the *Herald Tribune*, was most impressed by Anne's "careless gaiety," a proof to him that "Anne is not going to her death,"[14] a proof, that is, of what is perfectly false. (Even things that are true, Oscar Wilde once said, can be proved.) However extreme Bruno Bettelheim might have been in his harsh criticism of the Frank family for carrying on business as usual (instead of taking up arms, for example) he was surely right in his acrid analysis of the real reason for the play's huge popular success: "There is good reason why the enormously successful play ends with Anne stating her belief in the good in all men. . . . If all men are basically good . . . then indeed we can all go on with life as usual and forget about Auschwitz. . . . [Anne Frank's story] found wide acclaim because . . . it denies implicitly that Auschwitz ever existed. If all men are good, there was never an Auschwitz."[15] If there was, then Anne's indomitable spirit proved, in the words spoken by the Goodrich-Hackett travesty of Otto Frank, Anne's father, that a person "could be happy in a concentration camp" (Rosenfeld, 258).

The playwrights also thought that, in order to make Anne Frank's story conducive to the greatest happiness of the greatest number, she had to be stripped, as far as possible, of her specific Jewish identity. In the diary she is seriously engaged in trying to understand the tortured, paradoxical relation between the Jews having been chosen by God for exaltation and by history for degradation. Thus, on April 11, 1944 she writes:

> Who has inflicted this upon us? Who has made us Jews different from all other people? Who has allowed us to suffer so terribly up till now? It is God that has made us as we are, but it will be God, too, who will raise us up again. If we bear all this suffering and if there are still Jews left, when it is over, then Jews, instead of being doomed, will be held up as an example. Who knows, it might even be our religion from which

the world and all peoples learn good, and for that reason and that reason only do we have to suffer now. We can never become just Netherlanders, or just English, or representatives of any country for that matter, we will always remain Jews, but we want to, too. (*AF*, 221)

This passage, Anne's anticipation of some great, specifically Jewish, affirmation of life in the face of death, was expunged by Goodrich and Hackett, who substituted the following piece of "universalist" flummery, lacking any basis in the diary. "We're not the only people that've had to suffer. There've always been people that've had to . . . sometimes one race . . . sometimes another."[16] Anne's awareness of the distinctiveness of the Jewish catastrophe in the Holocaust and of the fact that Jews alone were singled out for total destruction, is blotted out and the Nazi murder of European Jewry, a crime of terrifying clarity, becomes an indiscriminate part of man's inhumanity to man.

The Ghost Writer, by Philip Roth

The disparity between Anne Frank's diary and the stage travesty of it that enraptured American audiences is alluded to with ironic understatement in Philip Roth's *The Ghost Writer* (1979)[17] in which he returned to the subject of the Holocaust over two decades after "Eli, the Fanatic." In fact, the hero of *The Ghost Writer* is precisely (or as precisely as can be in imaginative writing) Roth at the time he wrote that story. "I was twenty-three," says the narrator (the mature Nathan Zuckerman, Roth's *persona*), "writing and publishing my first short stories" (*GW*,3). One of his stories, not yet published, has given particular offense to his father, who sees in it a treacherous defamation of all Jewry and desperately asks a local eminence of Jewish Newark, Judge Leopold Wapter, to try to straighten out the wayward Nathan. The judge asks Nathan ten questions about himself and his story. Among them are: "What in your character makes you associate so much of life's ugliness with Jewish people?" and "Can you honestly say that there is anything in your short story that would not warm the heart of a Julius Streicher or Joseph Goebbels?"(*GW*, 103–04). But, along with the accusatory questions, the judge recommends a nostrum for Nathan's ailments: "If you have not yet seen the Broadway production of *The Diary of Anne Frank*, I strongly advise that you do so. Mrs. Wapter and I were in the audience on opening night; we wish that Nathan Zuckerman could have been with us to benefit from that unforgettable experience." Later we learn that Nathan "didn't see it. I read the book"(*GW*,107).

Although the judge does not explicitly recommend the diary as an example of how a Jewish *writer* can serve her people, his letter forces Nathan to think about Anne not only as (what she has certainly become) the most famous child of this century, but also as "of all the Jewish writers, from Franz Kafka to E. I. Lonoff, . . . the most famous." (*GW*, 152) This is the view of Amy Bellette, the main character (in a way) of *The Ghost Writer*. In the third chapter of the novel, "Femme Fatale," Nathan Zuckerman spends a sleepless night in the Massachusetts home of E. I. Lonoff, an older, modernist writer whom he (outwardly at least) reveres. He imagines that young Amy Bellette,* who may be Lonoff's mistress, is really Anne Frank. In this fiction within the fiction, Amy, after seeing *The Diary of Anne Frank* at the Cort Theatre, decides to tell her beloved Lonoff that she, the 26-year-old woman, is really Anne Frank.

Having survived Auschwitz, so her story goes, she was rescued by the British army from Belsen as the S.S. surrendered, then brought to England as a refugee. She changed her name in order to forget her past life, and not to hide her identity, for nobody yet knew of Anne Frank. She remembers being appalled by an English teacher who, after prying from Amy some recollections of the concentration camps, first wept and then asked "Why is it that for centuries people have hated you Jews?" Amy replied, quite properly, "Don't ask me that!—ask the madmen who hate us! " (*GW*,131). She then decided she had "had about enough of the snooty brand of sympathy the pure-bred English teachers offered at school" (*GW*,131), and took herself off to America. After ordering it from Amsterdam, Amy gets to read her own diary, and goes through a series of shifting feelings about it.

When she had written, in her diary entry for May 1944, that her "greatest wish is to become a journalist someday and later on a famous writer," (*GW*, 138) she could not imagine the circumstances that would make the diary itself the instrument of her fame. At first, she tells Lonoff, she thought the usefulness of her book depended on the (supposed) fact that she had not been merely hiding from the Nazis but had been

---

* Her first name, in Zuckerman's dream-vision, comes from *Little Women*, the surname from what her British nurses call her, "Little Beauty." But if the first name is read as a Hebrew word, its meaning is "my people." Bellette, of course, asks to be read as *belles-lettres*.

murdered by them. Here Zuckerman feels called upon to explain that the Frank family, with the exception of sister Margot, who hoped to emigrate to Palestine, had not (in his view) been very Jewish at all:

> once a year the Franks sang a harmless Chanukah song, said some Hebrew words, lighted some candles, exchanged some presents—a ceremony lasting ten minutes— and that was all it took to make them the enemy. It did not even take that much. And that was the truth. . . . Europe was not theirs nor were they Europe's, not even her Europeanized family. . . . This was the lesson that . . . she came to believe she had the power to teach. But only if she were believed to be dead. . . . Dead she had something more to offer than amusement for ages 10-15; dead she had written, without meaning or trying to, a book with the force of a masterpiece to make people finally see. (*GW*,144-46)

Soon, however, recognizing (quite rightly, in fact) that what would "happen" when people had "seen" was precisely "nothing," she decides that her diary's only mission was to memorialize the dead—her family and friends—in print, "for all the good that would do them." From this recognition of futility, she lurches to the impulse for vengeance: "an ax was what she really wanted, not print." Yet even this temptation quickly evaporates: "once she had it in her hands, whose head would she split open?" (*GW*, 182-83). She then seems to content herself with the knowledge that the world needs her forgiveness. "I was the incarnation of the millions of unlived years robbed from the murdered Jews. It was too late to be alive now. I was a saint"* (*GW*, 150).

In all of these shifting perspectives (and more is to come in the deflating revelation that Amy will keep Anne Frank dead so that she can seduce Lonoff), Roth is exploring not only the real meaning of Anne Frank's story, but the writer's relation to the Holocaust. If Amy Bellette is impersonating Anne Frank, then Nathan Zuckerman is impersonating Amy Bellette—as Anne Frank. In the shrewdest essay that has been written on Roth's artist figures, Donald Kartiganer asserts that "Zuckerman makes the central character in his story that Jewish writer whose credentials are indeed impeccable—what could please his father, or Judge Wapter, more?—but he has chosen to impersonate her through the

---

* In Latin America some organs of the Catholic church have suggested the suitability of Anne Frank for sainthood. Educational publications of the church in Argentina began in 1975 subtly to link Anne's fate with that of Catholic martyrs over the centuries, without bothering to mention either that she was Jewish or that the death she suffered was part of a vast operation of murder aimed at Jews. See, on this topic, Nissim Elnecave, "Por que la Iglesia esta especulando con los martires Judios para sanctifarlos como Catolicos?" *La Luz*, (20 July 1979), 12-15.

medium of another impersonator who is either crazy or wholly un-scrupulous."[18] Amy-Anne conceals herself (i.e., the fact that she is still alive) from her father, Otto Frank, as Zuckerman-Roth conceals himself from his father, ostensibly for the benefit of art—"the loving father who must be relinquished for the sake of his child's art was not hers; he was mine" (*GW*, 207)—but perhaps ultimately for the benefit of the Jews.

In the novel's final chapter, Nathan has awakened from his dream-vision, but its attendant fiction lingers with him as daydream, in which he outgrows his (Rothian) desire to *épater les Juifs* yet again and sees himself telling his parents he is engaged to marry a Jewish girl—Anne Frank, no less. How, in that case, could the Jewish writer, Zuckerman (or Philip Roth), be indicted for betraying his own people in his fiction? But Amy Bellette will not own up to being Anne Frank, and admits to no more than having "looked at" (*GW*,169) the diary, whose literary virtues Zuckerman extols to her. Unable to lift Anne from her sacred book and make her a character in "real" life, Zuckerman is left with a fiction (the "Femme Fatale" of chapter 3) that, far from exonerating him from the Jewish community's accusations, would make him guilty of a desecration more vile than the unpublished story they had read.

The "marriage" to Anne Frank remains metaphorical at the novel's end. Zuckerman as ghost writer binds himself to the most famous Jewish ghost writer of all, Anne Frank, the silenced diarist who, posthumously, restores a voice to the silenced millions of Jews. Anne was herself, Zuckerman now believes, dreamed into existence by Franz Kafka. "Kafka's garrets and closets, the hidden attics where they hand down the indictments, the camouflaged doors— everything he dreamed in Prague was, to her, real Amsterdam life. What he invented, she suffered" (*GW*,170). But can Roth retrospectively reinvent what she suffered? Is *The Ghost Writer* "about" the Holocaust or merely about Philip Roth's quarrel with the Jewish community over whether a writer should be a spokesman for his people? Has Roth compounded the moral immodesty of impersonating Anne Frank with the artistic immodesty of linking himself to Franz Kafka? Has he grappled with what Malamud's narrator called "ancient history" or merely with his "per-sonal" relation to the Holocaust?

Cynthia Ozick

Four years before Roth sought to resurrect Anne Frank in his nearly blasphemous elegy, Cynthia Ozick, in a foreword to the selected poems[19] of Gertrud Kolmar, a reclusive German Jewish poet murdered in Auschwitz in 1943, had also imagined a resurrection:

> A dream of reversal, of reconstruction: who has not, in the forty years since the European devastation, swum off into this dream? As if the reel of history . . . could be run backward: these mounds of ash, shoes, teeth, bones, all lifted up, healed, flown speck after speck toward connection, toward flowering, grain on grain, bone on bone, every skull blooming into the quickness of a human face, every twisted shoe renewed on a vivid foot, every dry bone given again to greening life. Ezekiel's vision in the valley of bones. . . . Who rises up, what? Populations; a people; a civilization. And everything unmade, undone, unwritten, unread. . . . Unwritten alphabets clog the breath of this dream like so many black hosts of random grit—letters still inchoate, not yet armied into poems, novels, philosophies. Torrents of black letters fill the sky of this imagining like a lost smoke. And singular voices, lost. (*AA*, 230)

The most famous voice actually to have come up out of the grave was, of course, Anne Frank's. But it was a voice never allowed to mature into its full range. "What," wonders Ozick, "would the mature Anne Frank's novels—she *would* have become a novelist—have turned out to be?" (*AA*,231).

In her 1975 essay on Bruno Schulz, another writer murdered by the Nazis, and most of whose work (though it did just barely survive) still remained inaccessible to American readers, she urged that we "think of what our notion of the literature of the Dark Continent of Europe would be like if we had read our way so late into the century without . . . *Red Cavalry*, or . . . 'Gimpel the Fool,' or . . . *The Metamorphosis*" (*AA*, 225). This hypothetical question epitomizes the conviction, which permeates Ozick's work, that what distinguished the Jewish tragedy was the loss not only of vast numbers of lives; it was the loss, probably irreparable, of a culture and a civilization. In criticizing William Styron for choosing a non-Jew as the central emblem of Nazi genocidal policy, Ozick has explained that her point is not that Jews suffered more than anyone else in the camps, or in greater numbers (even though they did make up the vast majority of the Auschwitz inmates). Rather, it is that European Jewish civilization was blotted out. "Catholic Poland, for instance (language, culture, land), continues, while European Jewish civilization (language, culture, institutions) was wiped out utterly—and that, for Jewish history, is the different and still more terrible central meaning of Auschwitz. It is, in fact, what defines the Holocaust."[20]

In her short story of 1969, "Envy; or, Yiddish in America," the obliteration of Yiddish, which had for a thousand years been a major language of Jewish creativity, epitomizes the Holocaust, the end of the old Jewish world. One of the story's protagonists, quixotically devoted to perpetuating Yiddish language and literature in America, declares his ambition: "In Talmud if you save a single life it's as if you saved the world. And if you save a language? Worlds maybe. Galaxies. The whole universe" ("Envy," 47). Compared with this, how trivial to him are the ambitions of "so-called Amer.-Jewish writers . . . boys and girls such as (not alphabetical) Roth Philip/Rosen Norma/Melammed Bernie/Friedman B. J./Paley Grace/Bellow Saul/Mailer Norman" ("Envy," 37).

Some of that quixotic passion to recover what appears lost is evident in Ozick's novel of 1987, *The Messiah of Stockholm*. The book's hero, Lars Andemening, orphaned in Poland in World War II and brought up in Sweden, believes he is the son of Bruno Schulz, who had been murdered by the Nazis before his major work, *The Messiah*, could come to light. Andemening devotes himself to research into his supposed father, hoping thereby to rescue from oblivion some of the writings of the murdered of Eastern Europe: "Rescue was the only thought he kept in his head—he was arrogant about it, he was steady, he wanted to salvage every scrap of paper all over Europe. Europe's savior! His head was full of Europe—all those obscure languages in all those shadowy places where there had been all those shootings—in the streets, in the forests."[21]

In this passion for rescue, Andemening is Ozick's surrogate. The book is pointedly dedicated to Philip Roth, apparently for two reasons. As general editor of Penguin's Writers from the Other Europe series, he had himself rescued Schulz, considered by many to have been Poland's leading writer between the two world wars, for American readers. But Ozick was also, it seems likely, expressing gratified recognition of the changed attitude towards Jewish tragedy and Jewish fate evinced in Roth's "Israeli" novel of the previous year, *The Counterlife*. Roth had, in that novel, come (like Ozick herself) to recognize that what an American Jewish writer might aspire to do by himself was being attempted on a much larger scale by the State of Israel.

The energy and courage with which Ozick has come to the defense of the State of Israel against the ideological aggression of anti-Zionism are fueled by her belief that Israel, more than being a haven for Jews in flight from persecution, is the effort to restore Jewish civilization. In 1983 she argued that much of Europe's growing fury at the state of Israel arose from the Europeans' sense that the Jews had reneged on the Napoleonic bargain, according to which they would pay for toleration as citizens by surrendering their distinct identity as Jews. So long as the Europeans believed— mistakenly—that Israel was essentially a haven for the shattered remnants of the Holocaust, she could be tolerated, even welcomed (when this did not impede good relations with the oil-producing Arab nations). But now that they have begun to recognize "that a more fundamental program is in hand, and that what the founding of Israel represents is . . . a declaration of the renewal of an entire civilization . . . the heirs of Napoleon detect insolence. The Jews are escaping from their normal condition and place into the transcendence of full national expression—a privilege owed to all peoples but the Jews" (*MM*, 232).

According to Ozick's conception of Jewish history, enlightenment and emancipation narrowed the inner world of Jews. Before they gained political emancipation in the nineteenth century, Jews lived in a confined, segregated society. But the Jewish *mind* was not confined; on the contrary, through "the all-inclusive reach and memory of Talmud," it ranged widely, from ethics to hygiene and law. She knows that many Jewish writers in whatever language they use—and this includes Hebrew— choose to pass into the majority civilization, severing their Jewish tie. All the while they delude themselves that they are choosing largeness over narrowness when in fact they are doing just the opposite: taking "the trodden path and the greased pole" (*MM*, 232, 237).

If even writers in Tel Aviv and Jerusalem can make themselves intellectually into Hebrew-speaking (and writing) gentiles, how much stronger the temptation to escape Jewish history and avert one's eyes from Jewish fate in the various corners of the Exile:

> . . . nothing is less original, by now, than, say, Parisian or New York novelists "of Jewish extraction" who write as if they had never heard of a Jewish idea, especially if, as is likely, they never have. "Be a man abroad and a Jew at home" is finally truncated to "Be a man abroad"—and of these there are a hundred thousand and more, all alike, all purged of Jewish understanding. . . . By now, for writers to throw themselves entirely into the arms of post-Enlightenment culture is no alternative at all. It is a laziness. It is the final shudder of spent thought, out of which no literature, Jewish or otherwise, can hope to spring. (*MM*, 234)

The Holocaust . . . and Me: Literary Latecomers

But even writers who never heard of a Jewish idea had, by the 1980s, heard about the Holocaust. What even the sharp-eyed Ozick could not foresee was that the Holocaust might come to serve as a kind of false Jewish consciousness for writers who knew nothing of the Jewish past *except* the Holocaust (and therefore could not truly know even that). The "personal impressions" of literary latecomers to the subject have been conveniently, if shamelessly, displayed in *Testimony: Contemporary Writers Make the Holocaust Personal*, edited by David Rosenberg.[22]

The egregious title of this very large book pretentiously appropriates an idea that has acquired historical and moral resonance for Jews. The book is lavishly illustrated, on dust jacket, title page, and chapter openers, with details from *Curtain for the Torah Ark* (Italy, 1643–44). The Torah ark curtain proclaims that this testimony has an almost sacred quality, intended to call to mind Exodus 25:16: "And thou shalt put into the ark the testimony which I shall give thee."

But what we actually find in this 500-page monument to egoism is (with a few exceptions) much closer to the profane than to the sacred, much more akin to the advertiser who offers "to personalize your paper towels" than to the moral heroism of which Hannah Arendt wrote when she referred to the testimony of "one man [who] will always be left alive to tell the story." The common reader's most frequent reaction to the responses given by Rosenberg's twenty-seven contributors to his questions about how their lives and writing careers have been shaped by the Holocaust will be: "Who cares?" Who cares about the failed marriages of Anne Roiphe or Alfred Kazin, or the Ashanti circumcision of Leslie Fiedler's grandson? Who cares that Leonard Michaels' "life was a mess" (*T*, 11) when he heard Arendt give a lecture, or that Daphne Merkin was hospitalized at age eight for psychiatric observation because she thought of her father (a German Jew) as "a Nazi manqué" (*T*, 18), and of her mother as Ilse Koch? Who cares that "God became the God of the Holocaust" for Anne Roiphe in "the year of my puberty" (*T*, 135), or that she thinks she married a non-Jew because of the Holocaust? Who cares that Fiedler resents people who wrongly assume that he is a Jew?

Worse still than the mawkish, self-pitying, licentious equations between their Lilliputian "personal" disturbances and the torture and murder of European Jewry are the "ideas" of these literary scribblers. Here ignorance and arrogance are in full flower. Most exploded fictions about the Holocaust—ranging from the notion that not only Jews but also Poles, Communists, and homosexuals were chosen by the Nazis for total annihilation, to the imbecile description (by Phillip Lopate) of the majority of the Jewish victims as "religious peasants" (*T*, 293) to the tale about body fat being reduced into soap—are dredged up repeatedly, apparently to the satisfaction of the book's editor. Contempt for Israel is rife among these writers, and, despite the fact that Israel is the only country in the world whose neighbors (with the relatively recent exception of Egypt) have for forty-five years denied her right to exist, many of Rosenberg's testifiers see another Holocaust in prospect for virtually every group except the Jews. Several "worry" about Latin America or the omnipresent "Palestinians"; and E. M. Broner's uncurbed benevolence embraces nothing less than "the earth . . . in mortal danger" (*T*, 279). Conjectural speculation about how Zionism *might* "grow into a fanatical passion" (thus Geoffrey Hartman [*T*, 431]) like the nationalism that laid waste European Jewry is more in evidence than simple respect for the Jews who actually died. One hopes that Daphne Merkin's tongue will cling to the roof of her mouth next time she wants to allude to "overweight Jewish women standing before open pits, covering their pubes with their hands" (*T*, 18).

Rosenberg reports that the working title for *Testimony* was "Sheltered Lives." Alan Lelchuk, in one of the few good essays in the book, modestly explains what this means: "Over here, in America, a small Jewish boy was following the Dodgers and listening to 'The Shadow' and 'The Green Hornet' and playing boxball on the sidewalk, while, over there, in Europe, the game was the killing of Jews. Such was history" (*T*, 254). The book's most riveting (and learned) essay, by Susanne Schlotelburg, rejects *Testimony's* premise, arguing that "to ensure remembrance the Holocaust would have to be made transpersonal rather than personal," and that those who are not bound by *akedah* or *brith* are no more likely to remember the Holocaust than the Crusades (*T*, 353). Most of the book's contributors, however, remain just as sheltered from the Holocaust now as their predecessors (and sometimes they themselves) were in the 1940s. Thus Leslie Fiedler, like some curious insect preserved in amber from the pre-Holocaust (or pre-Dreyfus) period, holds forth about how his "love of all humanity, including whose who have long persecuted us," leads him to urge Jews "to cease to exist in their chosenness for the sake of a united mankind" (*T*, 229). It never occurs to Fiedler that, as Emil Fackenheim has written, after the Holocaust a commitment to Jewish survival is precisely "a testimony to life against death *on behalf of all mankind.*"[23]

Outdoing even Fiedler in his mercifulness toward "those who have long persecuted us" and (no easy task) far outdoing all other contributors in the gross, the flagrant, the blatant, is the tooth-baring Phillip Lopate. Lopate seethes with hatred and rage—not against the Nazis (in fact, he speculates on the "youthful idealism" of the S.S. and praises Reagan's laying a wreath on the S.S. tombs at Bitburg as a gesture of "old-fashioned Homeric nobility" [*T*, 294]) but against the Jews. These include the middle-class victims, "lined up in their fedoras and over-coats" (*T*, 293), his own mother, who was "erotically excited" by blue numbers on the arms of survivors, and those he derides as "Holocaus-tians" (*T*, 287), including Yehuda Bauer, Elie Wiesel, and the late Lucy Dawidowicz.

Too obtuse to understand that the uniqueness of the Holocaust consists neither in the number of Jews killed nor in the degree of individual suffering but in the fact that Hitler's was a war against the Jews, that Jews occupied the central place in his mental universe, that Jews alone were singled out for total destruction, and that European Jewish civilization *was*—as Ozick keeps insisting—totally destroyed, Lopate keeps flailing away at Jewish "chauvinism" (*T*, 299), Jewish "ethnic muscle-flexing" (*T*, 296), Jewish "tribal smugness," Jewish "pushiness" (*T*, 307), and Jewish lack of compassion "for the other victimized peoples of this century" (*T*, 300). He recommends as ultimate wisdom on memorializing the victims of the Holocaust a passage from Avishai Margalit's "brilliant essay" (*T*, 298) in the *New York Review of Books*, on "The Kitsch of Israel." In this passage Margalit heaped scorn on the "children's room" at Yad Vashem with its "tape-recorded voices of children crying out in Yiddish, 'Mame, Tate.'" It was long ago pointed out by Reuven Dafni of Yad Vashem (and could be pointed out by anyone who had visited the place) that Margalit is a liar, that there is no "children's room" or taped children's voices at Yad Vashem. There is a memorial to the murdered children and a tape-recorded voice that reads their names. Apparently, Lopate's "aesthetic" sense of the fitness of things is more offended by Jewish mourning than by Jewish lying.

Lopate's description of the very word *holocaust* as a Jewish con-spiracy in which "one ethnic group tries to compel the rest of the world" to follow its political program, his voracious munching on the "grain of truth" in "the more moderate revisionist historians" (*T*, 294), and his allegation that Jews have been able to "own the Holocaust" only because of political clout ("There are many more Jews in the United States than there are Ibos or Bengalis" [T, 293]) bring him perilously close to the position of the neo-Nazis. "Before I give the wrong impression," he nervously announces, "let me interject that I am not one of those revisionist nuts who deny that the Nazis . . . exterminated millions of Jews" (T, 286). Lopate might have added that, despite appearances to the contrary, his essay could hardly be called antisemitic since it originally appeared in a Jewish magazine called *Tikkun*, of which, in fact, he was the literary editor.

The reason why so many of the essays in this volume are egocentric, mean-spirited, and vulgar is not far to seek. Most of these American Jewish writers are people for whom the post-Enlightenment Emancipation formula—"Be a man in the street and a Jew in your tent"—seems perfectly natural. Having accepted the disfiguring privatization of Jewish self-definition, they feel no shame in "making personal" a loss that was sustained by the whole Jewish people. When Jacob Glatstein, who was also safe in America while European Jewry was being murdered, wrote that "Just as we all stood together/at the giving of the Torah,/so did we all die together at Lublin," he immersed himself in the vast ocean of Jewish civilization. When the contributors to *Testimony* speculate about how the Holocaust has affected their sex life or their politics, they are navigating an enclosed basin.

Notably absent from this anthology of Jewish personalizers are Ozick, Roth, and Saul Bellow, the very writers who, in dealing with the Holocaust, have kept their eye unflinchingly on the subject of Jewish collective fate (even if, in the case of Roth, we too often hear the pen scratching in the background). If one were to generalize about the difference between these absent "older" American Jewish writers and the "contemporary" novelists and critics who are abundantly represented in this collection, one might conclude that the lessened sense of marginality (or greater sense of belonging) often claimed by or for recent, younger Jewish writers has been an expression neither of imagination nor of moral courage but of their opposites. It is not by accident that most of the writers who lazily embrace the Enlightenment dispensation and the majority culture and call their opportunism courage, also present themselves as brave dissenters from the American Jewish community when they attack Israel. The literary critic Ruth Wisse has penetrated this charade with moral exactitude: "This whole idea of dissent is fraudulent, and its popularity does not make it any less of a lie. The political community that American Jews actually inhabit is not the Jewish community but the North American community. . . . By substituting the Jewish community for Arab propagandists as their major antagonist, they wrap themselves in a mantle of free expression while justifying their withdrawal from the propaganda war into which the Jews have been drawn."[24]

Mr. Sammler's Planet, by Saul Bellow

To acquire some perspective on the self-deceptive flight from Jewish history inherent in the activities of these enlightened Jewish writers, one cannot do better than return to Saul Bellow's *Mr. Sammler's Planet* (1970),[25] which remains, over two decades after its publication, the most profoundly imagined exploration of the relation between American Jewish life and recent Jewish history. The book's central premise is that the Holocaust served as a metaphysical refutation of Enlightenment assumptions dear to Jewish (and other) progressives. Just as the hero of Bellow's first novel, *Dangling Man*, mentioned earlier in this chapter, had been writing a series of biographical essays on the Enlightenment philosophers when the war and induction into the U. S. army intervened, so Artur Sammler had, before the outbreak of World War II, devoted himself to scholarly study of the English expositor of Enlightenment principles, H. G. Wells. Both of these Bellow protagonists had been taught what the author calls (in *To Jerusalem and Back*, 1976) the Holocaust's "deliberate lesson or project in philosophical redefinition: 'You . . . Christians, Jews, and Humanists, you believers in freedom, dignity, and enlightenment—you think that you know what a human being is. We will show you what he is, and what you are. Look at our camps and crematoria and see if you can . . . care about these millions."[26]

Living in New York after surviving the Holocaust, Sammler is separated from the American Jews surrounding him by a knowledge of what death is. During the war, he and his wife had been deported to an open-air killing center in Poland from which he had barely managed to crawl out. But he had not been only a victim. Later in the war, as a partisan in the Zamosht forest, he had discovered a German soldier and twice shot the man through the head even as he pleaded with Sammler for mercy.

If his experience of the Holocaust and his knowledge of death separate Sammler from American Jews, they tend to unite him with people otherwise foreign to him: the Jews of Israel. First, there is his conviction that the Arab aggression of 1967, beginning with Nasser's closing of the straits of Tiran and the Arab armies' encirclement of Israel, is a historical repetition. Sammler has seen it all before: "For the second time in twenty-five years the same people were threatened by extermination: the so-called powers letting things drift toward disaster; men armed for a massacre" (*MSP*, 146). In such circumstances, Sammler cannot merely sit in New York reading the world press and listening to his trendily leftist young relatives "explaining" the psychological necessity that drives the Arabs to war. He gets himself (as did Bellow at the time) a special assignment as a journalist so that he can be there, in Israel, "to send reports, to do something, perhaps to die in the massacre" (*MSP*, 147).

Later in the novel, when Sammler seems in danger of forgetting his Holocaust experience and its lessons, he is reminded of them (albeit in extreme and radical form) by an Israeli, his half-mad son-in-law Eisen. Seeing his acquaintance Lionel Feffer being thrashed in the street by the very same pickpocket who had once assaulted him, Sammler enlists Eisen's help. After some hesitation, the Israeli pounds the culprit with blow after blow until Sammler begs him to desist from what a moment before he had implored him to do. "You'll murder him. Do you want to beat out his brains? . . . You're . . . crazy enough to murder him" (*MSP*, 294). But the retort of Eisen is devastating to Sammler because it wrenches him back to the painful truth that he had learned in World War II and then remembered at the time of the Six-Day War. "You can't hit a man like this just once. When you hit him you must really hit him. Otherwise he'll kill you. You know. We both fought in the war. You were a Partisan. You had a gun. So don't you know?" (*MSP*, 295). Shut your ears, Eisen in effect says, to the tempting voice of ethical "idealism" in which American Jews, impervious to history, like to speak. If, for two thousand years, the Jew had not stooped to weapons of violence, that was in large part because the weapons (and the decision to use them) were not available to him. To be "proud" of a history of pacific powerlessness, or to attribute it to a superior moral instinct, "makes as much sense," says the American-born Israeli writer Hillel Halkin, "as it does for a man starving for lack of money to buy food to boast of his self-control in keeping thin."[27]

If the self-deception of many American Jews did harm only to their reputation for intelligence, it would hardly merit the scrutiny of Bellow.

But he knows that those American Jews who think themselves ethically superior to people in general and to combative Israeli Jews in particular have led others to conclude that, if Jews really are better than everybody else, then they (and especially the state that is their collective representative) should be held to higher standards than everybody else. "Jews," Bellow has written, " because they are Jews, have never been able to take the right to live as a natural right. . . . At the same time Jews are called upon . . . and call upon themselves to be more just and more moral than others" (*TJB*, 26). Who can doubt that if Israel had lost the war forced on it in 1967, its moral standing in the world today would be infinitely higher, and its severest detractors would now be heaping praise upon the glory that was Israel and the grandeur that was Zion?

Conclusion

American Jews have in recent years often been faulted for living on borrowed experience, a European suffering that was not theirs, a Zionist struggle that, even though they might well have joined it, they observed (and still observe) from a distance. The scholar Jacob Neusner, for example, has deplored the fact that American Jewish life is based upon a myth of Holocaust and heroism that is suitable for Israelis but has no relevance to American Jews and therefore serves only to instill in them a sense of "dislocation" in a place where they ought to live "without apology or guilt." "Ours," he once wrote, "is a mythic situation in which we talk about what other people go through, but then we find ourselves unable to explain the world in which we live."[28]

At first glance, this seems a plausible criticism. American Jews, still more the writers amongst them, know that (like every other branch of Diaspora Jewry and unlike, say, the Jews of Galicia mentioned in the epigraph to this chapter) they no longer possess a culture and an inner world of their own. Therefore they nourish themselves on what Neusner calls myths about the murder of European Jews and the heroism of Israeli Jews. But if Norma Rosen was right in saying that the Holocaust is the central event of this century and if Winston Churchill knew whereof he spoke when he declared that "The coming into being of a Jewish state . . . is an event in world history to be viewed in the perspective not of a generation or a century, but in the perspective of a thousand, two thousand or even three thousand years,"[29] how can Jewish writers be criticized for placing these events at the center of their imaginative lives? As the narrator of Bellow's *The Bellarosa Connection* inelegantly says, "besides, damn it, you couldn't say no to Jewish history after what happened in Nazi Germany."[30] Moreover, the world in which American Jews now live is, after all, the world which witnesses a universal campaign of hate against four million Jews who have created a state on a territory smaller than the island of Sicily.

Finally, we should remember that life in exile has always depended upon "myths" about other Jews. The Haggadah commands that every Jew view himself as having gone forth from Egypt. Jewish folk identity in Eastern Europe was preserved by what Maurice Samuel described as "an ingenious charade, which governed their religious life, which in turn interpenetrated their secular life. They pretended they were still living in their ancient homeland" (Samuel, 7). We have already seen, in chapter two, how modern Yiddish poetry about the Holocaust, however "secular" in outward appearance, is entirely traditional in its insistence that all Israel was present in the death camps because every Jew was potentially present at Mount Sinai. Although we may not admire all, or even much, that they do, we must allow that the American Jewish writers who keep returning to the subject of the Holocaust and Israel are responding not only to their historical moment but also to an ancient Jewish impulse.

Notes

1. Philip Roth, *Deception* (New York: Simon and Schuster, 1990), 81–82.
2. Irving Howe, Introduction to *Jewish-American Stories* (New York: New American Library, 1977), 6.
3. Norma Rosen, "The Holocaust and the American-Jewish Novelist," *Midstream*, 20 (October 1974), 54. Subsequent references to this work will be cited in text.
4. David Wyman, *The Abandonment of the Jews: America and the Holocaust, 1941–1945* (New York: Pantheon, 1984), 189.
5. *Dangling Man* (New York: Vanguard Press, 1944), 120.
6. *The Magic Barrel* (New York: Farrar, Straus and Cudahy, 1958), 105. Subsequent references to this work will be cited in text as *MB*.
7. Alan Berger, *Crisis and Covenant: The Holocaust in American Jewish Fiction* (Albany, N.Y.: State University of New York Press, 1985), 156.
8. *Goodbye, Columbus and Five Short Stories* (New York: Houghton Mifflin, 1959), 253. Subsequent references to this work will be cited in text as *GC*.
9. See Deborah E. Lipstadt, *Beyond Belief: The American Press & the Coming of the Holocaust, 1933–1945* (New York: The Free Press, 1986).
10. "Popularization and Memory: The Case of Anne Frank," *Lessons and Legacies: The Memory of the Holocaust in a Changing World*, ed. Peter Hayes, 234–78 (Evanston,

Illinois: Northwestern University Press, 1991). Subsequent references to this work will be cited in text.

11. *New York Times Book Review* (June 15, 1952), 1, 22.

12. *The Works of Anne Frank* (Garden City, N.Y.: Doubleday & Company, 1959).

13. *Anne Frank: the Diary of a Young Girl*, translated by B. M. Mooyaart-Doubleday (Garden City, N. Y.: Doubleday & Company, 1952), 64–65. Subsequent references to this work will be cited in text as *AF*.

14. *Herald Tribune*, October 23, 1955.

15. "The Ignored Lesson of Anne Frank," *Harper's* (November 1960), 46.

16. *The Diary of Anne Frank*, by Frances Goodrich and Albert Hackett (New York: Random House, 1956), 168.

17. *The Ghost Writer* (New York: Farrar, Straus & Giroux, 1979). Subsequent references to this work will be cited in text as *GW*.

18. Donald M. Kartiganer, "Ghost Writing: Philip Roth's Portrait of the Artist," *AJS Review*, 13 (Spring–Fall 1988), 163.

19. *Dark Soliloquy: The Selected Poems of Gertrud Kolmar* (San Francisco: Seabury Press, 1975).

20. Cynthia Ozick, *Metaphor and Memory* (New York: Alfred A. Knopf, 1989), 43. Subsequent references to this work will be cited in text as *MM*.

21. *The Messiah of Stockholm* (New York: Alfred A. Knopf, 1987), 98.

22. *Testimony: Contemporary Writers Make the Holocaust Personal* (New York: Random House, 1989). Subsequent references to this work will be cited in text as *T*.

23. Emil L. Fackenheim, *The Jewish Return into History* (New York: Schocken Books, 1978), 54. Subsequent references to this work will be cited in text.

24. "Denizens of Dissent," *Forward*, May 31, 1991.

25. *Mr. Sammler's Planet* (New York: Viking Press, 1970). Subsequent references to this work will be cited in text as *MSP*.

26. *To Jerusalem and Back: A Personal Account* (New York: Viking Press, 1976), 58. Subsequent references to this work will be cited in text as *TJB*.

27. *Letters to an American Jewish Friend: A Zionist's Polemic* (Philadelphia: Jewish Publication Society, 1977), 94. Subsequent references to this work will be cited in text as *Letters*.

28. "Beyond Catastrophe, before Redemption," *Reconstructionist*, 46 (April 1980), 8–11.

29. See Dan V. Segre, "Is Anti-Zionism a New Form of Antisemitism?" in *Antisemitism in the Contemporary World*, ed. Michael Curtis (Boulder and London: Westview Press, 1986), 153.

30. *The Bellarosa Connection* (New York: Penguin Books, 1989), 28.

4

The Holocaust and the Israeli Imagination

> *To speak of the mystical course which, in the great cataclysm now stirring the Jewish people more deeply than in the entire history of Exile, destiny may still have in store for us . . . is the task of prophets, not of professors.*
> —Gershom Scholem (1938)[1]

> *We call you to vengeance. . . . This is our challenge to you, who have not suffered in Hitler's hell. This you are duty-bound to fulfill. Our scattered bones will not rest in peace, the scattered ashes of the crematoria will not lie still, until you have avenged us.*
> —Tzippora Berman (young member of the Zionist underground in Bialystok, writing to her comrades in Palestine)[2]

> *From the promised land I called you,/I looked for you/among heaps of small shoes/At every approaching holiday.*
> —Abba Kovner (1967)[3]

Forerunners

The place of the Holocaust in the imagination of Israelis generally and Israeli writers in particular cannot be fathomed without remembering the place of Eretz Yisrael (the Land of Israel), a Jewish homeland, in the imagination of those victims of Nazism who had been imbued with the idea of Zion reborn. These were people who knew something, often a great deal, about the developing institutions of Jewish Palestine, people who, had they lived, would never have been ensnared by the now

71

widespread and pernicious fiction that the State of Israel came into existence only because of Western bad conscience over the Holocaust. Nevertheless, they understood how deeply embedded in Jewish sacred literature was the sense of intimate connection between destruction and rebirth. In Ezekiel, the prospect that God will make "a full end of the remnant of Israel" is inseparable from the promise that "I will even gather you from the peoples, and assemble you out of the countries where ye have been scattered, and I will give you the land of Israel" (Ezekiel 11:13, 16). According to one Jewish legend, the Messiah was born on the day that the Temple was destroyed; and the Talmud proposes that the Messiah will come only in a generation totally innocent or—the far more relevant possibility in this bloodiest of all centuries—wholly guilty.

For Jews who found themselves in the depths of Nazi oppression the debate over whether the ingathering of the Exiles was to come only through messianic deliverance at the end of days or as the result of human effort seemed less immediate than the question of whether, despite the loss of millions of individuals, the Jewish *people* would survive. We see this clearly in the diary of Moshe Flinker, one of the most remarkable documents in the spiritual history of modern Jewry. It was composed in Hebrew in 1942-43 by a 16-year-old Dutch boy hiding in Brussels; he was murdered a year later in Auschwitz. The diary was published in 1958 at the urging of Israel's greatest imaginative writer, S. Y. Agnon. At the diary's center is the struggle of the religious will to preserve the idea of a just and merciful God in the face of soul- and body-destroying evil. Passionate for messianic redemption, sensing the difference between the present calamity and all the previous afflictions of the Exile, Moshe is contemptuous of those who pray for Allied victory and a return to the old life, the old separation from the Land and from God. He believes that this war against the Jews, and the unspeakable sufferings visited upon them can only be the birthpangs of the messiah, portending the end of Exile and the return to the Land of Israel.[4]

But Moshe's longing for the messianic transformation of the world as he had known it coexisted with shrewd, practical planning. His ambition was to become, once the Messiah had fulfilled *his* obligation, a statesman in Israel; and so, having already mastered Hebrew, he plunged into the study of Arabic. Although we may smile at Moshe's belief that messianic success in the new Jerusalem depends on the quality of Jewish states-manship, he understood (rather better than many innovative American-

Jewish mapmakers of recent years[5]) that normative Judaism never separated celestial from earthly Jerusalem. When Mahatma Gandhi made the fatuous suggestion that persecuted German Jews stay put rather than go to Palestine because true Biblical Palestine is not a "geographic tract" but a metaphor, Martin Buber replied: "Zion is the prophetic image of a promise to mankind, but it would be a poor metaphor if Mount Zion did not actually exist. This land is called 'holy'; but it is not the holiness of an idea, it is the holiness of a piece of earth. That which is merely an idea and nothing more cannot become holy; but a piece of earth can become holy just as a mother's womb can become holy."[6]

Despite his preparations for a statesman's career in Eretz Yisrael, Moshe did not believe in Zionism until he received what he calls "a letter from God" in the guise of a school almanac called "My Homeland." "How many times have I not said this word to myself . . . and each time it comes into my mind I am filled with yearning for it" (81). It is possible to dismiss Moshe Flinker's diary with the old quip that when a man is no longer capable of being a Jew, he becomes a Zionist. Yet it does suggest how, at the deepest level of Jewish imaginative experience in this century, the will to impose meaning on the terror of history leads to the desire for a Jewish national home. Like Zippora Berman, whose letter (never sent) appears at the head of this chapter, Moshe looks to the Palestinian *Yishuv* for revenge, which he defines as a redemptive mending of what has been shattered: "the return of our people to their homeland. That will be the greatest revenge that could ever happen" (118).

Moshe, writing in isolation from the masses of Jews under Nazi rule, viewed the paradoxical link between catastrophe and redemption through the lens of the spirit. Others responded to immediate, physical signs of the relation between despair and hope, degradation and reconstruction. When the Nazis promulgated their anti-Jewish boycott on April 1, 1933 Robert Weltsch, editor of the *Jüdische Rundschau*, wrote an editorial called "Wear the Yellow Badge with Pride!" The Nazis had intended to disgrace the Jews, especially those who no longer considered themselves to be Jews, by pasting the Magen David, the shield of David, on Jewish store fronts, business signs, and windows. Weltsch urged the Jews to be proud of that for which they were suffering: "Jews, pick up the Shield of David and wear it honorably!"[7]

This symbol also figures prominently in Chaim Kaplan's *Warsaw Diary*. Trapped in the ghetto, this Warsaw Hebrew teacher and author was both perplexed and tantalized by spurious, counterfeit fulfillments of God's promise that only after the Jewish people had endured the punishment of their iniquities and nearly perished would He remember His covenant and return them to the land of Israel. The ghetto now (in 1942) had Jewish tax officials, Jewish public utility officials, Jewish housing officials, even Yiddish-speaking policemen. "The residents of the ghetto," he writes in his diary, "are beginning to think they are in Tel Aviv."[8]

Of course Kaplan knows that this facade of a Jewish state exists to allow the Germans to destroy their victims more efficiently and economically. Nevertheless, when the Nazis order all Warsaw Jews to wear on their bodies and display on their shops the Star of David in the Jewish national colors of blue and white, Kaplan—a shrewd and skeptical observer—glimpses in this emblem of Jewish degradation a sign, from a realm beyond human experience, of Jewish national rebirth. "In the future," muses Kaplan, " everywhere we turn we shall feel as if we were in a Jewish kingdom . The national colors will flutter everywhere. From now on Jerusalem will not only crown our every joy, but also our ordinary weekdays, as we get up and as we lie down" (WD, 79). The Ingathering of the Exiles, the dawn of deliverance—gifts of the Nazis! Kaplan's tone in such passages is a turbulent mixture of genuine emotion and corrosive irony.

The very symbol that encouraged Weltsch and Kaplan to look forward, beyond humiliation and destruction, to the restoration of Israel, has for forty-five years spurred Israelis to look backward and reflect on the great impetus they received from the experience of the Holocaust—that is to say, of the German murder of the Jews, of the callous indifference of the nations of the world, and of their own responsibility to redeem the dead. No one has given more eloquent expression to the way in which this best-known symbol of Israeli civil religion conveys memory of the Holocaust to the popular imagination of Israeli citizens than the great scholar Gershom Scholem:

> The . . . Jewish star, as a sign of exclusion and ultimately of annihilation, has accompanied the Jews on their path of humiliation and horror, of battle and heroic resistance. Under this sign they were murdered, under this sign they came to Israel. . . . Some have been of the opinion that the sign which marked the way to annihilation and to the gas chambers should be replaced by a sign of life. But it is possible to think quite the opposite: the sign which in our own days has been sanctified by suffering and dread has become worthy of illuminating the path to life and reconstruction.

Before ascending, the path led down into the abyss; there the symbol received its ultimate humiliation and there it won its greatness.[9]

Since the establishment of the state of Israel in 1948, the Holocaust has played a central role in the public, political culture of the country, and also in the inner life of many of its citizens. Half a million of the first great wave of 600,000 postwar immigrants were survivors, who would become a major segment of the population. No sooner had the cultural and political center of world Jewry shifted from Eastern Europe to Palestine than the Jewish people found itself once again threatened with destruction. In 1948, what had seemed the desperately quixotic Jewish resistance in the Warsaw Ghetto five years earlier proved how, in the long run, nothing that is done for the sake of justice is practically useless. For when the invading Egyptian army appeared on the verge of breaking through the Negev to the cities of Ashdod and Tel Aviv, it was stopped at Kibbutz Yad Mordechai, the kibbutz which took its name and inspiration from the leader of the Warsaw Ghetto uprising, Mordechai Anielewicz. In fact, most of the defenders of Yad Mordechai, whose courage saved the newborn state, were veterans of the Warsaw uprising or other fighting against the Germans. "The battle for Yad Mordechai," the philosopher Emil Fackenheim has written, "began in the streets of Warsaw" (Fackenheim, 285). Moreover, the sense of having been once more targeted for annihilation— for what Arab leaders at the time called a massacre that would equal those perpetrated by Genghis Khan or the Crusaders—was sharpened by the awareness that many Arab potentates and in particular the leader of the Palestinian Arabs, Haj Amin al-Husseini, had actively supported Hitler and Himmler in their campaign of murder, urging the Nazis to (thus al-Husseini) "kill the Jews wherever you find them. . . . God is with you" (Fackenheim, 212).

Nowhere does the Holocaust generate such sympathetic interest and remembrance but also shame, revulsion, and controversy as in Israel. The majority of the survivors live there. The major centers of Holocaust research are in Israel. Many of the world's museums devoted to remembering the victims and their destroyed culture are in Israel. Israel must be the only country in the world in which a national television audience will have its attention riveted to a "This Is Your Life" program that re-creates the life of a survivor of Auschwitz and introduces, among the hero's old friends, a woman who recounts the slow killing of her child in one of Dr. Mengele's experiments. It is the only country in the world that annually honors, in formal ceremonies with flags lowered to half-staff in every city and village, the six million murdered Jews.

But there is another side to the picture. The subject of how much (or how little) effort had been invested by the Yishuv in the rescue of European Jewry has long been a matter of intense debate, a cacophony of accusing and self-accusing voices. The full litany of accusations against the Jews of Palestine for their alleged indifference to the fate of their European brethren may be found in the book *The Seventh Million: The Israelis and the Holocaust*, by Tom Segev.[10] As one might expect from a left-wing Israeli journalist, it purports to show that the Jews of Palestine callously went about their daily lives even after they became aware of the catastrophe that faced European Jewry, and that their alleged indifference was entirely in accord with the policy and priorities of the Jewish leadership, especially David Ben-Gurion, in Palestine. Segev never explains precisely what practical rescue action Palestinian Jewry should have undertaken in preference to carrying on with (more or less) normal life. "Would it," asks Hillel Halkin, "have saved a single life in Europe if they had gone about in sack cloth and ashes, as Mr. Segev, from the lofty perch of his own moral superiority, seems to think they should have done?"[11] Segev also is endlessly shocked by the fact that the Zionist leadership, which had always predicted that Diaspora Jewry would disappear either as a result of antisemitic violence or assimilation, did not now refrain from noting that the catastrophe it had warned of was taking place or from placing the preservation of the Yishuv first in its list of priorities.

Segev's title expresses his conviction that all Israelis, that is, the seventh million, were in a sense victimized by the Holocaust too. What he mainly means by this is that numerous Israelis have exploited the Holocaust for political ends, especially political ends that are not his own. The "exploiters" of the Holocaust for political purposes, according to Segev, are those who stress the infectious power of antisemitism and the necessity of Jewish political power and a Jewish state for Jewish survival. In his view, by contrast, contemplation of the Holocaust should follow an arrow-straight course from memory of the event to the policies of the Israeli left.

Although Segev's manipulative polemic has, not surprisingly, been trumpeted by the American press, the most authoritative and scholarly study of the subject of whether the Yishuv did all it could to help the Jews of Europe is Dina Porat's book *The Blue and the Yellow Stars of David*. In it she stresses that the Yishuv was a community, not an independent state, and that its leaders were not only genuinely concerned about the fate of Europe's Jews, but undertook various projects of aid and rescue. That they achieved little was not a reflection of their indifference but of that of the Europeans, the United States, most of all of the British mandatory power, which scuttled most of these projects. The Jews of Palestine also, she insistently demonstrates, had some problems of their own, including the possibility of a Nazi invasion through Syria. Her massively documented conclusion is that, despite instances of ideological disdain for European Jewry, "the Yishuv in fact did more than it was ever given credit for—either then or now."[12]

Six years after the war ended, in 1951, an offer by the West German government to pay reparations to Israel for Jewish survivors ignited a terrific controversy, with the late Menachem Begin on the right and Mapam on the left alleging that the Germans were buying Israeli silence, an allegation that was belatedly proved false when Israel captured Eichmann and brought him to trial in Jerusalem in 1961. Even the Day of Remembrance for Holocaust victims is entangled in controversy, for it is called not only Yom Hashoah (Holocaust Day) but also Yom Hagevurah (Heroism Day), as if the action of a substantial, yet relatively small, group of resistance fighters in the ghettos were needed to counterbalance the passivity with which the vast majority of the victims went to their deaths. For a long time, perhaps until the Eichmann trial, many sabras (native-born Israelis) thought of the European Jews contemptuously, as having gone like "sheep to the slaughter."

But it is worth remembering that this expression was first applied to the European Jews not by a Palestinian Jew but by a young activist and poet calling for Jewish self-defense in Vilna, Lithuania. On January 1, 1942, Abba Kovner read a proclamation to a meeting of 150 young Zionists that began: "Let's not allow ourselves to be led like sheep to the slaughter" (in the original Yiddish, "Lomir zikh nisht lozn firn vi shof tsu der shkhite!" [*HR*, 334–36]). Thirty-three years later, having become an Israeli poet of international reputation, Kovner told an American audience how much he regretted having put this derisive expression into circulation. "I never thought a woman who had her child taken out of her arms had gone like a sheep to the slaughter" (*New York Times*, March 6, 1975). The remarkable journey of Abba Kovner from European resistance fighter to Israeli poet is parabolically represented in the body of his writing, to which we now turn.

Abba Kovner

My place of work is a wooden hut between the graveyard and the children's house. There I am writing something that has no beginning and no end. But if there is a central thread that goes through the empty pages, it is the leitmotif of those who survived, those who were destroyed and those who come after them. (Abba Kovner, March 7, 1975)[13]

Abba Kovner's work and life were attempts to join together what had been separated by the Jewish history of expulsion, dispersion, oppression, Holocaust. He located the source of his creative work in a tension between two loves, his love of the Jewish people and his love of the land of Israel. He sought to bring together, as completing counterparts, those Jews who attached themselves to the Jewish people but had no experience of the living reality of the land, and those Israelis who saw themselves "as the first of a new humankind."[14] During the first half of his life, he gained honor and fame as a resistance fighter in Vilna and the surrounding forests and then as a leader in the Brichah (rescue) movement that brought the pitiful remnant of European Jewry to the homeland in Palestine. In this period he sought to bring the Jewish people to the land of Israel. But in his poetry he initiated a vast backward movement of recovery that was intended to carry the imagination of his contemporaries in Israel back to the Jewish people, back to a buried life they had either not known or had known and thought they had forgotten.

Kovner's poetry is based on the impulse to join people with land, matter with spirit, the living with the dead, past with present, life with literature. At any particular moment in his poems, we may be simultaneously at the foot of Sinai and at the edge of the shooting pits of Ponary, circling the walls of Jericho and the walls of a European convent or ghetto, defending Vilna (the "Jerusalem of Lithuania") and the Jerusalem of modern Israel, receiving the Covenant and giving it back. He is a writer whose imagination, like his life, may rise from the material to the spiritual, but may also return, for renewal, from the spiritual to the physical. Two examples of this forward and backward movement from Kovner's life underscore its centrality in his poetry.

At the war's end, he felt powerfully the need not only for rescue but for transformation of the Jewish people. He was shocked by the apathy of those small segments of the European Jewish population that had not suffered in the Holocaust, people who had lived through an event of biblical enormity without even pondering it. In a speech of 1945 he said, "There blew in our faces a chill cellar-wind of a community that goes on living as if nothing had happened, as it did before the deluge, as if there had been no deluge." His immediate goal was physical rescue, a task made difficult enough by allies as well as enemies in Europe, and by the British Mandatory Government in Palestine; but he could not conceive of physical rescue apart from spiritual renewal. Physical rescue of European Jewry might perhaps take place if the survivors could be moved from the displaced persons camps to America, but spiritual renewal required their reunion with the Jewish land. Yet it was not only the European survivors who needed spiritual rebirth after the great catastrophe: "We want," he continued, "to come to the Land of Israel, to its people, and by the force of our conviction, of our inquietude, our sense of the danger that hovers over us and is also latent within us, to change its ways of thinking . . . which is also largely the outcome of detachment, distance and indifference."[15] If the Jewish people were one—and, Kovner believed, they were—then Palestinian Jewry could not achieve its mission unless it absorbed into its consciousness the grim central experience of modern Jewish history. Just how true this was even Kovner could not know until the traumatic war of 1967 dramatically revealed how "young Israelis . . . in the most critical hours of their lives, found that their deepest feelings came into contact with that forgotten chapter . . . that seemingly repressed chapter, the destruction of our people in Europe" ("First Attempt," 2).

Kovner believed that literature and life were mutually dependent, that one fructified the other. He was fond of pointing out that in classical Hebrew there was no single word for literature; rather, it was called *hayim she-bikhtav* (life in writing). The rightness of this apparently cumbersome phrase was proved to Kovner by his experience in commanding resistance fighters in the Vilna ghetto. On September 1, 1943, the Germans surrounded the ghetto in order to remove the last thousands of Jews to the death camps. It was necessary to build defense positions with sandbags, but—irony of ironies—the people whose forefathers had for a thousand years built their homes of drifting sand could now find none with which to protect themselves against German bullets. Their salvation (temporary, to be sure) lay in "the great volumes of the Talmud in their brown leather binding," which were taken from the famous Jewish library of Vilna to serve in place of sandbags. The event was to remain with Kovner as a revelation of the complex possibilities of renewal in the interactions between matter and spirit, life and literature. From one point of view, it is possible to say that the Talmud was here degraded from a spiritual to a physical role; yet it is also clear that the degradation enabled a preservation of Jewish life through a transformation of the traditional Jewish passivity in the face of violent threat. "I propped up my rifle on the back of the books. Were the books a support for the rifle with its ten bullets? Or, at that hour, were they a support for something else?"[16]

The desire to overcome geographical and chronological discontinuity by joining Israel with Diaspora, present with past, is apparent in Kovner's account of the genesis of *My Little Sister*, published in 1967, almost a quarter of a century after the events of the Holocaust that form its center. He was walking late at night through the streets of a section of Tel Aviv when he heard the shrieks of a woman coming from a high window. Although his own attention was riveted on the terrible screams, neither the other passersby in the street nor the people behind the neighboring windows seemed to pay any attention. Kovner was at once carried back to the Holocaust years when the collective death rattle of the Jews of Europe failed to disturb the placidity or even attract the attention of the outside world.

> A cloister's wall is high.
> A wall of silence
> still higher. (*ACD*, 26)

This gave the first impulse toward recovery of the past. The second came from Kovner's discovery of the truth behind the appearances. In actuality, he had been hearing the cries of a woman in labor coming from a maternity hospital; those who knew the neighborhood paid no attention because they were familiar with such cries and knew their cause. Stirred by remembrances of the wartime isolation and abandonment, by particular memories of the agonies of mothers and children during the Holocaust, and by the paradoxical relation between torture and birth, Kovner embarked on what he called "an enduring attempt to turn ashes into an eternal light" (*ACD*, xvii).

The incident in Tel Aviv is specifically reflected in *My Little Sister* in several ways. The Dominican convent in which the little sister receives (temporary) shelter is shown to be out of touch with the human actuality and the horrors enveloping European Jewry by the fact that here "No woman has crouched to give birth / on the floor" (*ACD*, 29). The convent's mother is the Mother Superior, its ideal of motherhood the virginal mother of the infant Jesus, over whose image the nuns lovingly fuss. The contrasted ideas of motherhood give rise to the poem's contrasts between the sanctified Christian image of the crucified Jesus and "my crucified memory / outside the fence!" (*ACD*, 28), a memory of images themselves crying for sanctification: "ashes that speak" (*ACD*, 23) and "heaps of small shoes"(*ACD*, 57).

The mother's agony of which the cries from the lying-in hospital reminded Kovner is in *My Little Sister* illustrated in ways that, if considered logically, are mutually inconsistent; yet this inconsistency gives us a clue to the organizing idea of the poem. In the opening section of Part Four, the poet looks back "from the promised land" upon the carnage in Europe and searches among heaps of small shoes for his sister-bride. He then imagines all the little sisters who were killed, before their parents could say goodbye or explain that they had not really resented the extra burden of weight on the road to death. He wishes that he could have

> even in one word
> whispered
> that you were no burden to us.
>
> On the way. Mother walked heavy.
> I.
> All your brothers.
> And the desperate convoy. (*ACD*, 57)

In Part Five of the poem, however, the mother's agony arises not from her separation from her child on the way to execution in mass graves but from her infant never surviving the maternity hospital that was the starting point of Kovner's imaginative journey:

> The Bikur Holim Hospital
> walls soaked
> with the smell of sour urine
> and dying hopes.
>
> In the old hospital

> among walls of red brick
> my sister died.
> She was two hours old. (*ACD*, 68)

In the following section, the suffering mother is said to have mourned eight years (1940–48, when the State of Israel was established) "a daughter / who never came into the world"(*ACD*, 69).

This factual inconsistency in the narrative indicates that we are dealing not with a single sister-bride or a single mother but with a generalized account of the Holocaust. Kovner's mode of generalizing is something like Milton's; that is, he eschews abstract, generalized language and limits himself to specific images and concrete details, but says that the occurrence might have happened this way or that way or yet a third way—except that, unlike Milton, he omits the *or*. A hint of Kovner's intention is given in the poem's title itself. In grammatical strictness, the Hebrew title should be *Ahoti Haktana* rather than, as it is, *Ahoti Ktana*; the grammatical anomaly suggests that it is not a single little sister we are recalling but all the little sisters, born and unborn, who were devoured by the Holocaust.

Long before Kovner heard the shrieks from the Tel Aviv maternity ward, his imagination was captured by a little girl who had died, yet lived. She was one of the 47,000 Jews taken from Vilna to the shooting pits of Ponary. Incredibly, she managed to crawl out from among the thousands of dead and dying bodies to tell her story. Like a myriad of such survivor-witnesses whom we now know from the history and literature of the Holocaust, she was believed by no one—except for Abba Kovner, who proceeded to organize the armed resistance. "The central fact in Kovner's life," according to his translator Shirley Kaufman, "is his confrontation with the half-dead, half-crazed girl from the mass grave at Ponar. Her face haunts every line he writes" (*ACD*, xv).

The little sister of the narrative finds refuge in the convent but also "betrayal /—no island. / Only a folded sail in a storm" (*ACD*, 33). Unlike the group that took her to the convent and was itself later shot by the mobile killing units of the *Einsatzgruppen*, the little sister was "not privileged to be condemned to death" and "did not enter a covenant of blood" —just as later she is said to be "not privileged to see / the light of the day!" (*ACD*, 69). But Section 39 seems to say that she was turned over to the Germans by the nuns and eventually murdered. Her "shorn head" (*ACD*, 63) is both that of a nun and a death-camp inmate.

The little sister's varied and contradictory fate is most fully explored in Section 28, which describes the preparations for her wedding. The brother-narrator here stresses her identity as the "sister-bride" of the biblical Song of Songs. Many of the central images and motifs of Kovner's poem are to be found in Solomon's song, especially in its eighth and concluding chapter, where the speaker wishes that the beloved could be "as my brother, / That sucked the breasts of my mother!" The speaker subsequently says of the sister that "thy mother was in travail with thee, / There was she in travail and brought thee forth." Finally, he asks: "What shall we do for our sister / In the day when she shall be spoken for?" (a line Kovner quotes from in Section 36).

If, as traditional religious interpretation of Song of Songs holds, the sister-bride is no mere figure of romantic love poetry but a symbol of the people of Israel, then the little sister's wedding would be a reaffirmation of the covenantal relationship between God and his Chosen People. Kovner describes many of the customary appurtenances of the wedding ceremony, including the braided challah, the dish of honey, and the golden chicken soup. But an anomalous element intervenes: "The whole world drinks / kosher chicken soup." Chicken soup, however, is not supposed to be drunk until *after* the ceremony, and then only by the bride and groom. Yet the canopy, the covering that symbolizes the consummation of the marriage, is not present at all, and therefore the "whole world" would seem to be celebrating an event that has not taken place. The mystery of the world's presence at the prematurely celebrated Jewish wedding is resolved in the following lines:

> Our father took his bread, bless God,
> forty years from one oven. He never imagined
> a whole people could rise in the ovens
> and the world, with God's help, go on. (*ACD*, 49)

The world flocks to celebrate a Jewish marriage precisely because it is a marriage with death. The Covenant that was given at Sinai has been returned in Europe as the whole Jewish people returns—in smoke—to the God who did them the dubious favor of choosing them. The feeling at this point in Section 28 is similar to that in Glatstein's "Dead Men Don't Praise God," discussed earlier: "We received the Torah on Sinai / and in Lublin we gave it back." Both feel the immediacy of the biblical past and its painful and paradoxical continuity with the Holocaust present, but the Hebrew poet, unlike the Yiddish one, feels, and indeed embodies, the future, as well: after the giving back in Lublin, there is to be a retrieval in Sinai. Although "the marriage contract will be written in stone" (*ACD*, 49) for multitudes of little sisters, the canopy missing from this wedding of death will again be raised, and in the very place where the seemingly dissolved Covenant originated, the desert of Sinai.

The marriage contracts are written in stone, the whole vanished Jewish world has become "a choir of stones" (*ACD*, 63), a huge cemetery. After such material and spiritual ravages, is it possible to rebuild,

> to wipe from the lips
> the taste of hot ash.
> To bring back
> a world of innocence,
> as if to its socket a bone
> from the foot of the dead. (*ACD*, 53)

The contrast between the wholeness, unity, and coherence of the Dominican convent and Jewish Vilna, "a city thrust on its back / like a horse in blood, jerking its hooves / unable to rise" (*ACD*, 36), like the contrast in *Canopy in the Desert* between Saint Catherine's Monastery with its 3,000 steps to Sinai and "the kind of stuff / Jacob's ladder was made of " (*ACD*, 160), is at first dispiriting to the poet. He stands amidst the ruins of his world and asks,

> With what—
> with what, little sister,
> shall we weave and draw the dream
> now? (*ACD*, 55)

The question faced by Kovner was not very different from the one put to Martin Buber in 1933 by a Christian polemicist who asked whether the fulfillment of Jesus' prophecy that Jerusalem would be destroyed and never again come under Jewish rule did not prove that the Covenant between God and the Jews had been abrogated. Buber replied as follows:

I live not far from the city of Worms, to which I am bound by the tradition of my forefathers; and, from time to time, I go there. When I go, I first go to the cathedral. It is a visible harmony of members, a totality in which no part deviates from perfection. I walk about the cathedral with consummate joy, gazing at it. Then I go over to the Jewish cemetery consisting of crooked, cracked, shapeless, random stones. I station myself there, gaze upward from the jumble of a cemetery to that glorious harmony, and seem to be looking up from Israel to the Church. Below, there is no jot of form; there are only the stones, and the dust lying beneath the stones. The dust is there, no matter how thinly scattered. There lies the corporeality of man, which has turned to this. There it is. There it is for me. There it is for me, not as corporeality within the space of this planet, but as corporeality within my own memory, far into the depths of history, as far back as Sinai. I have stood there, have been united with the dust, and through it with the Patriarchs. That is a memory of the transaction with God which is given to all Jews. From this the perfection of the Christian house of God cannot separate me, nothing can separate me from the sacred history of Israel. I have stood there and have experienced everything myself; with all this death has confronted me, all the dust, all the ruin, all the wordless misery is mine; but the covenant has not been withdrawn from me. I lie on the ground, fallen like these stones. But it has not been withdrawn from me. The cathedral is as it is. The cemetery is as it is. But nothing has been withdrawn from us.[17]

Kovner, like Buber, refuses to see in Jewish defeat and suffering signs of the abrogation of the Covenant. The Covenant has not been withdrawn from the People Israel, but the covenantal relationship must be held in abeyance until the remnant of the Jewish people returns, spiritually as well as physically, from the Diaspora to the original source and site of the Covenant.

> There was no one
> with me there who spoke
> or understood my tongue
> cleaving to the roof of my mouth
>
> (if I forget thee Oh canyon!
> if I forget thee)
>
> On all my roads
> I imagined I'd find the road
>
> to you (*ACD*, 172)

This passage from *A Canopy in the Desert* suggests that the canopy missing from the little sister's wedding is to be found only in the homeland. The feeling with which we are left at the conclusion of *My Little Sister* has much in common with what we feel near the end of the book of Leviticus, when God announces that although he will bring his people to nearly total destruction in the lands of their enemies, while their own land "shall lie forsaken without them," he will not even then break His Covenant with them, or theirs with the land. They have rejected his ordinances and abhorred his statutes: "And yet for all that, when they are in the land of their enemies, I will not reject them, neither will I abhor them, to destroy them utterly, and to break My covenant with them." When Kovner returned to the liberated but destroyed Vilna, he found amidst the ruins only the eastern wall of the old synagogue, and on it an ancient inscription: "Lift up the miracle-banner for the ingathering of our exiles" ("A First Attempt to Tell," 32). At the end of *My Little Sister* the poet already seems to be embarking, with the imagined bier of his dead mother, on a ship that cracks through the ice floe of the vast cemetery of Europe on its journey south, out of exile and toward a renewal of life and the Covenant. The "First Gate" of *A Canopy in the Desert*, published three years later, is entitled "The Return to the South," suggesting both the trip to the Negev and Sinai, but also the larger return of the Jews of Europe from Exile to their homeland.

That rebirth in the homeland will be no clear and unambiguous resurrection of life and rediscovery of the Covenant is already implicit in *My Little Sister*. Part Four begins with the poet-survivor-brother calling from Israel to the unanswering corpse of his sister in Europe:

> From the promised land I called you,
> I looked for you
> among heaps of small shoes.
> At every approaching holiday. (*ACD*, 57)

Part Five concludes with the mother who both mourns her children and is herself mourned by the son who carries his mother's bier away from the ice fields of the European cemetery. The mother figure here represents Rachel weeping for her children, the centuries-old pain of the Jewish mother who bled and suffered in childbirth so that murderers should be amply supplied with victims for their knives, the shrieking mother in the Tel Aviv hospital, the Israeli mother who mourns her sons fallen in battle, and—not least of all—the poet's memory of his own mother.

When Kovner, in September 1943, ordered the headquarters of the Vilna resistance sealed off, his mother fell against the gate and asked her son in terror whether she should remain in Vilna or flee with him into the forests: "And I, the commander of the ghetto fighters, could not look into her eyes as I answered, 'Mother, I don't know!' And so to this very day I don't know whether I am worthy of the honor of a ghetto resistance fighter, or the curse of a son who abandoned his mother and did not go with her on her last road."[18]

In Section 46 of *My Little Sister* the mother whose memorial candles "ran out in the ghetto" carries her memories of the little sister elsewhere, kindling her "on all the seas." Her mourning continues until 1948, when the State of Israel is established. The speaker from the promised land asks her how she can mourn indiscriminately both her sons "who were cut down," apparently in the War of Independence, and the daughter "who never came into the world" (69). Here "never came into the world" seems to mean not only never was born but never entered into history, died, that is to say, from the point of view of many native-born Israelis, a death both passive and meaningless because it was not an integral part of world history.[19] In *Canopy in the Desert*, the poet himself speaks of the Sinai desert as "The one place in the world / where a man will not die alone" (*ACD*, 182) because here one fights and dies not for oneself but for the survival of the Jewish people. But here the mourning mother turns aside the accusatory question and repeats, with significantly altered words, her earlier reply: "my son—she was not privileged to see / the light of the day!" (*ACD*, 69). The little sister never saw either the actual light of day or the light of the new dawn that emerged in 1948; yet the mother insists that her aborted life and her many deaths in the Holocaust are inseparable from the life that seems to be starting *ab initio* in the homeland, in Israel.

In yet another story of mothers and sons disputing over the ashes of their destroyed past, Kovner told of

> a great fire in the house of the parents of the Maggid of Mezeritch, when he was only a child of ten. His father was not there. He saw his mother standing in the yard, wringing her hands as she watched the conflagration and weeping bitterly. "Mother," he said to her, "do this wooden house and this wooden furniture deserve to have you weep over them?" "Son," the mother replied, "it is not for the house or the furniture I am weeping. The scroll of our family pedigree has been left behind there in the fire." "Don't cry, mother," said the ten-year-old boy. "I'll write you a new pedigree, starting with me. . . . "
>
> It is said of the Maggid of Mezeritch that later when he was a grown man, he would hide his face in his hands, whenever he remembered what he had said to his mother.[20]

Part of Kovner's poetic effort to reunite what time and history had separated was his repudiation of what he called the "infantile" Israeli myth (especially prevalent in the Israeli left, to which Kovner belonged) of "It starts with me." The creative reunion of the People Israel with the land of Israel toward which *A Canopy in the Desert* moves cannot be realized unless those memorial candles of Section 46 of *My Little Sister* are replanted in the new soil. The dead sister who in the earlier poem was berated for the "offense" of her "scalding silence" at holidays now speaks in the desert:

> Don't hand me over to a mute wall
> embalmed in the sounds of words—
> I am the threshold of your holidays.
> I am the candles in your forgotten
> candlesticks . . . .
>
> Make me grow, my love, in soil as naked
> as it was created. (*ACD*, 200)

Thus the mother who insists on mourning not only the sons who were "cut down" but the daughter who never saw the light of day is vindicated. The continuity between the European past and the Israeli present and future proves to be stronger than the discontinuity. This is partly because the birth of Israel, like all birth, is inseparable from bloodshed and suffering: "Can there / be spring without the danger?" (*ACD*, 199). Thus the little sister who in the earlier poem is pitied because "she was not privileged to see / the light of the day" is now congratulated for having been saved from a terrible knowledge because she was "privileged not to know / a taste of return"(*ACD*, 108). The irony here flows from the recognition, present throughout the poem in its many references to the three wars Israel had already, by 1970, fought in the desert, that the pariah people has become the pariah nation, and that the Jews in Israel, like their Diaspora ancestors, are destined to be besieged and to live, if at all, under constant threat of destruction.

Rather than returning from darkness to "the light of day," the clarity and elevation of the Commandments, the Jewish people's return to Sinai to recover the Covenant involves a plunge into more darkness and ambiguity. When, in the Eighth Gate of *Canopy*, there is a disagreement between two visitors to Saint Catherine's Monastery about the wisdom of making the traditional early morning ascent of Mount Sinai, the one who refuses to climb says:

> There's nothing
> there. Nothing. Except what
> cannot be reached
> in the light. (*ACD*, 156)

The reason why God and his Covenant are said to reside only in darkness and mystery is that the Jewish people, having achieved its difficult return to the promised land, now finds itself "mixed up in an unfortunate / ambiguity" (*ACD*, 161). Having carried the letters of the Covenant back to their source for validation and reconsecration, the Jewish people finds itself caught in a conflict between the Covenant and the historical necessity to survive within history, whose overriding commandment is an inversion of the Sinai injunction, saying to the Jews of a beleaguered Israel: "You may attack your brother/(shalt murder /shalt murder)" (*ACD*, 166). Statehood may have brought a Jewish "return into history," but it has not released the Jews from the constant burden of peril they bore in the Diaspora. Having once believed—*faute de mieux*—in the virtue of powerlessness and the powerlessness of virtue, they must now face the difficult moral choices entailed by the use of power. That is one price of national sovereignty.

The reaffirmation of the Covenant in the Sinai, like its abrogation in Lublin or Vilna, is sealed in blood. This wedding, like the abortive one in *My Little Sister*, requires death as the bride-price:

> in sandstone still
> red from the drop of the covenant
> my voice is wrapped in a package of vows
> on a land in its time of bleeding:
>
> I will pay for a marriage contract with my best
> my chosen from the land. (*ACD*, 176)

Recognition of the grim continuity between Israeli experience and that of the Jews during the Holocaust compels the survivor to search in the sands of the desert for that buried life which is in truth his own and without which he cannot guarantee his survival.

> . . . I will dig with fingers
> down to the flesh the blood
> until I hear their voice a voice
> tearing the desert coming back
> split in long burrows
> in the dry waste
>
> that was not destroyed. That won't be destroyed
> again (*ACD*, 128)

Although not a religious writer like Moshe Flinker or Chaim Kaplan, Kovner too was possessed of a mystical sense of the linkage between Holocaust and national rebirth, indeed a mystical sense of Jewish existence itself.[21] In *The Seventh Day* (1967), a book of conversations with soldiers about the then recently concluded Six-Day War, Kovner observed how Israeli-born soldiers, who had thought nothing more foreign to themselves than the fate of European Jewry, kept associating themselves with it in the time of crisis. He came to the conclusion that the Six-Day War had been a turning point in history because it demonstrated to Israelis that their own fate was continuous with that of the Jews of Europe, that they too must live with the paradox of chosenness, must commit themselves to life in defiance of the omnipresence of death. "In the Diaspora," he wrote, "fathers didn't bring up their sons to commit suicide, or to despair. No one brought up his sons to abandon Judaism. They taught them that it was their destiny to be persecuted; but, at the same time, they educated them to life."[22] Kovner, participant in the two most important (and wildly improbable) events of modern, perhaps of all, Jewish history, seeks to join the Holocaust and the return to the homeland by a prodigious feat of poetic imagination, which steps into the void left by the divine silence to affirm that the Jewish people shall not die, but live: "I speak to/myself I speak and speak I'll return/I'll return here alive" (*ACD*, 205).

Dan Pagis

The only other Israeli poet who has produced a body of Holocaust poetry comparable to Kovner's in scope, ambition, and imaginative power is Uri Zvi Greenberg (1896–1981).[23] But relatively little of his work is available in English translation (most likely because of his own resistance rather than lack of interest). Although radically different from Kovner in religious background (Hasidic), he too was already in Europe immersed in the Socialist Labor stream of the Zionist movement (later in Palestine he would move to the right wing of Zionism) and was writing poems in both Yiddish and Hebrew. More typical of the next wave of Israeli Holocaust poets and novelists is Dan Pagis (1930–1986) who, unlike Kovner and Greenberg, but like the great majority of immigrants to Israel, was propelled to Zion not by idealism but by terrible historical circumstances. Pagis, as Robert Alter has remarked, "probably never would have known Hebrew, never have had any serious connection with

Israel or the Jewish cultural heritage,"[24] had he not been thrown into a Nazi concentration camp (from which he escaped in 1944) and then been expelled from the life of Europe into the haven of Palestine.

Like the poet Paul Celan, Pagis was born and brought up in a Germanized Jewish home in Bukovina (the town of Radautz) and survived the Nazi period in labor camps. Whereas Celan received some instruction in Hebrew as a boy, and had the benefit of an orthodox tradition against which to rebel, Pagis received neither. Eventually, he acquired a land and a language, the first by accident, the second by a conscious act of will. By the time of his death in 1986 Pagis stood at the center of Hebrew literary culture, both as a practicing poet and as the foremost living authority on the poetics of medieval and Renaissance Hebrew literature. No one need expend energy or ingenuity arguing the question of whether he is a "Jewish" poet, or whether, as Celan said of his own work, his poems "imply" his Judaism. Celan, ten years older than Pagis, told his Israeli colleagues in his 1969 address to the Hebrew Writers Association, that "I need Jerusalem, as I needed it before I found it."[25] Pagis may not have needed Jerusalem but he did live in it and write his poetry in the colloquial diction of his ordinary neighbors. He complained, in one of his poems, of not knowing "Where to begin? / I don't even know how to ask. / Too many tongues are mixed in my mouth" (*PD*, 33). Nevertheless, the fact remains that his life as a poet began with a conscious decision to express himself in Hebrew rather than in his native German: less than four years after he began to study Hebrew, he was publishing poetry in the holy tongue.

Like Kovner, Pagis was a European-born Israeli poet who wrote about his experience of the Holocaust; also, like Kovner, he wove biblical and rabbinic motifs into the texture of his verse. But his present had no Israeli dimension. With Kovner we move, despite immense difficulties, toward the sense of a meaningful continuity between past and present, of a joining together of what has been separated by history, of a redemptive scheme that will forge a meaningful historical (if not theological) pattern uniting Holocaust and rebirth, murder in Europe and creation in Israel. But Pagis typically shows us life interrupted, cut short, aborted; its only continuity is in fratricide. Probably his best-known poem about the Holocaust is the six-line monologue spoken by the mother of mankind:

Written in Pencil in the Sealed Railway-Car
here in this carload
i am eve
with abel my son
if you see my other son
cain son of man
tell him that i (*PD*, 23)

No distinctive personal voice, this, but one of the many imaginary voices and personalities not his own, that Pagis temporarily adopts in his effort imaginatively to grasp the Holocaust. Here Pagis is Eve, confounded by the permanent division between victim and murderer in her own progeny, and unable even to convey her desperation. In another poem, called "Autobiography," Pagis temporarily becomes the victimized Abel, member of a family that has become famous because his "brother invented murder," his parents invented grief, and he invented— silence. Abel, whatever his long history of misfortune, can at least claim a Malthusian advantage over his murderous brother, for the number of victims has multiplied more rapidly than have Cain's offspring. Thus Abel can boast: "you can die once, twice, even seven times / but you can't die a thousand times. / I can. / My underground cells reach everywhere" (*PD*, 3).

Sometimes the attempt to recover the past goes no farther back than the 1930s. It is abortive partly because it is conducted not by a comprehensive historical imagination like that of Abba Kovner, but by a series of ordinary, time-bound people incapable of imagining the extraordinariness of their historical plight. In a poem entitled "Europe, Late," the speaker is a frivolous, flirtatious, optimistic fellow who tries to divert his girl friend's attention from the worrisome newspapers of summer 1939 to the delights of the tango (that once popular dance that provided the original title for Celan's poem "Todesfuge," "Todestango"):

what year is it?
Thirty-nine and a half, still awfully early,
you can turn off the radio.
I would like to introduce you to:
the sea breeze, the life of the party,
terribly mischievous,
whirling in a bell-skirt, slapping down
the worried newspapers: tango! tango!

He, in his attempt to reassure, like Eve in her attempt to warn and dissuade, is stopped by the enormity of history, which cuts off syntax and paralyzes expression:

> You'll see, madame,
> that everything will be all right,
> just heavenly—you wait and see.
> No it could never happen here,
> don't worry so—you'll see—it could (*PD*, 23)

If the poetic imaginations of writers like Kovner (or the German-born Nelly Sachs) try to fathom the Holocaust by viewing it under the aspect of a paradoxical history that makes tragedy indispensable to redemption, Pagis's imagination toys with the reversibility of history, but in a more mordant manner than Cynthia Ozick's "dream of reversal" discussed in the previous chapter.[26] In a poem called "Draft of a Reparations Agreement," he starts with a series of acrid analogies to the idea of physical restitution that was at least implicit in the German-Israeli reparations agreement, which in effect penalized the postwar German regime because its Nazi predecessors had not quite completed their murderous work: had the Nazis killed more, Germany would have paid less to survivors. Suppose, says the poet, we could have restitution: "the scream back into the throat. / The gold teeth back to the gums. / . . . The smoke back to the tin chimney . . . and already you will be covered with skin and sinews and you will live, look, you will have your lives back, sit in the living room, read the evening paper." It's never too late, thinks the speaker. As for that little matter of the yellow star, all the way back at the beginning of the process, however, "It will be torn from your chest / immediately / and will emigrate / to the sky" (*PD*, 27). That is to say, something more than worldly *historical* reversibility would be required for a full reparations agreement. This unpleasant business began in "the sky": the blessing and the curse of chosenness, as the Yiddish poets saw, were inseparable. "O God of Mercy," wrote Kadia Molodowsky, "For the time being/Choose another people./We are tired of death, tired of corpses" (*TYP*, 289-90). Like her, Pagis sees the heavens themselves implicated at the inception of the history of anti-Jewish terror.

Pagis may start with history, but usually his imagination forces him to metahistory, and when this happens he is working in the realm of Nelly Sachs, who imagined the sufferings of the Jewish people to have been "constellated" in the heavens themselves. Her sense of a radically disoriented universe, torn loose from ordinary modes of time and space, and viewed from a perspective that is not earthly but intergalactic, is often echoed in Pagis's verse. So too is her sense of transformation, metamorphosis, and even reciprocity between the realms of death and life.

In a lengthy poem called "Footprints," we find Pagis again impersonating—but impersonating a creature who is at once a Holocaust victim, a cloud, a wreath of smoke; an earthly figure mired in mud and a heavenly one whose appearance in their realm confounds the angels. The circumstantial reality of the Holocaust permeates the poem in references to refugees, "unloading of cattle-cars," the speaker's body mistakenly forgotten in a sealed car, passports showing double citizenship called into question at the border, shoes piled up in "a great gaping heap," "bayonets rising / to fulfill their role" in a victim, pits for bodies, and "convoys of smoke." The footprints of the title, like the global wounds Nelly Sachs envisioned, have permanently scarred "this ball of the earth." Therefore the poetic imagination can only express its sense of the enormity of the crime by trying to pass from historical fact to superhistorical truth. Ordinary distinctions between this world and the next, between body and soul, between man and nature, between man and God, are suspended. The speaker, dead yet alive, has been perpetuated, albeit against his will, in a restless cloud. Old problems of dual citizenship continue to plague him now that he is a new kind of refugee, one who wonders: "Can I pass from my body and onwards—" (*PD*, 31). Will bribes to the officials be any more useful than they were in the terrestrial world in effecting escapes across borders? If he is now an element, maybe he can steal across the border just the way the rain does. If he is still alive in some form, then he must be diligent and immerse himself "in the laws of heavenly grammar," learn "the declensions and ascensions of silence." (*PD*, 33) By dint of such diligence, he does attain to heaven, but when the angels behold a body—the body, now, not just of a single self but of a whole collectivity—"Frozen and burst, clotted, scarred,/charred, choked" (*PD*, 33), they expel him and he is forced to descend rung by rung on an endless ladder until he falls back into the world, the same wretched "ball of the earth, / scarred, covered with footprints"(*PD*, 37). Here the contrast with Nelly Sachs is at least as striking as the similarities have been: Pagis delves into transformation, metamorphosis, reversibility, obliteration of all distinctions, even between life and death, this world and the next: but he does not admit resurrection and restoration, whether particular or general, national or celestial.

One of the few poems in which he *appears* to come close to such a consolatory note is "Testimony." The poem begins with the speaker pondering the relation between himself and the Nazi murderers, but then moves on to the still more paradoxical similarity between himself and the creator. How odd that he should be related by his humanity to murderers. How much odder that he should be related by the particular manner in which he was murdered to his creator:

> No no: they definitely were
> human beings: uniforms, boots.
> How to explain? They were created
> in the image.
>
> I was a shade.
> A different creator made me.
>
> And he in his mercy left nothing of me that would die.
> And I fled to him, floated up weightless, blue,
> forgiving — I would even say: apologizing—
> smoke to omnipotent smoke
> that has no face or image. (*PD*, 25)

Here Pagis's compulsion towards transformations and metamorphoses leads him to the fiercely ironical suggestion that man is not created but only murdered in the image of God. Such paradoxical consolations, at once theologically sound and blasphemous, exact a price the poet is unwilling to pay, just as Glatstein, in "Smoke," would not aspire to unity with a God reached only through transfiguring death in the ovens and chimneys of Auschwitz.

Pagis's work is valuable not only because of its intrinsic merits but because it suggests the extent to which the dominant patterns of Holocaust poetry, in Israel and elsewhere, patterns forged by writers with ambitious historical and prophetic aspirations, could impose themselves even on younger writers who viewed history as a nightmare and prophesy as a risky business best left to fools and professors.

Aharon Appelfeld

Like Dan Pagis, two years his senior, Aharon Appelfeld was born in Bukovina and brought up in a Germanized Jewish home. His mother was murdered by the Nazis and he, at age eight, was sent to a concentration camp. He managed to escape and then spent three years hiding in the Ukrainian countryside before joining the Russian army. Like Pagis, he made his way to Palestine in 1946. Among Israeli novelists who deal primarily with the Holocaust, he is now the best-known and most highly esteemed. Irving Howe has called him "one of the best novelists alive."[27]

Despite the instant and universal association that now exists between Appelfeld's name and the Holocaust, the relation between his fiction and historical reality is curious. Its special quality is epitomized in his most widely read novel, *Badenheim 1939*. Appelfeld believes that he need only specify the year in his title to get the reader to supply the historical background, texture, and focus that, with a kind of reticence resembling that of Victorian novelists about sex, he resolutely declines to supply in the story itself. "In *Badenheim 1939* I completely ignored the historical explanation. I assumed that the historical facts were known to readers and that they would fill in what was missing."[28]

This reticence about history is, then, partly a matter of spare, understated technique, but also a means of suggesting that the Jewish catastrophe in World War II was more than historical. Rather, the Jews were overwhelmed by "archaic mythical forces, a kind of dark subconscious the meaning of which we did not know, nor do we know it to this day" (Roth 1988, 28). In *Badenheim 1939* we hear that "some other time, from some other place, had invaded the town and was silently establishing itself."[29]

Outwardly, the book is an unsystematic collection of laconically recounted incidents in a Jewish resort town in Vienna shortly before World War II. Badenheim is a vacation retreat for cultivated, middle class Jews. Appelfeld has said that such resorts "occupied a particular place in my memories. . . . Every time I tried to reconstruct those forgotten resorts, I had visions of the trains and the camps, and my most hidden childhood memories were spotted with the soot from the trains" (Roth 1988, 29).

Badenheim offers the attractions of a music festival, poetry readings, excellent pastry, transient romance. As spring returns, so do the regular vacationers. But this year, instead of the seasonal signs of renewal, hidden fears and ominous disturbances, internal as well as external, threaten the old atmosphere and comfort. The pharmacist's wife Trude watches the visitors arrive, and thinks they all resemble patients in a sanatorium (as if they had wandered in from a Thomas Mann novel). She, the novel's Cassandra, is stirred by memories of Jewish life on the banks of the Vistula in the Poland of her birth. The reader not only shares her sense of doom; he knows exactly what it is to be. Another character, Frau Zauberblit, really has escaped from a sanatorium for a few weeks in the hotel. The premonitions of the vacationers begin to be confirmed (and reenforced) by the announcement that the jurisdiction of the Sanitation Department has been extended: it has been "authorized to conduct independent investigations" (*Badenheim*, 11). Soon, as a result of these investigations, the sanitary experts order that all citizens who are Jews must register with the Sanitation Department "no later than the end of the month" (*Badenheim*, 20).

We then get a full range of responses to this order issued by a department that is busily putting up fences, planting flags, unloading cement pillars and rolls of barbed wire—all in apparent preparation for "a public celebration." At least they are as full a range of responses as can be expected from assimilated Jews who have been blinded by the certainty that they are no longer Jews, so that what applies to "the Jews" does not apply to them. Dr. Pappenheim, the impresario of the arts festival, hastens to reassure worriers by speculating that "the Sanitation Department wants to boast of its important guests and is thus writing their names down in its Golden Book." Others, in what must be construed as a mordant comment by Appelfeld on incurable Jewish optimism, admire the efficiency of their persecutors: "Nothing like it [the Sanitation Department] for order and beauty" (*Badenheim*, 15, 23, 24). The most sanguine, encouraged by the posters heralding the wonderful fresh air in Poland, think about soon returning there.

Many who have never thought of themselves or been recognized by others as Jews at all "began unburdening themselves to each other as if they were speaking of an old illness which there was no longer any point in hiding." Still others, displeased by the order, blame it on the *Ostjuden*, the uncouth Jews from the East. The antisemitic Jewish doctor Langmann, for example, regards himself as a free Austrian citizen— "'Let them send the Polish Jews to Poland; they deserve their country. I landed in this mess by mistake.'" Frau Milbaum, an even grander personage than Dr. Langmann, senses a conspiracy against her. Despite having had two husbands with titles, she could not prevent the Sanitation Department clerks from attending exclusively to her father's name. She considers the other Badenheim guests to be riff-raff, and shuts herself in her room to write letters "about those clowns, the *Ostjuden*, who had taken over Badenheim and were dragging every bit of true culture through the dirt." Yet even the most ardent devotees of "true culture," the most committed participants in European Christendom's high artistic forms, are not immune from the taint of easternness. One character, in fact, blames all the Jews' misfortunes on "Dr. Pappenheim, the arch *Ostjude* and source of all our troubles. Who invented the Festival if not Pappenheim? Who filled the town with morbid artists and decadent vacationers?" (*Badenheim*, 21, 45, 80, 113–14).

As in so many Jewish stories of impending catastrophe, whose forebodings yield their significance to everyone except the doomed victims, a messenger comes to warn that the world they know will soon disintegrate. We hear a vague story about a man who a few years earlier had shouted at the Badenheimers: "Save your souls while there is still time!" (*Badenheim*, 41), but he found few disciples, and was discredited by rumors of personal scandal.

Soon the town is quarantined, for this vacation resort is also a home of that disease called Jewishness. Then deportations to Poland begin. Some of the Jews do object to these "inconveniences," but they do so in a legalistic, formal way that reveals their incomprehension of the extremity of their situation. "The words *procedure* and *appeal* seemed to satisfy him. . . . The contact with the old words restored him to his sanity" (*Badenheim*, 70, 99). Like soft snow, these words conceal the ugly actuality of the Jews' peril.

Appelfeld has often expressed his indebtedness to Kafka, whom he began to read in Israel during the 1950s. This novel expresses Kafka's sense of the intrinsic link between bureaucratic processes and an all-encompassing metaphysical web of death. Still more, it shows Kafka's keen sense of the victims' endless capacity for complicity through self-delusion. In Kafka's story "An Old Manuscript," for example, ferocious nomads descend on a nameless town, steal what they need from local merchants, and behave with utmost savagery toward the inhabitants. And what do the townspeople do? They pool resources to subsidize the predators' principal victim, and then, faced by imminent ruin, feebly conclude that "this is a misunderstanding of some kind." Similarly, Appelfeld's Badenheimers, rather than recognize the murderous enmity directed against them and consider means of opposing it, seek refuge in the by now familiar formulas of evasion and self-deception: "It's not a question of a crime, but of a misunderstanding. We too . . . are the victims of a misunderstanding" (*Badenheim*, 98–99).

What these Jews misunderstand, moreover, is not just the ultimate design of the Sanitation Department, but the uniqueness of their situation, its unprecedented character, which makes it as difficult for the victim to imagine as for the artist to represent. Two of Pappenheim's musicians, puzzling over their impending deportation to Poland, produce one of the most poignant and haunting snatches of dialogue in all of Holocaust literature:

> "What will they do with us there in Poland?"
> asked one of the musicians.
> "What do you mean? You'll be a musician, just as
> you've always been," said the friend sitting half
> asleep next to him.
> "In that case why send us there at all?"
> The friend sought an impressive formula. "Historical
> necessity," he said.
> "Kill me, I don't understand it. Ordinary common sense
> can't comprehend it."
> "In that case, kill your ordinary common sense and
> maybe you'll begin to understand." (*Badenheim*, 70)

To understand what was happening to them, the Jews would have had to kill their common sense. Hannah Arendt, in the concluding volume of *The Origins of Totalitarianism*, argued that "There is a great temptation to explain away the intrinsically incredible by means of liberal rationalizations. In each one of us, there lurks such a liberal, wheedling us with the voice of common sense" (Arendt 1951, III, 137–38). This wheedling voice of common sense pervades *Badenheim 1939* in the ingenuousness, the frank and artless and naive character of the clownish Jewish victims of misfortune. "Isn't it fascinating," Appelfeld has written, "to see how easy it was to fool the Jews? With the simplest, almost childish tricks they were gathered up in ghettos, starved for months, encouraged with false hopes and finally sent to their death by train" (Roth 1988, 28).

Appelfeld, in comments about his work, has always professed love for the very weaknesses of such Jews as he depicts in *Badenheim*, but some of his critics contend that his professions are belied by the works themselves, that in fact he scorns these people. Ruth Wisse, for example, has charged that Appelfeld's mode of presenting the "ugly, assimilated Jews" in his novels is "more damning of the victims than of the crime committed against them." The reason why this is so, she alleges, is that the novel, like its characters, seems to equate the Germans and Austrians with fate itself, implying that the westernizing, assimilated Jews accepted their deportation in cattle cars to the Poland of their origin as their destiny. "In this way," she concludes, "*Badenheim 1939* spares its readers any confrontation with history, a process determined by the choices of living persons."[30]

Yet the dialogue in which the two musicians debate the reason for their deportation to Poland suggests that Appelfeld does know perfectly well what is at stake here, and mocks the characteristically modern notion of historical inevitability.

> "In that case why send us there at all?" The friend sought an impressive formula. "Historical necessity," he said. (*Badenheim*, 70)

Here Appelfeld subtly intimates that after things have happened they may appear (especially to generations reared on "social science") inevitable, but that, of course, they were not inevitable until they happened.

The book ends with the Jews being ordered into the filthy freight cars that will carry them to death. Dr. Pappenheim contrives an optimistic explanation even for this: "If the coaches are so dirty it must mean that we have not far to go" (*Badenheim*, 148). This may represent the acme of his incurable self-delusion; but it may also represent the brave front assumed by someone who really does know just what terrible fate awaits him, for two chapters earlier the narrative unobtrusively noted the fact that Pappenheim took no luggage with him. In either case, only a foolishly self-confident reader will conclude that he, in the same circumstances, would have acted better, more wisely, more bravely, than Pappenheim and the other doomed Jews.

Although less well known than *Badenheim 1939*, *The Age of Wonders* is the most representative and also the most powerful of Aharon Appelfeld's novels. It epitomizes his conviction that the Holocaust cannot (indeed, must not) be approached directly in literature. In his numerous Holocaust fictions, Appelfeld stops before, or begins after, the killings of the Jews. In this novel, he does both. The first part of the book, narrated by its hero, recounts, from both the child's eye view of a twelve year old and the mature perspective of an adult, the disintegrating life of an assimilated Jewish family in Austria just before the war. The second part, presented (surprisingly) in third person narration, takes place "many years later, when everything was over,"[31] and describes the hero's return visit, as a 42-year-old Israeli citizen, the only one of his immediate family to survive the war, to his native village (belatedly identified as Knospen). The ostensible motive for his homecoming is a publisher's invitation to assist in the reissuing of his murdered father's writings, in which there has been a renewed interest.

Outwardly, Appelfeld's novel seems to follow a well-established pattern for the Israeli Holocaust novel in sending a European-born but largely Israeli-bred hero back to Europe (especially Germany or Austria) to confront his past. Yehuda Amichai's novel of 1963, *Not of This Time, Not of This Place*,[32] is among the earliest examples of this genre. Typically, such Israeli novels explore the following themes: the hero's desire to avenge the murder of his family and friends; the frustration of his revenge by the Jewish incapacity for "normal" hatred; sabra (native-born Israeli) shame for the "passivity" of European Jews who seemed to have gone "like sheep to the slaughter," and disgust for the few Jewish survivors who have chosen to remain in Europe; the conflict between the longing to forget, and the compulsion to remember, the past; the paradoxical link between German death factories producing Jewish corpses and peacetime German industries producing the German "economic miracle"; the nature and extent of German (and Austrian) guilt. But Appelfeld shows little, if any, interest in these themes. His overriding, even obsessive, concern is with antisemitism, most especially the antisemitism of assimilated Jews, the geography of whose inner world he tries to map. The story begins by juxtaposing the expulsion of the young hero, Bruno, and his mother from a summer resort because they are Jews with the father's absorption in his literary triumphs in Vienna and Prague. The expulsion and the subsequent order that Jews register fail to concentrate the father's mind on the growing danger (this is 1938) to Jews of Austrian antisemitism. An intimate family friend is fired from her acting job at the National Theatre because she is Jewish, yet the father is delighted to have the same institution dramatize one of his stories. The main effect of rising official antisemitism on the father is to exacerbate his hatred for the objectionable Jews—the vulgar ones, the bourgeois businessmen, the new arrivals from the east, the religious ones—who have incited the resentment of the gentiles. When he learned from his wife about the strange night train that had stopped to have its Jewish passengers registered, he at first denounced the bureaucracy, "but immediately added that ever since the *Ostjuden* had arrived things had gone haywire." He criticizes little Bruno's violin teacher for susceptibility to "Jewish anxiety" and "Jewish sentimentality." Still worse are the unsentimental and materialistic Jews. "Father cursed the liitle Jews who could think of nothing but money and who stirred up strife wherever they went." His proposed "solution" for Jewish businessmen is precisely that of the Nazis: "Jewish entrepreneurs should be wiped off the face of the earth." Jewish religion is equally objectionable. "Believe me," he tells a prospective convert, "Judaism has nothing to offer you, or me either. It simply doesn't exist. But for the anti-Semite it would have vanished long ago." He quarrels fiercely with a rabbi who administers a Jewish almshouse, and predictably concludes: "No wonder people hate them .. . infesting Austria like rats, infesting the whole world, to tell the truth" (*AW*, 24, 29, 53, 54, 83, 103, 133).

The father is by no means an anomaly in the world of assimilated Jews that Appelfeld portrays. His lawyer Landmann stridently denies his Jewishness by insisting "I'm a human being." The family doctor Mirzel keeps warning young Bruno that if he doesn't toughen himself by field sports he will end up "a little Jew"; for good measure he—a physician and "a Jew born and bred," author of "The Destruction of Judaism—Relief and Recovery"—asserts that Jews have "no talent for art" and can produce nothing but cantors and comedians. A cousin publishes "an attack on Judaism as a religion without divine grace" (*AW*, 37, 49, 44, 79, 85).

The "defenders" of Jews and Judaism in young Bruno's family circle are the real anomalies: his father's 93-year-old blind stepmother Amalia and the half-Jewish sculptor Stark, who wants to return to Judaism. Amalia surprises these Jews (whose mode of assimilating is precisely to become antisemitic) by praying, and shocks them by declaring her conviction that apostates (including her two daughters) "would never be at peace. Not here and not in the worlds to come." Stark, moved by an "obscure passion to return to the crucible of his origins," the faith of his mother's forefathers, studies Bible and midrash with a rabbi. He, being one of them, really knows Austrians and tries to convince the besotted A. that "a Jewish pedlar hawking his goods in the streets of Vienna is more beautiful to me than an Austrian cadet" (which Stark had been [*AW*, 48, 103, 108]). But the superannuated relic and the eager convert are lonely voices where Jewish antisemitism is rank orthodoxy.

Jewish antisemitism has often been given the name, perhaps too clever, of Jewish self-hatred. The downward progress of A.'s career epitomizes this. Like other Jewish antisemites, he has conveniently opted out of the real battle to be fought—that is, the battle against the Jew-hatred of the gentile majority (of Austria in this case) by substituting for it the sham battle against other Jews, who of course lack all power to coerce or harm him. But in the course of the novel he is forced to decide not merely whether he will abandon the defense of other Jews—that cowardly decision was easy for him— but the defense of himself.

After his early literary triumphs and praise for bringing to Austrian literature "a beauty that was sickly, but nevertheless new" (58), A. begins to be subjected to critical attack of a venomous kind. His heroes, the critic points out, are not even Austrians, but Jews—and Jews "who had lost all semblance of humanity and were now useless, corrupt, perverted; parasites living off the healthy Austrian tradition." Whatever beauty might lurk in this subject, or in the writer's treatment of it, was "the unhealthy beauty of the parasite." The articles demanded that the Jewish parasite be rooted out of Austrian life and literature. Vicious and slanderous as the articles were, however, "we couldn't even argue that the articles were written by an anti-Semite. The critic, as his name showed, was a Jew" (AW, 58, 72–73). Since none of A.'s literary friends comes to his aid, it is fortunate that his critical enemy dies.

But the enemy's accusations outlive him: they are perpetuated by A. himself. "When Mother tried to refute one of the obscure critic's contentions, Father would say indignantly, 'I don't know what you're talking about. Can't you see that he bases everything on the texts themselves?'" So completely does P.A. internalize the slanders of his late enemy that his young son gains the impression that the critic did not really die young but "took up residence amongst us as an adopted member of the family." Bruno's father does, however, cling to his enmity against, indeed sues, two literary journals that accuse him of a crime so unspeakable that even his self-hatred balks at admitting it. "'I deny,' thundered father, 'the Judaism others attribute to me'" (AW, 76, 94).

The fact that the father, feeling a "guilt for which he could never atone" (101), turns the rage which should be directed against Austrian Nazis against himself does nothing to slow the process whereby his old school-mates and friends and colleagues among the gentiles abandon and isolate him. Literary societies cease to invite him to their meetings. The Jewish-

Christian League, whose journal he had edited, closes its offices. Although twelve-year-old Bruno senses that "the bitter smell of the approaching end was already in the air," his 43-year-old father scorns an invitation to escape to South America, for this would imply admission that his faith in reason and literature had been misplaced. "Father kept his literary delusions to which he continued to cling even when everything teetered on the edge of the abyss." In Book Two we also learn that when a well-meaning Zionist Catholic priest urged emigration to Palestine, P.A. indignantly retorted: "I am an Austrian writer" (*AW*, 101, 154, 134, 107, 163–64, 257).

He does, however, escape as far as Vienna (and a mistress), leaving his wife and son to be rounded up with all the other Jews of Knospen in the synagogue (a building few have entered before). Even here, Jewish disunity is rife. Anger is directed against "decadent artists," still more against the rabbi himself, who is cursed and beaten—"but for him, for his sermons, his nagging and demands for money and activity, no one would have known who was a Jew." The dismal spectacle of Jewish self-hatred is ended only by the Jews' murderers: "By the next day we were on the cattle-train hurtling south" (*AW*, 217, 174).

There can be no doubt that Book One of *The Age of Wonders*, moving between the innocent impressions of the child and the mournful wisdom of the adult, is partly a representation of Appelfeld's own experience.

> What has preoccupied me, and continues to perturb me, is this anti-Semitism directed at oneself, an ancient Jewish ailment which, in modern times, has taken on various guises. I grew up in an assimilated Jewish home where German was treasured. . . . The attitude toward German culture was virtually religious. . . . I grew up with the feeling that anything Jewish was blemished. . . . It took years to understand how much my parents had internalized all the evil they attributed to the Jew, and through them, I did so too. . . . The change took place in me when we were uprooted from our house and driven into the ghettos. Then I noticed that all the doors and windows of our non-Jewish neighbors were suddenly shut, and we walked alone in the empty streets. . . . I was 8 years old then, and the whole world seemed like a nightmare to me. . . . Anti-Semitism directed at oneself was an original Jewish creation. I don't know of any other nation so flooded with self-criticism. Even after the Holocaust Jews did not seem blameless in their own eyes. On the contrary, harsh comments were made by prominent Jews against the victims, for not protecting themselves and fighting back. The Jewish ability to internalize any critical and condemnatory remark and castigate themselves is one of the marvels of human nature. (Roth 1988, 30)

How much of this dubious "marvel" passes from P.A. to his surviving son is among the questions posed in Book Two of the novel.

At first, Bruno, now an Israeli adult, seems to have inherited his father's ugly legacy. Meeting an elderly, religious Jewish survivor on the local train to Knospen, he is revolted by the man's "self-satisfaction, grossness, and ugliness." Of the intellectuals who once upon a time frequented a still popular Knospen cafe, he ruminates, "Naturally, they were mainly Jews, dragging their restlessness behind them wherever they went" (AW, 178, 188). But now, although the town's landmarks are unchanged, virtually the only Jews left in Knospen are a group of "mongrels," including the illegitimate daughter of his roué uncle, Salo.

The gentiles, however, no longer look as "natural" and "beautiful" as Bruno's father had led him to believe; or if they do, their looks belie the actuality. "Strange," thinks Bruno as he looks at the new owners of what had been Jewish shops, "they don't look like murderers." The family maid Louisa, whom he had loved as a boy, confesses that she had refused to shelter Uncle Salo when the deportations took place: "May God forgive me" (AW, 226). The sole survivor of a family of Jewish converts to Christianity also confesses to Bruno. He alone of his brothers is still alive because he "did not have the courage" (AW, 245) to follow them in joining the Jewish victims. After so much ugliness, the image of moral beauty that captures Bruno's inward eye at this moment is overwhelming:

> The Fursts were honest people. A strange honesty. . . . And in the evil days they stood up to be counted and joined the queue with all the other deportees. The way they stood by themselves in the locked temple stirred the hearts of the beaten people with wonder for the last time. There were four of them and all the way to Minsk they did not remove their caps. Not all the Fursts possessed the same strength, however. August stayed in his shop. And he was still sitting in it. And all night long Bruno continued to see the converts standing at attention in the temple like reprimanded soldiers. And afterward too, in the cold and close to death, they did not utter a sound. (AW, 246–47)

Thus is P.A. confuted.

But his legacy is not laid to rest until Bruno confronts one Brum, who had saved himself in the last days before deportation by marrying his maid and totally transforming himself from a bachelor of "delicate and morbid sensibilities" into "the likeness of an Austrian cattle farmer." Since it is generally understood that "the old Brum was dead" and "the new one wasn't Brum any more," the old cripple at first refuses to acknowledge Bruno. But then he expresses his loathing for the returned Jew, his repudiation of "everything that you refer to as old times," and his hatred of the Jews generally. Bruno, instead of reenforcing Brum's contempt and hatred by mimicking them, throws the old man to the ground, declaring: "Anti-Semitism from you is something I won't permit. From you I expect a little remorse." And when Brum persists by defiantly announcing that "My hatred for Jews knows no bounds," Bruno hits him again. A hatred so boundless that it cannot be satisfied by the destruction of European Jewry deserves some reason, some pretext for existing. "Now," says the hero, "it will be easier for you" (AW, 201–02, 267–68).

In Book Two, then, the hero can avenge his father's murder only by repudiating his father's creed of self-hatred, the antisemitism of Jews. The reader senses a movement in the novel, however hedged and guarded, from doubt to faith. In Book One Bruno is asked by an orphan whom his family has adopted whether "you people believe in God?" and promptly answers "No" (AW, 159). In Book Two, a Japanese studying in Austria asks him (after having heard that Bruno is from Jerusalem, the holy city), "Do you believe?" and gets the reply: "I believe" (AW, 212). The affirmation is of faith not in God so much as in the ability of a Jew from restored Jerusalem to cast off the Diaspora heritage of self-contempt and self-hatred.

Yehoshua Sobol and the Haifa Municipal Theater

Appelfeld is too shrewd an observer of Israeli life to assume that Diaspora deformities would be corrected simply by breathing the invigorating air of Zion. Were his hero to have followed the path of least resistance, he, like many other Israeli intellectuals desirous of emulating the prevalent idolatries of their European counterparts, might have perpetuated his father's Jewish antisemitism in the land of Israel itself. Once upon a time, such a paradox as Israeli antisemitism would have seemed inconceivable. The Zionists did recognize that the normalization of Jewish existence to which they aspired would be accompanied by many things less intrinsically desirable than happiness and national independence: Jewish prostitutes, Jewish thieves, Jewish political parties and their attendant insanities. Few Zionist theorists, however, anticipated that the normalization of Jewish existence would bring with it, along with the other vices, crimes, and historic hatreds of European societies, antisemitism. Yet as early as 1936, twelve years before the state was founded, Berl Katznelson, the Labor Zionist leader, warned (in a May Day speech) that the poison of Jewish self-hatred could spread to Zion itself: "Is there another people on earth whose sons are so emotionally and mentally twisted that they consider everything their nation does despicable and hateful, while every murder, rape and robbery committed by their enemies fills their hearts with admiration and awe? As long as a Jewish child, nurtured by generations of pain and hope, can come to the Land of Israel, and here catch the virus of self-hate . . . let not our conscience be still."[33]

In the May 22, 1987 issue of the Israeli newspaper *Ma'ariv*, the humorist and cartoonist Dosh drew a picture of a shopper in a supermarket that specializes in antisemitic merchandise reaching for the top shelf carrying the most expensive package, which is adorned by a Stuermer-like caricature of a Jew and prominently labeled "Made in Israel." The article that this cartoon illustrated spoke of Israel's need to increase exports by embellishing products available elsewhere in the world with unique local characteristics. Israel had done this with certain fruits and vegetables in the past, and now she was doing it with defamations of Israel, produced *in* Israel. Market research had shown a strong demand for documentary material to justify hostile attitudes to the Jewish state; but it also showed that customers were becoming more selective, and would no longer be satisfied with grade B merchandise produced by British leftists or French rightists. No, these discriminating buyers wanted authentic material from local sources; and Israeli artists, intellectuals, and most of all playwrights, aware of the tremendous opportunities for exporting antisemitism from Zion itself, were responding with alacrity to the opportunity. Dosh singled out, as the most consistently successful exporter of Israeli antisemitism to a world eager for something better than the shoddy goods turned out by Europeans, the Haifa Municipal Theater.

Productions of the Haifa company have been received with acclaim in Berlin, Chicago, Washington, and Edinburgh, despite the fact that no serious literary critic would place the company's playwrights on a par with Israel's many distinguished poets and novelists. The reasons why these theatrical productions find favor with foreign audiences eager for new ammunition to fire at Israel are not far to seek. Regardless of their ostensible subject, they tend to promote the Israeli-Nazi equation discussed at length elsewhere in this book. The company's most prominent playwright, Yehoshua Sobol, contributed mightily to this effort with his 1982 play, *The Soul of a Jew*, which recounted the career of an Austrian-Jewish antisemite named Otto Weininger, with *Ghetto* in 1984, and with

The Palestinian in 1987. The second and third members of this triad merit some attention from the student of Israeli writing, especially bad Israeli writing, about the Holocaust. They are prime examples of writing that takes the Holocaust as its subject yet remains unaware of and untouched by the moral, historical, and metaphysical uniqueness of the event.

The hero of *Ghetto*, which is a Holocaust "musical," is an anti-Zionist Jew named Herman Kruk who belongs to the socialist Bund party. The play's chief Nazi, Kittel, turns out to be not just a great admirer of Jews (Gershwin is his favorite composer), but a Talmudic scholar whose mind was formed not in Tubingen or Heidelberg but in the Hebrew University of Jerusalem. He is also, needless to add, a devotee of Zionism, particularly of the Revisionist or "right-wing" Zionism of Zeev Jabotinsky. The Jews of the Vilna Ghetto are depicted by Sobol as eager to develop a commercial enterprise out of mending German uniforms, and to carry out round-ups (*Aktionen*) and selections. Jacob Gens, the Nazi-appointed Jewish chief of the ghetto, offers the following apologia for his conduct: "In order to spare some Jews their clear conscience I had no choice but to plunge into the filth, leaving my own conscience behind."[34] For the Bundist librarian Kruk, the clear sign that Gens is the dutiful puppet of the Nazis' evil intentions is his "Zionist" speech requiring Hebraization of the ghetto. Any such encouragement of Jewish national feeling demonstrates that the Nazis have "succeeded," since "Nationalism breeds nationalism" (*G*, 77–78). (Here it might be worth noting that the English text of *Ghetto* is introduced by an Israeli critic named Uri Rapp who declares that "historical inaccuracy is unimportant in a work of art" [*G*, 6]).

Sobol's musical was, soon after its April 1984 debut in Haifa, exported to Germany and performed at the Freie Volksbuhne of Berlin in June. It was nominated by the German Critics Poll of *Theater Heute* as best foreign play of the year in 1985, and Peter Zadek's German production was chosen as best show in Germany for 1985. Many German reviewers spoke gleefully of how the play depicted Jews as "accessories to the Holocaust," and one wrote that "*Ghetto* depicts how incredibly easily the Jews allowed themselves to be pushed into the role of victims, sometimes to the point of virtually obscene collaboration with the perpetrators."[35] At the party celebrating the premiere of *Ghetto* in Germany, the hosts showed an unerring instinct for the level of taste displayed by Sobol himself: they served cupcakes in the form of the yellow star. At another reception for Sobol during his company's 1985 tour of Germany, the director of a leading German theater thanked his Israeli guests for having appeared there: "The works of Yehoshua Sobol," he asserted, "will help us to better forget Auschwitz." But then, caught by the embarrassment of unintended candor in words too true to be good, he corrected himself: "better understand the meaning of Auschwitz" (Broder, C).

Having done so much to assure Europeans that the Jews of Europe had cooperated actively in their own destruction and were not morally distinguishable from the Nazis, who were themselves crypto-Zionists, the Haifa Theater had now to demonstrate that the evil spirit of Nazism found its continuator not in Europe at all but in the very state that had given lodging to those who survived the Holocaust, the state of the Jews themselves. Sobol's *The Palestinian* (1987) deals with a favorite cliché of contemporary Israeli writing, a love affair between an Arab and a Jew that is doomed to sterility and failure because of the prejudices and hostility of that convenient culprit "society"—especially of the Jews in that society. The Jews in the play are depicted as, for the most part, ugly, bigoted, brutal, "fascistic." The Palestinian Arab girl in the title role has been so atrociously treated by these Jews that, when asked for her address, she replies, "Nuremburg Avenue, corner of Auschwitz" (Broder, B). The incipient Nazi tendencies of the Jews in the earlier play's concentration camp have now reached their full flowering in Israeli "Nazism." When invited by morbidly curious journalists to interpret his own play, Sobol, with characteristic intellectual delicacy, said that he was warning of the "danger of fascist tendencies in Israeli society" and, in a rhetorical question meant to implicate everyone but himself, asked "How much anti-Semitism do we carry within ourselves?" (Broder, C). If we were to generalize from the example of Sobol, the answer would have to be: plenty.

In Germany, once again, many critics interpreted the play in the spirit of the Zionism-Racism resolution passed by the U.N. when Kurt Waldheim directed that august body; and they drew from it the lessons that Sobol intended. One praised it for showing "the existing reality of Zionism" and the way in which "the Israelis behave as a master race . . . towards the Palestinians." Another thanked Sobol for having boosted German morale by "knocking the Jews from their pedestal of being taboo" and "showing them without their halo." Sobol had, according to this writer, courageously displayed the "ugly" Israeli and had been unabashed about having this nasty specimen "express his fascist attitudes." Henryk Broder, in his excellent discussion of the play's reception in Germany, described how, at the premiere in the newly renovated Bonn theater, the audience burst into frenzied, frantic ovations and "showered Sobol with cries of bravo" (Broder, C). Were they in ecstasy over the dramatic or lyric power of a play that the more sophisticated and reserved German critics variously described as "artistically and politically mindless, even embarrassing," "sentimental and trivializing," and "spewing kitsch" (Broder, B)? Or were they expressing their gratitude for being released at last from whatever burden of responsibility they might have felt over their country's role in the greatest crime in history, released, moreover, by an Israeli Jew who assures them that the spirit of Nazism has moved to the Middle East and taken up residence among the Jews themselves?

Some Germans, to be sure, were less grateful for a play that presented Jews in something like the way they had once been depicted in Nazi propaganda: all-powerful, aggressive, greedy, brutal. These ungrateful Germans were, of course, the German Jews. The Jewish community of Dusseldorf, which had already protested vociferously in 1985 against the antisemitic flavor of *Ghetto*, now appealed to the Haifa Municipal Theater not to perform *The Palestinian* there. Antisemitism, they argued, was already doing very well in Germany, and there was no need to carry coals to Newcastle. The theater's board of directors, after much wrangling, finally acceded to the Dusseldorf Jewish community's request in May of 1987. But while the Dusseldorf Jews were wondering whether it was for such things as the Haifa Theatre that they needed a Jewish state, the play was being performed elsewhere in Germany, as well as in Holland and Belgium.

We ought not to be entirely surprised to see that the centuries-old tradition of Jews who internalize the hatreds and fantasies of antisemitic gentiles and then project them onto other Jews did not automatically cease when the Jews returned from Diaspora to Zion. Amos Oz, the Israeli novelist, once wrote that "I am a Zionist because I cannot live and have no desire to live like the reflected image of a symbol imprinted in other peoples' imaginations, neither as symbol of a crafty and diabolic vampire nor as the symbol of a piteous victim to whom one must offer compassion and compensation. That is why there is no place in the world for me other than the country of the Jews."[36] Now we know that Oz was too sanguine. Even in Israel one can find anxiety-ridden Jews eager to substantiate the most outlandish allegations brought against the Jewish people by antisemites. Such Israelis are an aberration, to be sure, when viewed against the dominant patterns of Israeli Holocaust writing established by Kovner, Pagis, Appelfeld, and many younger writers. But they help us to understand what Gershom Scholem, with whose pre-Holocaust forebodings this chapter began, meant when he wrote in 1970 that "It is not surprising that there are as yet no signs of a reaction, of one kind or another, to the profound shock of the Holocaust. Such a reaction, when it comes, could be either deadly or productive. We hope it will be productive; that is why we are living here, in this Land."[37]

Notes

1. *Major Trends in Jewish Mysticism* (New York: Schocken, 1973), 350.
2. Bronia Klibanski, "The Underground Archives of the Bialystok Ghetto Founded by Mersik and Tenenbaum," *Yad Vashem Studies*, 2 (1958), 322–24.
3. *My Little Sister*, in *A Canopy in the Desert*, translated from the Hebrew by Shirley Kaufman with Ruth Adler and Nurit Orchan (Pittsburgh: University of Pittsburgh Press, 1973). All quotations from Kovner's poetry come from this volume, which contains Shirley Kaufman's translations of *My Little Sister, A Canopy in the Desert*, and other poems. Subsequent references to this work will be cited in text as *ACD*.
4. *Young Moshe's Diary: The Spiritual Torment of a Jewish Boy in Nazi Europe*, edited by Shaul Esh and G. Wigoder (Jerusalem: Yad Vashem, 1971), 27–29. Subsequent references to this work will be cited in text as *YMD*.
5. See, e.g., Leonard Fein, *Where Are We?* (New York: Harper & Row, 1987).
6. *The Writings of Martin Buber*, edited by Will Herberg (New York: Meridian, 1956), 281.
7. Quoted in Lucy S. Dawidowicz, *A Holocaust Reader* (New York: Behrman House, 1976), 148. Subsequent references to this work will be cited in text as *HR*.
8. Chaim Kaplan, *The Warsaw Diary of Chaim A. Kaplan*, translated by Abraham I. Katsh (New York: Collier Books, 1973), 234. Subsequent references to this work will be cited in text as *WD*.
9. *The Messianic Idea in Judaism* (New York: Schocken Books, 1971), 281.
10. *The Seventh Million: The Israelis and the Holocaust* (New York: Hill and Wang, 1993).
11. "Did the Yishuv Turn Its Back?" *Forward*, April 16, 1993.
12. *The Blue and the Yellow Stars of David* (Cambridge: Harvard University Press, 1990), 262.
13. Quoted in Fern M. Eckman, "Holocaust: Who's to Blame?" *New York Post*, March 7, 1975.
14. Abba Kovner, Introduction to "A First Attempt to Tell" (typescript of an unpublished memoir), 1–2. Subsequent references to this work will be cited in text as "First Attempt."
15. "The Mission of the Survivors," translated by Moshe Louvish (typescript of a speech of July 17, 1945, in the Moreshet Archives at Givat Haviva), 2, 13.

16. MS of a speech (translated by H. M. Daleski) prepared as an address to the PEN Club in New York in February 1975, but never delivered.

17. Quoted in Frank Talmage, "Christianity and the Jewish People," *Commentary* 59 (February 1975), 59.

18. Quoted in *New York Times* article of March 4, 1975 on the Holocaust Conference of the Institute of Contemporary Jewry held in New York.

19. See Joseph Dan, "Will the Jewish People Exist in the 21st Century?" *Forum*, 23 (Spring 1975), 61-67.

20. "Threnody for a Movement" (typescript of an unpublished lecture of 13 May 1973), 45. Subsequent references to this work will be cited in text as "Threnody."

21. That such a mystical sense can emerge in Jewish writers of the most rationalist cast of mind is evident in the work of the Jewish historian, Simon Dubnow, who insisted that "Jewry at all times . . . was preeminently a spiritual nation, and a spiritual nation it continues to be in our own days, too. . . . Bereft of country and dispersed as it is, the Jewish nation lives, and will go on lving, because a creative principle permeates it . . . an indigenous product of its history." (Dawidowicz 1967, 233)

22. *The Seventh Day: Soldiers' Talk About the Six-Day War* (Harmondsworth, Middlesex, England: Penguin Books, 1971), 230.

23. A sampling of Greenberg's poetry, in translation, may be found in Ruth Finer Mintz's *Modern Hebrew Poetry* anthology, cited in note 8 of the Introduction. See also Robert Alter, "A Poet of the Holocaust," *Commentary*, 56 (November 1973), 57-63.

24. Introduction to Dan Pagis, *Points of Departure*, translated from Hebrew by Stephen Mitchell (Philadelphia: Jewish Publication Society, 1981), i. Subsequent references to this work will be cited in text as *PD*.

25. Letter quoted in John Felstiner, "Translating Paul Celan's 'Jerusalem' Poems," *Religion and Literature*, 16 (Winter 1984), 41.

26. The English writer Martin Amis, in *Time's Arrow* (1992), has tried to construct a whole novel on the idea of conjuring, by a reversed arrow, live Jews out of ashes and mutilated corpses. See also the scene of posthumous mass healing in D. M. Thomas' *The White Hotel*.

27. See paperback edition of *The Age of Wonders*.

28. Philip Roth, "A Talk With Aharon Appelfeld," *New York Times Book Review*, February 28, 1988, 28. Subsequent references to this work will be cited in text.

29. *Badenheim 1939* (Boston: David R. Godine, 1980), 38. Subsequent references to this work will be cited in text as *Badenheim*.

30. Ruth R. Wisse, "Aharon Appelfeld, Survivor," *Commentary*, 76 (August 1983), 76, 74.

31. *The Age of Wonders*, translated by Dalya Bilu (Boston: David R. Godine, 1981), 175. Subsequent references to this work will be cited in text as *AW*.

32. Yehuda Amichai, *Not of This Time, Not of This Place*, translated by Shlomo Katz (New York and Evanston: Harper and Row, 1968). See also Haim Gouri, *The Chocolate Deal* (New York: Holt, Rinehart and Winston, 1968).

33. Berl Katznelson, *Kitvei B. Katznelson* (Tel Aviv: Workers' Party of Israel, 1961), VIII, 18.

34. *Ghetto* (Tel Aviv: Institute for the Translation of Hebrew Literature, 1986), 72. Subsequent references to this work will be cited in text as *G*.

35. Henryk M. Broder, "Sobol: Making a Scene," *Jerusalem Post Magazine*, 6 February 1987, Entertainment Guide, B. Subsequent references to this work will be cited in text.

36. Amos Oz, "Homeland," in *Under This Blazing Light* in Hebrew (Tel Aviv: Sifriat Poalim, 1979), 75.
37. "Reflections on the Possibility of Jewish Mysticism in Our Time," *Ariel*, 26 (Spring 1970), 46.

5

In the Shadow of the Vatican:
The Path from Italy to Auschwitz

The Jews of Italy

"They were always hopeful. They used to say: 'But the pope . . . the Vatican . . . open city. Here they wouldn't dare touch anyone.'" "Supported by that high sense of civilization that comes from having grown up in our beautiful Italy, mother of morality and law that from eternal Rome has illuminated the whole world, they refused to believe that the thugs of Hitler would dare repeat the incredible barbarities they had committed in Poland, Germany, Holland and Belgium." "We were very incredulous. German refugees who had escaped into Italy would take every opportunity to warn Italian Jews about what was happening to Jews in Germany, but we always said, 'What happened in Germany can never happen in Italy.' You heard that phrase constantly, up until the end." These are the voices of three of the Italian Jewish survivors interviewed by Alexander Stille in *Benevolence and Betrayal*[1] concerning the vain illusions that aggravated their vulnerability to the racial laws of 1938-40, and then to the depredations of the German occupiers in 1943.

Italy's Jews had better reasons than those of other European countries, including France and England, to feel safe in their native land. Although Italy did not eliminate the ghetto until 1870, its Jews quickly thereafter achieved a level of acceptance unmatched in other European countries. While mobs of Frenchmen, agitated over the Dreyfus Affair, were marching through French cities shouting *"Mort aux Juifs,"* Italian Jews were serving as generals, cabinet ministers, and prime ministers. Not even the advent of fascism disturbed their complacency, for Mussolini seemed to go out of his way to mock the racial theories of the Nazis.

"National pride," he insisted, "has no need of the delirium of race." In 1934 he said of Germany that "It would mean the end of European civilization if this country of murderers and pederasts were to overrun Europe. . . . Hitler is . . . a horrible sexual degenerate, a dangerous fool" (*BB*, 22, 55).

These admirable sentiments did not prevent Italy from becoming, in June 1940, Germany's only real European ally in the war. But even in war the Italians acted in such a way as to confirm their Jewish citizens in the conviction that they belonged to a national culture more civilized than Germany's. Up until the German occupation of September 1943 Mussolini allowed Jewish relief organizations to receive and assist refugees. More importantly, the Italian army protected Jews in Italian-occupied territory in southern France, Yugoslavia, and Greece from deportation to Nazi death camps. The Italian general, Roatta, for example, declared that it was "incompatible with the honor of the Italian Army" to deliver the Jews from Italian-occupied Yugoslavia to the German authorities. In fact, Italy's sabotage of the "Final Solution" assumed such serious proportions that Dome Sztojai, the Germans' puppet prime minister in Hungary, whenever he was given new anti-Jewish measures to carry out, would resentfully ask the Germans whether the Italians were being required to do the same. One of the tragic paradoxes of the war was that the surrender of Italy in September 1943, a triumph for the Allies, was a catastrophe for the Jews, who now found themselves, in Italy and formerly Italian-occupied territories, in the hands of the Germans.[2]

But the distinction between Italian fascism and German Nazism, though real, was not sufficient to save the more than 7000 Italian Jews who were deported to Nazi death camps or killed on Italian soil. Compared with their German allies, the Italians may have been notable for benevolence and rescue; but they also were guilty of sufficient betrayal and persecution to destroy or cripple or poison the lives of countless Jewish families, such as the five whose stories are so powerfully conveyed by Alexander Stille through deftly handled interviews, letters, and diaries. Although his book includes many moving and memorable accounts of the generosity and bravery of non-Jewish Italians, it concludes with a lengthy denunciation (by the Buchenwald survivor Franco Schönheit) of the Italian fascists who provided German occupiers with the lists of Jewish community members. "Even though I returned to

Italy," he tells Stille, "I no longer identify myself with the country. It no longer says anything to me" (*BB*, 349).

To no group of Italian Jews had Italy "said" more than the fascists who idolized Mussolini and nearly all that he represented—"Fatherland, Faith and Family." Out of a Jewish population of 47,000 in 1938, more than 10,000, that is, one-third of the adults, belonged to the Fascist Party. Many, perhaps the majority, joined for practical reasons, and it was a standing joke that PNF, the initials of the Partito Nazionale Familiare, really stood for *per necessita familiare*. But a still substantial number who found that their Jewish patriarchalism and Piedmontese military tradition blended perfectly with fascism joined Mussolini from passionate conviction. Their story is embodied in the tragic and terrifying career of Ettore Ovazza.

A hero of World War I and an active fascist, Ovazza saw no contradiction between being president of the Turin Jewish community and genuflecting before Mussolini as if before a god: "We have come, he wrote of his 1929 audience with Il Duce, "to express our gratitude for the fascist laws that recognize the love of country and the sacrifices of those who belong to religious minorities. . . . On hearing my affirmation of the unshakable loyalty of Italian Jews to the Fatherland, His Excellency Mussolini looks me straight in the eye and says with a voice that penetrates straight down to my heart: 'I have never doubted it'. . . . Such is The Man that Providence has given to Italy." (Rabbi Bolaffio of Turin outdid Ovazza by calling Mussolini "a spiritual heir of the prophets of Israel," gifted with "divine qualities" [*BB*, 47,53].)

Such oily sycophancy, to say nothing of the fact that Jews volunteered for World War I in disproportionate numbers (there were fifty Jewish generals in the Italian army), raises the question of whether the Italian Jews were really as free as they claimed to be. When two Jews were arrested in March 1934 for an "antifascist plot" (smuggling leaflets from Switzerland into Italy), Jewish fascists panicked, and Ovazza founded *La Nostra Bandiera* (Our Flag), which devoted its considerable polemical energies to lambasting the Italian Zionists (who had had nothing to do with the "plot") for dividing their loyalty between two fatherlands and thereby meriting expulsion from Italy (a measure that Ovazza fell just short of endorsing). In search of a still more impressive display of undivided loyalty to the fascist regime, Ovazza proposed to lead a squad of Jewish fascists to burn down the Florence office of *Israel*, the Zionist newspaper. At this point, a fellow Jewish fascist (father of the Israeli writer Dan Vittorio Segre) issued the fitting rebuke: "To attack other Jews in such hard times . . . in order to ingratiate ourselves with a regime that has betrayed us [is] to act as slaves, not as free men" (*BB*, 76).

Ovazza's relentless attacks on Italy's small Zionist movement seemed to afford him the protection of powerful friends even as the regime, in deference to its German ally, adopted antisemitic racial laws. Stille paints a vivid picture of the warm personal relations between Ovazza and Paolo Orano (rector of the University of Perugia), who in May 1937 published a book called *The Jews in Italy*, which instantly became the Bible of Italian fascist antisemitism and the preamble to its racial laws. When Ovazza was recovering from a calamitous automobile accident, this antisemitic ideologue inquired after his health every day. In the very month that Orano published the book that laid the groundwork for the persecution of Italian Jewry, he wrote to commend his "dear and noble friend" for "your position in relation to the Zionism of the Italian 'fascists' of the Jewish faith" (*BB*, 66).

Stille interprets the intimacy between this leader of the Jewish community and one of Italy's leading antisemites as emblematic of the "paradoxical" nature of the relationship between Jews and fascist Italy. Perhaps this is so, but one may also view the episode as evidence that the history of the past is often the history of our buried life, whose study may involve us in shocking scenes of recognition. In February 1992, for example, Michael Kinsley of *The New Republic* defended his friend Patrick Buchanan from charges of antisemitism by saying that a person who has "warm personal relations" with Jews is most unlikely to be an antisemite.[3] The similarity between Ovazza and contemporary Jews who find that some of their best friends are antisemites is, of course, broad rather than exact. Ovazza did not hesitate to call Orano an antisemite and to reply, publicly, to his slanders, even though he ultimately accepted the premise that the regime was justified in distinguishing between good Jews and bad, Zionist Jews. In the end, to be sure, the regime did not so distinguish. Ovazza's great services to fascism availed him nothing. His pleas for continued recognition as a "discriminated," that is, privileged, Jew were ignored by the Italian bureaucracy; he was betrayed by fellow Italians to the SS; at the conclusion of Yom Kippur in October 1943, he, his wife, and his daughter were summarily shot in the back of the neck by the Germans, who then burnt them in a furnace.

Although the tragic irony of the Ovazza story is not equaled (how could it be?) by those that follow, the respect and even affection that Stille bestows upon this self-deceived figure sets the tone for all of his book. Fascist or antifascist, religious or secular, rabbi or airplane designer or street peddler, these Italian Jewish victims of fascism and Nazism are accorded a democratic equality of sympathetic understanding that is a chief virtue of Stille's method. The only Jews who remain outside the range of his imaginative sympathy are the outright spies, traitors and informers, such as Pitigrilli (the pen name of Dino Segre) and Celeste Di Porto ("La Pantera nera," or Black Panther), who turned in fifty of her fellow Jews of the Rome ghetto to the Germans; both converted to Catholicism after the war.

Pitigrilli figures prominently in the second story of the book, about the Foa family of Turin and the activities of the antifascist (and, after 1933, largely Jewish) organization, Giustizia e Libertà. The interest of the Foa story arises partly from its depiction of underground activities, partly from its account of how Pitigrilli—a bastard (in both senses of the term), a half-Jew, a writer of salacious and cynical fiction—expressed his resentment of his Jewish relatives and friends by betraying them to the police, and partly from the way it prompts us to ask what was Jewish about these Jewish antifascists. On the one hand, they would ostentatiously affect detachment "from anything smelling of Judaism" (*BB*, 125), but on the other they would conceive their antifascist schemes in study groups meeting on Friday nights and called Oneg Sciabbath (Sabbath pleasure). Describing the Foa Passover seder, Stille remarks that "for these highly integrated, completely Italian citizens, the verses read at Passover . . . seemed a quaint and infinitely distant legend of long-forgotten troubles" (*BB*, 101). But even if they were so obtuse about the Festival of Freedom as Stille here suggests, fascist persecution might lift the blinders from their eyes. Vittorio Foa, serving a fifteen-year prison sentence after Pitigrilli had betrayed him, wrote to his pregnant sister in order to allay her doubts about the wisdom of bringing a Jewish child into the Europe of 1937: "These deterministic ideas lose all meaning in the face of our Jewish family life, which in its unifying and cohesive force survives every assimilation and, against rational argument, continues to see in each new child the blessing of the Lord. If a shadow of doubt had overcome them, in the centuries of infinite suffering, how would they have survived?" (*BB*, 144). Thus does the ostensibly anti-

Jewish secularist demonstrate his understanding that there are innumerable sacrednesses in what people call "secularity," and that the Jews continue, despite appearances to the contrary, to be a community of faith.

Although Stille's main concern is the "world of subjective personal experience" (*BB*, 13), he subsumes his five stories within a chronological progression of historical events in the wider world. After recounting the main events in the rise of fascism and Jewish antifascism in the first two stories, he turns in the third to the great roundup in the Rome ghetto of October 16, 1943, and how it ravaged the Di Veroli family. These shopkeepers, salesclerks, and peddlers had been left relatively unscathed by the 1938 racial laws that devastated the Jewish professional classes; their doom came with the wave of antisemitism that followed Italy's entry into the war in June 1940. Perhaps more than any other Italian Jews, those of Rome were lulled by the illusion that they would be safe. Had they not lived in this city for two thousand years? "Everybody," Silvia di Veroli recalls, "talked about the pope, about how in Rome the Germans would never do anything" (*BB*, 199). The reasons why the Italian Jews were mistaken in their expectations of papal protection will be explored in the next part of this chapter. They were also mistaken in their expectations of the Germans. Italian antifascists who had come to the Rome synagogue to show their solidarity with the Jews warned that they had seen the Germans kill two or three hundred people an hour in Russia. "He had seen it with his own eyes. But no one believed him" (*BB*, 197).

The book's fourth section begins two weeks after the Rome deportations, with the Jews of Genoa preparing for the Germans' next move. Stille's emphasis here is on the cooperation between the Jewish community and the local Catholic Church in hiding and rescuing Jews. In accord with his announced intention of using the stories of individuals as antidotes to overly broad generalizations, Stille describes the work of Jews and Christians in DELASEM, Delegazione Assistenza Emigranti Ebrei (Delegation for Assistance to Jewish Emigrants) to confute the image of Jewish passivity before the Nazi predators. "In places where Jews had the freedom to organize and help themselves, they did so" (*BB*, 232). The key figures here are Massimo Teglio, a Jewish aviator of astonishing ingenuity, bravery, bravado, and humor; Rabbi Riccardo Pacifici, the chief rabbi of Genoa, who would not go into hiding and forsake his duty to the refugees because "with the Torah under my arm,

I can go safely anywhere"(*BB*, 238); and Don Repetto, a Catholic priest who courageously took over the work of DELASEM after the armistice of 1943. Nowhere is the truism that generalizations about groups tell us nothing about individuals more memorably illustrated than in this chapter. The devotion and love of the Mother Superior of the convent in which the rabbi's wife Wanda took refuge permeate her account of the Germans' invasion of the sanctuary and capture of their Jewish prey: "We gave each one the most affectionate sisterly embrace possible; it was a scene to make the stones cry, but those hearts hardened by hatred seemed to feel no pain. . . . Just and Merciful God, have pity on your chosen people." But it is the same Sister Esther Busnelli who reports with shame that the German hunters "seemed to know exactly where to look—a clear indication of betrayal" (*BB*, 254–55).

The book's concluding narrative commences in November 1943, describes the final deportations from Italy, and the fate of the Schönheit family in Buchenwald and Ravensbruck. The Schönheits of Ferrara are, apart from Rabbi Pacifici, the most religious Jews in Stille's book, and they are precisely the ones exempted from death by the Germans because both Gina and Carlo Schönheit had Catholic mothers, and in this instance the Germans temporarily spared Jews of "mixed race" from deportation to Auschwitz. Father and son spent eight and a half months at Buchenwald, when conditions there were at their worst. The story of how they survived only because they had each other provides a striking counterpoint to the famous account by Elie Wiesel in *Night* of relations between fathers and sons in Auschwitz. Upon their liberation in 1945, Carlo, who had been the cantor of Ferrara's synagogue, recited the Kaddish (memorial prayer) at the camp's crematorium.

In his epilogue Stille briefly recounts the story of the remnant of each family since the war's end. The most telling and distressing segment of this coda is the description of Rabbi Pacifici's surviving son Emanuele. His throat is badly scarred where one of his vocal cords was removed, and he wears a medical brace under his shirt to replace the stomach muscles that were destroyed by a bomb. These injuries were not, however, the work of the Germans from whom he had endured so much, but of an Arab terrorist who threw a bomb into a Rome synagogue in 1982, killing a small boy and wounding forty other people. At about the same time, the plaque honoring Rabbi Pacifici in Genoa was defaced by a swastika. Pacifici's assertion that there is more antisemitism in Italy now than in the fascist period can be supported by ample evidence from recent years. Demonstrations by Italian leftists against the war in Lebanon or in favor of the *intifada* took place not in front of the Israeli embassy but in front of the synagogues. In April of 1987 the walls of the University of Bologna were adorned with posters urging "Cannibals, Bedouins, Rabbis, Out of Italy!" In November of the same year, a Catholic magazine in Brescia republished excerpts from *The Protocols of the Elders of Zion*, with a preface by a priest who called for continued struggle "against that minority of ultrapowerful Jews who conspire to divide the church of Christ." These dismal incidents afford one consolation: they shed light on the dispute, usually centered (as in Hannah Arendt's work) on German Jewry, over whether it is power or powerlessness that provokes antisemitic hatred. The minority group that once gave Italy all those generals, cabinet ministers, and prime ministers without provoking resentment now has disappeared from the corridors of power. According to the Florentine Jewish writer Ugo Caffaz, "now there are virtually no Jews in public life at a national level."[4]

The Deputy, by Rolf Hochhuth

> *We have not yet had the consolation of hearing Simon Peter's successor clearly and sharply condemning, without a trace of tactful circumlocution, the crucifixion of these countless "brothers of Christ." One day during the occupation I asked Cardinal Suhard, who worked so hard for them behind the scenes, to "order us to pray for the Jews"; and he threw up his arms. No doubt the occupying forces were able to bring irresistible pressure to bear, no doubt the silence of the Pope and his cardinals was a most terrible duty; the important thing being to avoid even worse misfortunes. Nevertheless a crime of such magnitude falls in no small measure to the responsibility of those witnesses who never cried out against it—whatever the reason for their silence.*
> —Francois Mauriac

The condemning voice of the Catholic novelist Mauriac appears as one of the epigraphs to Rolf Hochhuth's historical drama of 1963, *The Deputy*,[5] and is a reliable key to the judgement of Pope Pius XII rendered by the play. Hochhuth sought to answer the question that, as we have seen, oppressed the Jews of Italy, and especially of Rome, after October 16, 1943. How could the Germans have carried out the arrest and deportation to almost certain death of people innocent of any crime (except that of being born Jews) under the ever-watchful eye of the Pope, the deputy of Christ in the eyes of hundreds of millions of Roman Catholics, including 100 million ruled by Hitler? How could the Jews, in the words of the historian Gerald Reitlinger, "be herded to their death from the very shadow of St. Peter's"?[6]

Natural and inevitable as these questions might be to some, they struck many others as blasphemy, especially when accusingly posed by a thirty-two-year-old West German Protestant. Here is a description of some of the reactions to *The Deputy* from the time it was first performed in West Berlin in early 1963. "Nightly riots, the throwing of stink bombs, and actual fist fights between actors bent on giving a performance and demonstrators equally intent on preventing it marked the Parisian run of this work." In London, efforts were made to have the official censor prevent the show's opening; when these measures failed, a printed rebuttal to the author's thesis was included in each program. In New York, pickets carrying banners with the slogan "THIS IS A HATE SHOW" appeared on opening night. The West German government deemed it necessary to apologize for being the country of origin of "this desecration of the sacred memory of Pope Pius XII." Pope Paul VI, while still a cardinal, wrote a letter condemning the play both as history and as literature.[7] Cardinal Spellman, whose archdiocese included Broadway, called the play "a slanderous . . . outrageous desecration of the honor of a great and good man."[8]

Although *The Deputy* is a historical drama, it is little interested in what social scientists often take to be the stuff of history, that is, impersonal sociopolitical forces and patterns which determine human actions. The drama of individual decision is at its center. What the Pope will do, or fail to do, at this historical crisis in 1943 is a matter of free will, not inevitability. The moral tension of the play rests on the author's belief (similar to that ascribed to Appelfeld in the previous chapter) that it is only after things have happened that they appear to have been "inevitable"; they were not inevitable until they happened. It is because he believes the Pope was free to act on behalf of the Jews that Hochhuth judges him so severely for having failed to act.

In an essay he appended to the play entitled "Sidelights on History," Hochhuth explained that he had in his play adhered only "as far as possible to the facts" (*D*, 287). (This "only" does not mean that he followed the path of, say, the Nazi filmmaker Leni Riefenstahl, whose productions were combinations of half-truths and outright lies, or of the notorious contemporary American filmmaker Oliver Stone, whose polemical licentiousness is on a par with Riefenstahl's. Compared with them, Hochhuth is a sober, diligent chronicler of facts.) He justified his departures from fact—that is, from memoirs, biographies, diaries, letters, records of conversation and court proceedings, all amply mined—in three ways. Reality had to be respected, but its "slag" had to be removed in order to transform the raw material of history into drama. In other words, as Aristotle long ago maintained, poetry has a greater power of generalization than history, which is in bondage to particular facts. Secondly, art cannot and should not compete with the newsreel because the latter can present the raw stuff of the world far more drastically and completely than can the stage; hence the futility of the naturalistic method in dealing with modern historical events.

Finally, and crucially, this particular historical event—the destruction of European Jewry—cannot, Hochhuth asserts, be represented by the imagination. "The most momentous events and discoveries of our time," Hochhuth writes in introducing Act Five, " . . . place too great a strain upon the human imagination. We lack the imaginative faculties to be able to envision Auschwitz. . . . For that reason the question of whether and how Auschwitz might be visualized in this play occupied me for a long time. Documentary naturalism no longer serves as a stylistic principle. . . . No matter how closely we adhere to historical facts, the speech, scene and events on the stage will be altogether surrealistic" (*D* 222–23). In the third act of the play, depicting the round-up of Rome's Jews, the author notes that the treatment of the Jews who were arrested in other countries was so much more beastly that it "could not be represented on any stage" (*D*, 174). Even so, Hochhuth insists—with just how much prescience we are only now beginning to recognize—that he has deliberately *understated* the horrific character of Hitler's war against the Jews because "there is little prospect that in time to come, when all eyewitnesses are dead, the historical truth will be believed in its full ghastliness" (*D*, 293).

Hochhuth's solemn justifications for departures from historic fidelity in telling the story of the Papacy and Italian Jewry were part of a subtle

strategy for adjusting or accommodating an intrinsically incredible actuality to fit the limited human capacity for imagination (*D*, 293). But by
granting that he had departed from "the facts," he provided his critics
with an opening they readily exploited. Since so many of the characters
of Hochhuth's play were historical personages, with numerous colleagues, friends, and relatives still living, he ought not to have been
surprised that many critics accused him of selective manipulation of facts
to support his charge of moral dereliction against the Pope.

Most major figures in the play—the Pope, Kurt Gerstein (whose
Christian principles—so we are asked to believe—led him to join the
S.S. in order to help Jews), the Satanic Doctor Mengele, Eichmann—are
actual historical personages. The notable exceptions are the young Italian
Jesuit Riccardo Fontana and his father, the count, counsel to the Holy
See. Even the young Jesuit, who identifies with, champions, and is finally
martyred for, the persecuted Jews, is based on an actual person, Provost
Bernhard Lichtenberg of Berlin Cathedral, who prayed publicly for the
Jews, was sent to jail, and died en route to Dachau. Naturally Hochhuth
would want an Italian rather than a German priest at the center of his
play. Thus, when Gerstein opens the play by reporting to the papal nuncio
in Berlin the fate of the Polish Jews, from arrest and deportation to
killings by gas, Riccardo responds patriotically:

What you tell me is shattering,
Herr Gerstein—and nevertheless,
as an Italian and as a priest
I have to disagree. At home in Rome
(*with pride, slightly declamatory*)
such things would be impossible. From the Holy Father
down to the chestnut peddler in the piazza,
the entire nation would rise up
against such cruelties, if Jewish fellow citizens
were arrested. (*D*, 81)

But Riccardo's confident guarantee that, as soon as he transmits (via
his father) a letter containing Gerstein's information, the Pope will protest
eventually proves to be unjustified.

The scene shifts in Act II to Rome, February 1943. Here Riccardo, in
the course of painful discussions with his father, Count Fontana, a
high-ranking layman in the service of the Holy See, begins to lose his
confidence in the papacy as a moral bulwark against the Nazis in Italy
and in Europe as a whole. To the father it seems perfectly sensible that a

protest against Hitler should not be attempted until "reasons of state" permit it, that is, until it can be made without putting the Church in peril. He also reminds his son of the policy of papal neutrality between the Allies and the Axis powers, a policy which he interprets as prohibiting protest against Hitler's deportation of the Jews. This means that priests who do protest, who already have protested, are acting in violation of Vatican policy. In other words, or so Hochhuth would have us construe the situation, priests who followed the promptings of conscience would be committing the sin of disobedience.

The idea that a papal protest against Hitler would be a quixotic gamble, a risk undertaken without any guarantee of its practical usefulness, is put forth in more extreme form by a cardinal who joins the debate. "The Chief," he insists repeatedly, "would lose a great deal of prestige if he endangered his position for the Jews." Riccardo tries to rebut this argument by recalling how the Church in Germany, led by Bishop Galen, had in 1941 successfully protested against Hitler's gassing of the sick. "Only one bishop had to stand up and Hitler retreated. Why? Because he fears the Pope—the Pope who did not even back up Galen's speeches!" (D, 99, 120). But Riccardo in effect answers his own criticism by adding the lament that Galen did not come forth to defend the Jews.

If young Riccardo had a fuller knowledge of the position of his Church, still more of his own order, the Society of Jesus, toward the Jews than he demonstrates in the play, he might be less shocked by the unwillingness of his religious superiors to "risk" the Church on the Jews' behalf. Pius XII's predecessor in the papal chair, Pius XI, like the Catholic bishops in Germany, protested against Hitler's anti-Jewish campaign only on behalf of baptized Jews, that is, "non-Aryan" Catholics. In 1934 the Jesuit magazine Civiltà Cattolica, published in Rome and usually close to Vatican thinking, in effect criticized the Nazis for giving antisemitism a bad name. The antisemitism of the Nazis, the Jesuits complained, "did not stem from the religious convictions nor the Christian conscience . . . but from . . . their desire to upset the order of religion and society. . . . We could understand them, or even praise them, if their policy were restricted within acceptable bounds of defense against the Jewish organizations and institutions."[9] In 1936 the same journal warned that opposition to Nazi racism should not be interpreted as a rejection of antisemitism and argued that Christians must defend themselves against the Jewish threat by suspending the civic rights of Jews and sending them back to the ghettos.[10]

Guenter Lewy, the premier authority on the relations between the Catholic Church and Nazi Germany, has pointed out that the Church had no objection in principle to subjecting the Jews to a policy of discriminatory legislation. This became clear in June 1941 when Marshal Pétain's Vichy government introduced a series of "Jewish statutes." The French Cardinals and Archbishops expressed strong disapproval of these measures, but Leon Berard, the Vichy ambassador at the Holy See, reported to Pétain, after consultation with high officials in Rome, that the Vatican did not consider such laws to be in conflict with Catholic teaching (Lewy, 31).

By the end of Act II, Riccardo, Hochhuth's protagonist, fears that he is debating with men for whom great power politics and "practical value" count for more than recognition of common humanity and the intrinsic value of justice. The practical result of their allegedly practical policies is depicted in *The Deputy's* third act, which takes place in Rome on October 16, 1943, the day of the great round-up of the city's Jews by the Italian militia and the S.S. Apprised of the outrage, Riccardo upbraids his chief adversary, the cardinal:

> Your Eminence, we now have come to this!
> Citizens of Rome—outlaws!
> A manhunt for civilians underneath
> the windows of His Holiness! Will
> no action be taken even now, Your Eminence? (*D*, 146)

Even the cardinal, though he believes that Hitler is a divine instrument for preserving the West from Bolshevism, is sure that the Pope will take action to protect Rome's Jews. Indeed, he points out that the Pontiff has already given refuge to some Jews within the Vatican itself. But Riccardo returns to the challenge of risk: "the doctor or the businessman,/the workingman who gives asylum to a Jew,/risks beheading. What does the Pope risk?" (*D*, 151). Now on the defense, the cardinal conjectures that the Pope will do no less, in his capacity as Bishop of Rome, than other bishops in Europe have done.

The cardinal here alludes to what had occurred in France, where the bishops took a firm and vocal stand against deportations of Jews in their cities. Hochhuth, in allowing even his repellent cardinal to anticipate a papal protest, seems to have caught perfectly the mood of October 15–17 in Rome, when even the most cynical expected and feared that the Pope would protest. While the round-up was going on, a letter from Bishop Hudal, the head of the German Church in Rome, was delivered to General Stahel, the German military commander of Rome. It said the following:

> I have just been informed by a high Vatican office in the immediate circle of the Holy Father that the arrests of Jews of Italian nationality have begun this morning. In the interest of good relations which have existed until now between the Vatican and the high German military command . . . I would be very grateful if you would give an order to stop these arrests in Rome and its vicinity right away; I fear that otherwise the Pope will have to make an open stand which will serve the anti-German propaganda as a weapon against us. (Lewy, 32)

On October 17 Ernest von Weizsäcker, the German Ambassador to the Holy See, told Berlin that the Vatican was upset because the deportations had taken place virtually under the Pope's window: "The people hostile to us in Rome are taking advantage of this affair to force the Vatican from its reserve. People say that the bishops of French cities, where similar incidents occurred, have taken a firm stand. The Pope, as supreme head of the Church and Bishop of Rome, cannot be more reticent than they" (Lewy, 32). But these German Catholics fretted needlessly. As Riccardo says in despair, hopes that the S.S. and the Vatican would, after three months of German occupation, finally clash violently, were dashed. On the contrary, laments the young priest, "They live together, harmoniously,/in the Eternal City— because the Pope/does not forbid the murderers of Auschwitz/to herd their victims into trucks/beneath his very windows" (D, 163).

After three acts of speculation about the Pope's intentions and motives, we meet "the Chief" himself in the fourth and decisive act of the play, set in the Papal Palace. He is introduced as "less a person than an institution," full of "burning concern for Italy's factories," angry at President Roosevelt for his bombings, and more concerned over buildings than Jews, although he does think it "tactless" (D, 195, 198) of Hitler to be deporting them from Rome at this particular moment. He expresses contempt for Roosevelt's emissary who (as we know from historical documents) had pointed out to the Vatican that its silence was "endangering its moral prestige and . . . undermining faith both in the Church and in the Holy Father himself" (Lewy, 31). Why, asks the Pope, should the Vatican condemn German atrocities when it is the Americans who are bombing churches?

Hochhuth presents Pope Pius XII as someone so obsessed with global political strategy and the balance of power in Europe than he can barely become interested in this little matter of the murder of the Jews. He sees Hitler as the sole defender of Europe against the depredations (and militant atheism) of Stalin. Repudiating the war aims of the Allies, he prefers "accommodation" with Hitler to the demand for his unconditional surrender; he does not wish to alienate the German nation.

When the Pope does finally issue a statement deploring the "sacrilege beneath Our very windows," he declines to mention either the arrests or the Jews specifically, obfuscating the scandal of that particularity with inflated, ambiguous language. To mention them "would amount to taking a position on military events. The Holy See must continue to shelter the spirit of *neutrality*." Finally Riccardo responds to what Hochhuth derisively calls "words, words, a rhetoric totally corrupted into a classic device for sounding well and saying nothing," with a powerful piece of symbolic action. He attaches a yellow Star of David to his cassock, a desecration and "blasphemy" to the Pope and his cardinal, but a symbol of civil courage in the mind of Riccardo. "No, Your Holiness. The King/of Denmark, a defenseless man,/threatened Hitler that he would wear this star,/along with *every member* of his house,/if the Jews in Denmark were forced to wear it./They were not forced" (*D*, 211–13, 218). To the man who is believed by members of the Roman Church to speak with infallible authority on matters of faith and morals, the young Jesuit is constrained to point out that the moral action must be undertaken because it is just, not because it is useful; but he then adds, with the Danish example to support him, that in the long run the intrinsic value of a moral action proves to have extrinsic, practical value as well.

In the last act of the play, set in Auschwitz itself, but also at various points earlier in the action, Hochhuth presents "evidence" that Hitler was so fearful of alienating the Roman Church before his anticipated final victory over the Allies that he would have deferred to the Pope's protests. "Why," Hitler had written as early as 1937, "is the Vatican so important to us? . . . They rule nearly four hundred million 'faithful' throughout the world; they control an amount of property of inconceivable proportions distributed over the whole globe; they influence a press such as no great Power possesses. . . . We National Socialists know better than anyone that the faith that moves mountains makes history. . . . Therefore we can recognize the importance of a power which has a different faith from ours" (*D*, 302).

The Vatican, of course, had the same fear of the Nazi "faith," knowing from long experience the fearsome potency of devil-worship. It would not risk losing the allegiance of German Catholics because it could not be sure that their fear of a papal interdict or even excommunication was greater than fear of (and belief in) Hitler. When an Italian journalist , Edoardo Senatro, asked the Pope whether he would protest the murder of the Jews, he is reported to have replied: "Dear friend, do not forget that millions of Catholics serve in the German armies. Shall I bring them into conflicts of conscience?" (Lewy, 33). Could any Pope risk a mass desertion of the faithful from the Church for a gamble, especially one whose practical purpose was rescue of the very group of "infidels" whose oppression the church had long countenanced, if not actually encouraged?

In evaluating the dilemma of Hochhuth's Pope, as indeed of the actual Pius XII, we need to remember the circumstances in which the bull of papal infallibility (not to be confused with the ancient dogma of the Church's infallibility) had been promulgated at the Vatican Council of 1870. John Henry Newman, one of the great minds of modern Catholicism, described in 1864 the state of the modern world as rushing hellbent toward atheism. "In these latter days . . . outside the Catholic Church things are tending,—with greater rapidity than in that old time from the circumstance of the age, to atheism in one shape or other." Since, so he argued, only an infallible Church could stand as a bulwark against the deluge, obedience to that Church must take precedence over every other consideration, however humanitarian and brotherly it might seem. Therefore "the Church must denounce rebellion as of all possible evils the greatest. She must have no terms with it; . . . she must ban and anathematize it.'" This, says Newman, is the meaning of a statement for which he had been widely criticized but which he is glad to repeat and endorse once again: "The Catholic Church holds it better for the sun and moon to drop from heaven, for the earth to fail, and for all the many millions on it to die of starvation in extremest agony, as far as temporal affliction goes, than that one soul, I will not say, should be lost, but should commit one single venial sin, should tell one wilful untruth, or should steal one poor farthing without excuse."[11] Espousing such doctrine can make one cavalier about the "temporal affliction" of others.

Apologists for the Pope, in the course of the the violent controversies that *The Deputy* ignited, maintained that public protest by the Pope might have worsened the situation of Catholics under Nazi rule, of the Vatican, even of the Jews. They cite, for example, the case of Holland, where the

Catholic Archbishop of Utrecht explicitly and forcefully denounced the actions against the Jews. The Germans responded by seizing and deporting all non-Aryan (i.e., Jewish-born) Catholics, whom they had previously agreed to spare on condition that the Church remain silent about the anti-Jewish campaign. No less a figure than Cardinal Montini, Archbishop of Milan, wrote in June 1963 (the very month he was elected to become Pope Paul VI) that "An attitude of protest and condemnation such as this young man [Hochhuth] blames the pope for not having adopted would have been not only futile but harmful: that is the long and the short of the matter."[12] No doubt Montini here had in mind his own role as Undersecretary of State in the Vatican during the deportation of the Jews from Rome. At that time Weizsäcker told him that "any protest by the Pope would only result in the deportations being carried out in a thoroughgoing fashion" and —so he reported later—"Montini saw the point" (Schmidt, 206). No doubt Montini and the Pope he then served felt relieved by Weizsäcker's warning. But since the Roman Jews were already being loaded into boxcars when it was given, one wonders what exactly they took this threatened worse fate for the Jews to mean. *The Deputy*, whatever its shortcomings, invites stern judgment on the bystanders during the Holocaust who solaced themselves by averting their eyes from the fact that the war against the Jews could not have been more "thoroughgoing," since it already portended for them the end of the world.

Primo Levi

Primo Levi, an Italian Jewish chemist from Turin, was arrested December 13, 1943, at age twenty-four, by the Fascist Militia, sent to the Fossoli detention camp at the end of January 1944, and from there to Auschwitz, more specifically to Monowitz-Buna, an *Arbeitslager* (work camp) near Auschwitz. Its 10,000 prisoners worked in a factory assigned to produce a type of rubber called Buna, from which the camp took the second half of its name. (Ultimately, Buna's only product was corpses; it failed to produce a single pound of rubber.) Italian Jews were even more disadvantaged than other Auschwitz inmates. They did not speak either German or Yiddish, the camp's second language. For the S.S. they were "Badoglios" (after the man who dissolved the Fascist Party and arrested Mussolini in 1943) and for the French, Greeks, and political prisoners "Mussolinis." Eighty percent of the more than 600 Italian Jews who arrived in Auschwitz with Levi were dead within two days, but he managed to survive until he was liberated from Auschwitz by a Soviet military unit in January 1945.

The first of the many books in which Levi recalled, examined, and analyzed—often with the detached scientific curiosity of his trade—his year in hell appeared in Italian in 1947 with the title *If This Is a Man* in a run of 2500 copies. Although well-received by critics, only 1900 copies of it were sold; the remaining 600, stored in a warehouse in Florence, were drowned in the flood of 1969. But the book returned to life in 1957, under the auspices of the Einaudi publishing company. Since then it has been translated into eight languages, adapted for radio and theater in Italy and elsewhere. It was republished as *Survival in Auschwitz* in English in 1961.[13]

From Levi's sombre narrative one gains a detailed, restrained, discerning, relatively undramatized account of the unspeakable horrors of Auschwitz: its filth, starvation, isolation, humiliations; its beatings, sadism, selections, and executions. Levi views Auschwitz as a unique horror in the world, at once ancient and new, a primal sin of biblical origin and antiquity, but also a fiendishly original experiment in the application of modern technology. The Germans who ran Auschwitz were for Levi something like the administrators of Kafka's penal colony, who used an elaborate, shiny, mechanical apparatus to enforce—on the bodies of the guilty (and "guilt is never to be doubted")—an ancient legal code, which was an end in itself. Even before his arrival at Auschwitz, Levi recognized that the Germans—he almost always uses this label in preference to the narrower "Nazis"—were in the service of some idol that extradited them beyond ordinary moral considerations and also made their actions incomprehensible to ordinary human understanding: "Here we received the first blows: and it was so new and senseless that we felt no pain, neither in body nor in spirit. Only a profound amazement: how can one hit a man without anger?" (*SA*, 12).

Soon he discovered that the Germans fancied themselves servants of History, an idol which declares that good and evil have no intrinsic or present meaning or value, since morality is only a consideration of the long run: good is that which forwards the historical process; bad is that which retards it. Levi's stunning ability to extract a general moral truth from a specific event first appears in his picture of how life and death were doled out to new arrivals in the camp. "Those who by chance climbed down on one side of the convoy entered the camp; the others went to the gas chamber. This is the reason why three-year-old Emilia died: the historical necessity of killing the children of Jews was self-demonstrative to the Germans" (*SA*, 16).

Levi views Auschwitz as both a vast laboratory experiment in the reduction of man to a species of the human animal, and as the modern expression of the sin of human presumption epitomized in the biblical story of the tower of Babel. The Germans wanted to be more than human, and to prove that the Jews were less than human. The Lager is "a perpetual Babel, in which everyone shouts orders and threats in languages never heard before, and woe betide whoever fails to grasp the meaning" (*SA*, 33). But it is not only the fifteen or twenty languages spoken in Buna that recall Babel. "The Carbide Tower, which rises in the middle of Buna and whose top is rarely visible in the fog," expresses "the insane dream of grandeur of our masters, their contempt for God and men, for us men" (*SA*, 66). This dream is a gigantic biological and social experiment conducted "to establish what is essential and what adventitious to the conduct of the human animal in the struggle for life" (*SA*, 79). Morbid curiosity led the Germans to impose on the Jews as many physical disabilities and psychological tortures as they could invent in order to discover the point at which human beings will forsake their social habits and instincts, and, in effect, cease to be human. When he recognized that the "funereal science" (*SA*, 23) of the German effort to destroy European Judaism was the modern expression of a primordial sin, Levi hoped that it would meet its traditional end: "And today, just as in the old fable, we all feel, and the Germans themselves feel, that a curse—not transcendent and divine, but inherent and historical—hangs over the insolent building based on the confusion of languages and erected in defiance of heaven like a stone oath" (*SA*, 66). Levi considered it one of his tasks, in the numerous books he wrote between 1946 and his death in 1987, to carry to the world "the evil tidings of what man's presumption made of man in Auschwitz" (*SA*, 49). In the conclusion of his last book, this rigidly irreligious man declared his belief that "the German people suffered a Biblical 'massacre' of the first born that decimated a generation and a partition of their country that put an end to century-old German pride."[14]

But at many times during his year in Auschwitz, Levi felt that the Germans had succeeded in demolishing not only men but man himself.

In the nineteenth century, gloomy writers like Carlyle, suspicious of the atheistic direction of modern thought, would complain that deism and rationalism had deprived them not merely of their belief in heaven but even of the prospect of hell: "In our age of Down-pulling and Disbelief," shouted Diogenes Teufelsdrockh, Carlyle's alter ego, "the very Devil has been pulled down, you cannot so much as believe in a Devil."[15] The Germans helpfully brought back what the rationalists had banished. "This," thinks Levi upon entering the camp after four days without water to drink, "is hell. Today, in our times, hell must be like this. A huge, empty room: we are tired, standing on our feet, with a tap which drips while we cannot drink the water, and we wait for something which will certainly be terrible, and nothing happens and nothing continues to happen. . . . It is like being already dead" (SA, 18).

The Germans did their best to eradicate all semblance of the ordinary moral world in the camps. They forced the inmates to devote all their mental and physical energy to the struggle for survival, which had to go on without respite because everyone was "desperately and ferociously alone" (SA, 80). To survive at all was rare; to survive without renouncing any part of your own moral world was conceded, Levi confesses, "only to very few superior individuals, made of the stuff of martyrs and saints" (SA, 84). Only those who believed in something, either a religious or a secular faith, could resist the seductions of power in the camps. The law of the Lager said "eat your own bread, and if you can, that of your neighbor" (SA, 145). That perhaps is why Levi in his later years declared that "The worst survived, that is, the fittest; the best all died" (DS, 82).

Yet this harsh judgment seems belied by Levi's story of his own survival, based on the miracle of the ordinary. In a place where "everything was forbidden" (SA, 25), ordinariness was to be cherished as a means both of defiance and survival. Levi recalls the system recommended to him by a fellow prisoner named Steinlauf. Why bother washing, Levi wanted to know, in turbid, filthy water? Washing, replied the veteran prisoner, was done not for its practical usefulness but for moral survival. "Precisely because the Lager was a great machine to reduce us to beasts, we must not become beasts; . . . even in this place one can survive, and therefore one must want to survive, to tell the story, to bear witness; and . . . to survive we must force ourselves to save at least the skeleton, the scaffolding, the form of civilization" (SA, 35–36). The fragility of personality was greater than that of life itself. You would lose the latter if you were foolish enough to carry out orders, eat only the official ration, and observe work and camp discipline; you would lose the former if you acquiesced in the countless schemes of the Germans to inure you to their senseless rules, rites, even cultural adornments and homiletic pieties. These assaulted you everywhere. On the walls of the huts in which men slept two to a bunk were great sayings, proverbs and rhymes in praise of order, discipline and hygiene, and also—Levi's wit is at its most mordant here—"two rubber truncheons . . . to enforce discipline should the proverbs prove insufficient" (*SA*, 27). The wash-room of the camp is dark, drafty, muddy; its water is undrinkable and malodorous when it flows at all. But its walls offer consolation in the form of "curious didactic frescoes" (*SA*, 34) enjoining good hygiene upon the inmates.

Music too played a large role in the Germans' annihilation plans. One of the many respects in which Auschwitz proved to be hell was its capacity to go on and on, to permit even those who survived it no escape from its dominance. Nowhere was this more true than in the way that the "infernal" music played by the band permanently embedded itself in the minds of the prisoners. Marches and popular songs dear to every German, laments Levi, "lie engraven on our minds and will be the last thing in Lager we shall forget: they are the voice of the Lager, the perceptible expression of its geometrical madness, of the resolution of others to annihilate us first as men in order to kill us more slowly afterwards. When this music plays we know that our comrades, out in the fog, are marching like automatons; their souls are dead and the music drives them, as the wind drives dead leaves, and takes the place of their wills. . . . The Germans have succeeded" (*SA*, 45). Their "success" lay in watching this choreography of their own creation, this dance of dead men that offered them proof of the success of their great experiment. That is why, although Levi managed, especially during his stint in the Ka-Be (the sick ward), to elude the pull of "this monstrous rite," his blood would freeze in his veins over a decade later when he remembered some of those songs.

"No one can boast of understanding the Germans" (*SA*, 126), says Levi after describing the chemistry examination administered by a German Dr. Pannwitz to the author and several other starved, filthy, half-naked prisoners. One of the striking features of *Survival in Auschwitz* is its depiction of the Germans as members of a different species from all others, almost like Martians. Early in Levi's narrative, he describes their behavior during a round-up of Italian Jews. They give "outlandish orders in that curt, barbaric barking of Germans in command which seems to give vent to a millennial anger." When a young man lingers to bid his fiancee goodbye, the Germans knock him to the ground as if doing "their everyday duty" (*SA*, 15). Much later in the book, when everybody but the Germans is aware of their impending defeat, they announce that the production of synthetic rubber will begin on February 1, 1945, and "they repair the damage, they build, they fight, they command, they organize and they kill. What else could they do? They are Germans. This way of behaviour is not meditated and deliberate, but follows from their nature and from the destiny they have chosen. They could not act differently" (*SA*, 127–28). The Germans are prisoners of their own nature, incurable lovers of order, systems, bureaucracy, classification, and murder (*SA*, 133–34, 142).

This is an element of *Survival in Auschwitz* that will not sit well with enlightened contemporary readers taught to bridle at the ascription of group characteristics, especially bad group characteristics. In Levi's final book, *The Drowned and the Saved*, the final chapter, called "Letters from Germans," quotes a correspondent who objects to his references to "the Germans" as a single entity, and pleads with him "to remember the innumerable Germans who suffered and died in their struggle against iniquity." Levi replies by allowing that it is indeed dangerous to speak about any people as of a single undifferentiated entity, yet insists that there is such a thing as a spirit of each people, a national character. "Therefore, while I consider insensate the syllogism, 'All Italians are passionate; you are Italian; therefore you are passionate,' I do however believe it legitimate, within certain limits, to expect from Italians taken as a whole, or from Germans, etc., one specific, collective behavior rather than another. There will certainly be individual exceptions, but a prudent, probabilistic forecast is in my opinion possible" (*DS*, 183–84). In other words, generalizations about groups may, if cautiously reached, be valid and yet tell us nothing about individuals in that group. But Levi never, during the more than forty years he brooded over this subject, relented in his judgment of the Germans. In *The Drowned and the Saved*, he recalls his feelings when, in 1959, he learned that *Survival in Auschwitz* would be published in Germany:

> Yes, I had written the book in Italian for Italians, for my children, for those who did not know, those who did not want to know, those who were not yet born, those who, willing or not, had assented to the offense; but its true recipients, those against whom

the book was aimed like a gun were they, the Germans. Now the gun was loaded. . . . I would corner them, tie them before a mirror. . . . Not that handful of high-ranking culprits, but them, the people, those I had seen from close up, those from among whom the SS militia were recruited,[and Levi later adds that "enrollment in the SS was voluntary"] and also those others, those who had believed, who not believing had kept silent, who did not have the frail courage to look into our eyes, throw us a piece of bread, whisper a human word. (*DS*, 168–69)

How, finally, did Levi manage "survival in Auschwitz"? Partly, as noted above, it was by consciously setting himself in opposition to the devices intended to turn men into beasts. Partly, and Levi makes no attempt to disguise this, it was a matter of luck. This good fortune included the strong possibility that "a simple mistake" (*SA*, 117) during a selection sent another inmate to the death for which Levi had been chosen. It also included his accidental meeting with Lorenzo, an Italian civilian worker who brought him a piece of bread and the remainder of his ration every day for six months, and who wrote a postcard to Italy on Levi's behalf. "For all this he neither asked nor accepted any reward, because he was good and simple and did not think that one did good for a reward" (*SA*, 109). The reminder that disinterested virtue could still exist, even in Auschwitz, enabled Levi to hang on. "However little sense there may be in trying to specify why I, rather than thousands of others, managed to survive the test, I believe that it was really due to Lorenzo that I am alive today; and not so much for his material aid, as for his having constantly reminded me by his presence, by his natural and plain manner of being good, that there still existed a just world outside our own, something and someone still pure and whole, not corrupt . . . something difficult to define, a remote possibility of good, but for which it was worth surviving" (*SA*, 111). If there is a "lesson" derivable from Auschwitz, apart from the lesson that free men should "take care not to suffer in your own homes what is inflicted on us here," (*SA*, 49), it is the lesson that morality must not be based on the notion of usefulness, that the moral act must be done for the sake of justice, even if nobody is watching (though somebody usually is).

Levi does not attribute his survival to divine forces, and is impatient with those who do. When he sees a prisoner named Kuhn praying passionately in thanks to God because he was not chosen in the selection, Levi declares the man out of his senses, stupidly blind to the unpardonable, inexpiable abomination in which he is implicating the Almighty. "If I was God, I would spit at Kuhn's prayer" (*SA*, 118).

Levi was a secular Jew, and his profoundest reflections remain outside the premises of Jewish religion and language. Yet his secularism is neither immaculate nor dogmatic. Early in the narrative, he describes his fellow Italians lighting Yahrzeit (memorial) candles on the eve of their deportation to the camps, and he experiences "the ancient grief of the people that has no land, the grief without hope of the exodus which is renewed every century" (*SA*, 12). Later, he comes to view his own ordeal and that of his fellow prisoners under the aspect of the Hebrew Bible itself. In an age that has seen an Auschwitz, no one, he bitterly insists, should speak of Providence; "but without doubt in that hour [when the Germans fled from the camp] the memory of biblical salvations in times of extreme adversity passed like a wind through all our minds" (*SA*, 143). Though Levi would have been revolted by the notion of something "sacred" about Auschwitz itself, he comes close to ascribing such a character to the hundreds of thousands of sorrowful, cruel, and moving stories of the Auschwitz prisoners:

> . . . all different and all full of a tragic, disturbing necessity. We tell them to each other in the evening, and they take place in Norway, Italy, Algeria, the Ukraine, and are simple and incomprehensible like the stories in the Bible. But are they not themselves stories of a new Bible? (*SA*, 59)

Auschwitz nearly deprived Levi of his life, but writing about Auschwitz gave him a reason for life after his liberation. Although he resumed his career as a chemist and relegated his writing to Sundays, he went on telling the tale and reasoning about it in book after book, under a compulsion that he likened, in the epigraph to his final book, *The Drowned and the Saved* (1986), to that of Coleridge's Ancient Mariner: "Since then, at an uncertain hour,/That agony returns,/And till my ghastly tale is told/This heart within me burns." Because Levi died as an apparent suicide the year after he wrote this summation of his work and thought, the book has generally been viewed as proof that his heart was indeed finally burned out, and that he had no more to tell. The question of whether this is really so is by no means the only, or even the main, consideration in examining this book, but it can never be far from our minds.[16]

Through four decades Levi always maintained that he had preserved of Auschwitz "a total, indelible memory" (*DS*, 130). This was his personal act of defiance against the Third Reich, whose entire history was "a war against memory, an Orwellian falsification of memory, falsification of reality, negation of reality" (*DS*, 31). This began with Hitler's denying his subjects any access to truth, especially about the mass murders. In the autumn of 1944, Levi points out in his preface, the Nazis blew up the gas chambers and crematoria at Auschwitz; the Warsaw ghetto, after the spring 1943 uprising, was razed to the ground; all the archives in the Lagers were burned during the final days of the war. The "apparently insane transfers" in 1945 of the survivors of Maidanek to Auschwitz, of Auschwitz to Buchenwald and Mauthausen, of Buchenwald to Bergen-Belsen, and so on, can be explained only by the Nazis' desire to dispose of this army of ghosts who might reveal the story of "the greatest crime in the history of humanity" (*DS*, 14).

For Levi, the failure to divulge the truth about the death camps constitutes "one of the major collective crimes of the German people" (*DS*, 15). That the German civilian community did indeed know what was going on is taken for granted by Levi. The concentration camps and death factories were not a closed universe. They had links with industrial companies, agricultural combines, and arms factories, all of which drew on the plentiful supply of free labor or profited by supplying the camps themselves. Nowhere is Levi's talent for shocking us into recognition with a single, telling detail more evident than in his reference to the Topf company of Wiesbaden, which designed, built, assembled, and tested the crematoria ovens: "*it was still in operation in 1975, building crematoria for civilian use, and had not considered the advisability of changing its name*" (*DS*, 16 [my italics]). The collective crime spreads its taint long after it has occurred.

Exploitation of the intrinsic incredibility of the Holocaust (discussed later in this book) in order to deny that it occurred at all seems to Levi perfectly in consonance with the Nazis' primal war against memory. Nor is it only Germans who understand that the more events fade into the past, the easier it is to reconstruct truth according to self-serving convenience. He gives as an instance the statements made in 1978 by Louis Darquier de Pellepoix, former commissioner of Jewish affairs in the Vichy government in 1942, and thus responsible for the deportation of 70,000 Jews. According to Darquier, the photographs of piles of corpses are montages; the statistics of millions of dead are Jewish fabrications; the deportations (difficult for him to dispute since his signature appears on the deportation orders) were perhaps for benign purposes; the gas chambers existed to kill lice or else (a foolish consistency is the hobgoblin of little minds) were built for propaganda purposes after the war was over; and so on *ad nauseam.*

Criminals more subtle than Darquier, rather than attempt to deny their crimes, have sought to blur the distinction between themselves and their victims, especially the sizable number who inhabited what Levi calls "the gray zone" of privilege ("protektsia") and collaboration. By definition, an infernal system such as National Socialism does not sanctify its victims or allow them the opportunity for martyrdom; rather it does its best to make them resemble itself. This demonic technique was carried to its extreme form in Nazism's formation of the *Sonderkommandos*, the Special Squads, that group of prisoners entrusted with running the crematoria. "One is stunned by this paroxysm of perfidy and hatred: it must be shown that the Jews, the subrace, the submen, bow to any and all humiliation, even to destroying themselves" (*DS*, 52). By shifting onto others, and specifically the victims, the burden of guilt, the Nazis proved, to their own satisfaction at least, that they were truly the master race, for they could destroy not only Jewish bodies, but also Jewish souls.

Levi does not deny that culpability may attach to those prisoners who, for a variety of motives, collaborated in the Lager with the Nazis, but he knows of no human tribunal fit to judge them. "If it were up to me, if I were forced to judge, I would lightheartedly absolve all those whose concurrence in the guilt was minimal and for whom coercion was of the highest degree" (*DS*, 44). Although Levi was often referred to, especially by the writer Jean Améry, as "the forgiver" (*DS*, 137), he makes it clear that he does not forgive the Nazi killers. The state of compulsion faced by the Jewish prisoners was of an entirely different order from what their killers faced and impudently invoked when later called before war crimes tribunals. The Jews had to choose between immediate obedience or death; the Nazis had to choose between obedience to orders or "some slowdown in career, moderate punishment, or, in the worst of cases, the objector's transfer to the front" (*DS*, 60). In fact, Levi is overly generous to the Nazis and their apologists. It has been demonstrated by numerous historians that, as one scholar puts it, "not once in the history of the Holocaust was a German killed, sent to a concentration camp, or punished in any serious way for refusing to kill Jews."[17]

The good faith of accused war criminals who claim to have been coerced is also open to question because enrollment in the S.S. was voluntary (and, of course, all Germans who had voted Hitler into power in the first place knew very well what his ideas about Jews were). All of Levi's intellectual lucidity and moral passion inform his conclusion on this subject: "I know that the murderers existed, not only in Germany, and still exist, retired or on active duty, and that to confuse them with their victims is a moral disease or an aesthetic affectation or a sinister sign of complicity." Levi also knows that the impulse to declare that everybody is innocent is but the other side of the banality that everybody is guilty. That is why he declares that "I do not know, and it does not much interest me to know, whether in my depths there lurks a murderer, but I do know that I was a guiltless victim and I was not a murderer" (*DS*, 48–49). Between the actuality of what the Germans did and the potentiality of what another people might do lies the margin of hope which enables us to go on believing, even after Auschwitz, that this is a livable universe.

Levi cannot insist too strongly on the distinctiveness of the Nazi crime. In a lengthy chapter called, provokingly, "Useless Violence," he argues that what distinguished the Nazis even from their own spiritual guides such as Nietzsche was their "deliberate and gratuituous viciousness." What motive, for example, did they have in forcing people to evacuate in public?

> The SS escort did not hide their amusement at the sight of men and women squatting wherever they could, on the platforms and in the middle of the tracks, and the German passengers openly expressed their disgust: people like this deserve their fate, just look how they behave. These are not *Menschen*, human beings, but animals; it's clear as the light of day. (*DS*, 111)

What motive did the Nazis have in the coercion of nudity, depriving victims of clothing, shoes, and all hair? Was it because, as Shakespeare demonstrated in the "stripping away" scenes of *King Lear*, clothes are a defense against dehumanization, and one who no longer has them perceives himself as a worm, not a human being?

A whole range of Nazi brutalities can be imputed solely to the desire to humiliate and debase, to make sure not only that your "enemy" dies, but that he dies in torment. Why did the Germans drag two dying ninety-year-old women from the infirmary in Fossoli onto the trains to die in far away Poland on the threshold of the gas chambers instead of letting them die, or killing them, in their beds? Why were Auschwitz inmates deprived of spoons for their soup when thousands of spoons lay unused in the camp warehouses? What was the practical purpose of the tattoo, the numbers burned into the skins of all prisoners at Auschwitz and camps under its jurisdiction starting in 1942 ? "The violence of the tattoo was gratuitous, an end in itself, pure offense: were the three canvas numbers sewed to pants, jackets, and winter coat not enough? No . . . something more was needed, a non-verbal message, so that the innocent would feel his sentence written on his flesh. It was also a return to barbarism, all the more perturbing for Orthodox Jews: in fact, precisely in order to distinguish Jews from the barbarians, the tattoo is forbidden by Mosaic Law (Leviticus 19:28)" (*DS*, 119).

Levi's question echoes through a chamber of horrors. Why were Jews locked into decompression cubicles "to establish at what altitude human blood begins to boil: a datum that can be obtained in any laboratory at minimum expense and without victims, or even can be deduced from common tables"? (*DS*, 124). Why was this stupid, yet symbolic violence extended even to human remains, as when women's hair was sold to the German textile industry for mattress ticking, or human ash from the crematoria was used instead of gravel to cover the paths of the SS village near the camp, "whether out of pure callousness or because, due to their origins, they were regarded as material to be trampled on, I couldn't say" (*DS*, 125). One who could say was Franz Stangl, who had been commandant of the Treblinka death camp. When asked by Gitta Sereny what, "considering that you were going to kill them all . . . was the point of the humiliations, the cruelties," Stangl, imprisoned for life in the Düsseldorf jail, replied: "To condition those who were to be the material executors of the operations. To make it possible for them to do what they were doing." The purpose, in other words, was to degrade the victim before he dies in order to lighten the murderer's burden of guilt. This, concludes Levi, "is the sole usefulness of useless violence"(*DS*, 126).

The penultimate chapter of *The Drowned and the Saved* is addressed to arguments that seek to inculpate the victims rather than exculpate the criminals. Levi epitomizes their level of moral maturity by recalling an incident in a fifth-grade classroom, to which he had gone to comment on and answer questions about *Survival in Auschwitz*. A little boy asked him: "But how come you didn't escape?" Levi explained the barbed wire barriers, the electric grill, the patrols, the surveillance of the guards armed with machine guns in the towers, the dogs ready to pounce. He further pointed out that even if the Jews passed all these barriers, they had nowhere in the outside world to turn for shelter, since they no longer had citizenship in their own countries or homes, or families; and the Germans hated Jews as the enemy of their country and the human race. Levi also told of what happened to one Jewish woman, Mala Zimetbaum, who did manage to escape from the women's Lager at Auschwitz-Birkenau. After reaching the Slovak border, she was betrayed by customs agents to the police, taken back to Birkenau and trampled to death by the S.S. as she was trying to take her own life. The little boy, nothing daunted, asked Levi to sketch the camp on the blackboard and then presented him with the plan he had worked out for escape. "If it should happen to you again," advised the boy, "do as I told you. You'll see that you'll be able to do it" (*DS*, 157).

This boy affords a comic representation of all those who, fatally entangled in simplifications and stereotypes, persist in assaulting the Jews with questions about why they didn't run away "before" or why they didn't flee imprisonment and rebel against oppression. Some did run away, some did flee, some did rebel; but the persistent reiteration of the obtuse questions (never asked about, for example, captured Soviet soldiers, who behaved no differently from the Jews though far better prepared and able to resist and rebel) betrays a stereotyped and anachronistic conception of history, an ignorance and forgetfulness likely to increase as events recede still further into the past.

We return, finally, to the question of whether *The Drowned and the Saved* is, in fact, what one critic called "a sort of suicide note."[18] The subject of suicide already appears in *Survival in Auschwitz*, where Levi says that to fall ill of diphtheria in the camp "was more surely fatal than jumping off a fourth floor"(*SA*, 145)—precisely what the Italian police believed he did over forty years later, in April 1987. He also says that while in Auschwitz he was "not even alive enough to know how to kill myself" (*SA*, 130). In his last book, similarly, he points out that suicides in the camps were extremely rare primarily because "suicide is an act of man and not of the animal" (*DS*, 76), and the Lager inmates had been reduced to the condition of enslaved animals. Nevertheless, it would be perverse to suppose that Levi, forty years after his liberation, would commit suicide to affirm his untrammeled humanity. Besides, his chosen foil in *The Drowned and the Saved* is Jean Améry, an Auschwitz survivor who was not only a theoretician (and practitioner) of suicide, but who embodied a morality of "returning the blow" of the aggressor that, Levi insists, is alien to him, precisely because it leads to self-destruction:

I admire Améry's . . . courageous decision to leave the ivory tower and go down onto the battlefield, but it was and is beyond my reach. . . . This choice, protracted throughout his post-Auschwitz existence, led him to positions of such severity and intransigence as to make him incapable of finding joy in life, indeed of living. Those who "trade blows" with the entire world achieve dignity but pay a very high price for it because they are sure to be defeated. (136)

Was Levi, long burdened with the title of "the forgiver," now paying the predicted price for trading blows, something he does plentifully in this last book, with the enemy? Perhaps. But insofar as there is any readily available explanation of Levi's apparent suicide (or, for that matter, the suicides of such survivor-writers as Paul Celan, Tadeusz Borowski, Piotr Rawicz, and Jerzy Kosinski) it may lurk in his statement that "If we had to suffer the sufferings of everyone, we could not live" (*DS*, 56).

Notes

1. *Benevolence and Betrayal: Five Italian Jewish Families Under Fascism* (New York: Summit Books, 1991), 191, 200, 283. Subsequent references to this work will be cited in text.
2. Hannah Arendt, *Eichmann in Jerusalem*, Revised and Enlarged Edition (New York: Viking Press, 1965), 176-77. Subsequent references to this work will be cited in text as *EJ*.
3. Michael Kinsley, "TRB," *New Republic*, February 24, 1992.
4. Alexander Stille, "A Disturbing Echo," *Atlantic Monthly*, February 1989, 20-29.
5. *The Deputy* (New York: Grove Press, 1964), 8.
6. Gerald Reitlinger, *The Final Solution* (New York: A. S. Barnes, 1961), 353.
7. Introduction to *The Deputy: Studies in Moral Responsibility*, ed. Dolores B. and Earl R. Schmidt (Chicago: Scott, Foresman and Co., 1965), vii. Subsequent references to this work will be cited in text as *Schmidt*.
8. Tom Prideaux, "Homage and Hate for 'The Deputy,'" *Life*, March 13, 1964, 28D.
9. Daniel Carpi, "The Catholic Church and Italian Jewry under the Fascists (to the death of Pius XI)," *Yad Vashem Studies*, 4(1960), 51-52.
10. Guenter Lewy, "Pius XII, The Jews, and the German Catholic Church," *Commentary*, 37 (February 1964), 30. Subsequent references to this work will be cited in text.
11. John Henry Newman, *Apologia Pro Vita Sua*, edited by A. D. Culler (Boston: Houghton Mifflin, 1956), 234.
12. "Letter from Pope Paul VI," *The Commonweal*, February 28, 1964, 651-52. (Originally published in *The Tablet*, June 12, 1963.)
13. *Survival in Auschwitz: The Nazi Assault on Humanity*, translated by Stuart Woolf (New York: Collier Books, 1961). Subsequent references to this work will be cited in text as *SA*.
14. *The Drowned and the Saved* (New York: Vintage Books, 1989), 202. (Originally published in Italian in 1986.) Subsequent references to this work will be cited in text as *DS*.
15. Thomas Carlyle, *Sartor Resartus* (London, 1833-34), Book II, Chapter vii.

16. A doctor who was a friend of Levi's claimed that the authorities reached the wrong conclusion when his body was found at the foot of the stairwell in his family home in Turin. Far more likely, claimed Dr. David Mandel, was that Levi fell over the bannister accidentally after a bad reaction to anti-depressant medication. See Esther Fein, "Book Notes," *New York Times*, December 11, 1991.

17. Daniel J. Goldhagen, "The Evil of Banality," *New Republic*, July 13 & 20, 1992), 49. Subsequent references to this work will be cited in text.

18. Cynthia Ozick, "The Suicide Note," *New Republic*, March 21, 1988, 32.

6

Crime and Punishment

*"Gentlemen," said the officer with a friendly
smile, "I know, of course, that after what you
have gone through and after what you have seen,
you must feel a deep hatred for your tormentors.
But we, the soldiers of America, and you, the
people of Europe, have fought so that law should
prevail over lawlessness. We must show our
respect for the law. I assure you that the guilty
will be punished, in this camp as well as in all
the others." Not until after [the American of-
ficer] had visited all the blocks and returned with
the soldiers to his headquarters did we pull our
[SS] man off the bunk—where covered with
blankets and half-smothered with the weight of
our bodies he lay gagged, his face buried in the
straw mattress—and dragged him on to the cement floor under the stove, where the entire
block, grunting and growling with hatred,
trampled him to death.*
                    —Tadeusz Borowski, "Silence"[1]

Historical Introduction

   The Nazis committed their crimes on the most wildly improbable scale
for three reasons. First, the annihilation of a whole people numbering, in
Europe, eleven million and scattered throughout the continent, was a
tremendous task. Second, they believed that the very improbability of the
scale of slaughter would make it difficult, perhaps impossible, for people
to believe that the slaughter had ever occurred. Third, they assumed that,
should they be defeated and brought to trial in the court of the victors,

147

no existing legal system could provide punishments commensurate with the scale of their crimes, and so the principle of making the punishment fit the crime might be abandoned altogether.

To a considerable extent, the Nazis were correct in their last assumption, about the inadequacy of the legal system to punish their crimes. Relatively few Nazis were brought to trial by the victorious Allies, and few of those who were found guilty received sentences even remotely proportionate to the heinousness of their crimes.

In spring 1945, when German atrocities began to receive wide publicity, Allied sentiment for massive punishment was strong. In May, Joseph Pulitzer, editor of the *St. Louis Post-Dispatch*, said that justice could not be done unless about one and a half million Nazis were shot. He was supported by Representative Dewey Short of Missouri, who demanded mass execution of S.S. men (*New York Times*, May 23, 1945). In August 1945 the Allies established an International Military Tribunal with power to try defendants for "crimes against humanity." It tried twenty-one major criminals, including Goering, Hess, Streicher, Ribbentrop, and Frank, handing down its verdicts, including ten death sentences, on October 1, 1946.

By August 1946 the American Subsequent Proceedings Division, headed by General Telford Taylor, had compiled a trial list of close to 5,000 names of those who had composed the central core of the destruction machine. But limits on "time, staff, and money" kept the number of accused criminals brought into court under 200, divided into twelve groups for arraignment. Thirty-five were declared not guilty, ninety-seven received prison terms up to twenty-five years, twenty-five were condemned to death. But no sooner had the judgments been written than the reduction process began. A special Clemency Board was despatched from the United States to review all decisions for High Commissioner John J. McCloy. By the time McCloy had finished his work on January 31, 1951, the 142 convicted defendants had shrunk to less than half; and seventy-seven were freed altogether (among those freed were all the convicted industrialists [Hilberg, 687-97]).

A typical instance of the work of the Clemency Board involved one Ernst Biberstein, a Protestant pastor and theologian. He had given up his congregation to work in the Church Ministry, from which he moved to the Reich Security Main Office and then the Gestapo. He had joined the Nazi party in 1926 and the S.S. in 1936, all the while remaining a man of the church. As chief of the local Gestapo office, he took charge of the deportation of Jews from the city of Oppeln to the killing centers in the East. In spring 1942 he was transferred to the field to head one of the mobile killing units in southern Russia, Einsatzkommando 6 in Russia. After the war, he was condemned to death by the Military Tribunal, but McCloy's Clemency Board commuted his sentence to life. "Regular church attendance" was one of the traits in a war criminal's life which earned him special consideration, and Biberstein, for obvious reasons, had done exceedingly well in this department.

The Germans themselves were forbidden by the victorious Allies from prosecuting their own war criminals, for the good reason that, given the pervasive corruption of the German judiciary by Nazism, such trials would generally have had Nazis sitting in judgment on their fellow Nazis. But the Allies' own good faith in this matter was called into question when in 1954 they approved what became the West German constitution and failed to object to a provision that forbade extradition of German citizens. As a result, for a considerable number of years, many hundreds of criminals wandered about free and happy in Germany, beyond the reach of the law in their own country and not liable to be extradited to others interested in prosecuting them. When West German prosecutors eventually brought criminals to trial, they were few in number, and very few of that small number were convicted. Of the thousands of German Order Policemen involved in the Final Solution, for example, only a handful were brought to trial. A sentence of more than three or four years meted out to such men was considered unusually heavy.

The effort to capture, try, and punish Nazi war criminals is not, of course, exclusively a German story. At the war's end Nazis fled for refuge to the Arab countries, especially Syria, to Argentina and Brazil, even (more surreptitiously) to Canada, England, and America. Nor were Germans and Austrians the only war criminals: major contributions to the organized murder of the Jews were made by Lithuanians, Ukrainians, and Frenchmen, among others. Nazism, far from being an exacerbated form of old-fashioned nationalism, was an international movement, and the pursuit of the criminals has also been international in scope. In 1960, the State of Israel captured Adolf Eichmann in Argentina, where he had been living since 1946. Josef Mengele, the physician of Auschwitz nicknamed the Angel of Death for the experiments (discussed later in this chapter) that he ordered to be performed on prisoners, lived from 1949 to 1960 in Argentina until, fearing capture, he fled to Paraguay and eventually to Brazil, where he died. Josef Schwammberger, who organized the death of thousands of Jews in the Polish town of Przemsyl, lived in Argentina until 1990, when he was extradited to Germany, where, in May 1992, he was sentenced (at age eighty) to life imprisonment.

Resistance to the pursuit and trial of Nazi criminals is also a story of international scope, and one by no means limited to countries which participated in the "Final Solution." Argentina agreed to open its file on Nazi war criminals only in 1992, after the new, democratic regime of President Carlos Saul Menem had come to power. In June of 1990 the British House of Lords rejected a Government bill that would have permitted the prosecution of suspected Nazi war criminals living in Britain for offenses committed in the Baltics, Byelorussia, and the Ukraine a half-century earlier. The vote (207–74) left Britain as the only one of the World War II allies without laws to prosecute suspected war criminals. Almost a year later the House of Commons invoked a rarely used constitutional procedure to overrule the House of Lords and pass the bill. (Canada and Australia changed their laws to allow trials, but Australia announced that it would close down its Nazi-hunting agency, the Special Investigations Unit, on June 30, 1992, after which date it seemed unlikely that any Nazi living in Australia would ever be held accountable for his crimes.[2] The United States has deported suspects for trial in other countries.)

When the Soviet Union disintegrated in 1991, newly created countries such as Lithuania, Latvia, Estonia, and Ukraine could, if they so wished, bring their own nationals to justice or cooperate with Western authorities holding criminals from these areas in which so many of the crimes had been committed. Yet one of the first acts of the newly independent government of Lithuania was to begin issuing certificates of exoneration for thousands of people who had been condemned as Nazi war criminals by Soviet courts. (Lithuanians and people from other Baltic states took part in some of the most heinous war crimes, including operation of the death camps and destruction of the Warsaw Ghetto.) When, in April 1992, a French court dropped charges of "crimes against humanity" brought against a Frenchman (Paul Touvier) for killing Jews in Nazi-occupied France, the world was again reminded of the fact that so far no French citizen has been brought to trial specifically for anti-Jewish crimes. A yet more dramatic reminder came in June 1993 when René Bousquet, a former Vichy official who was facing charges of crimes against humanity for deporting Jews to Nazi death camps was, at age eighty-four, shot dead by a gunman at his home. About 76,000 Jews, including 11,000 children, were deported to Nazi death camps from France, yet it was not until the 1980s that the French public became aware that French police and other collaborators killed Jews and organized deportations.

Although the opposition to pursuing Nazi criminals sometimes hinges on technical considerations or a kind of immoral thoughtlessness or the view that, as one of the British Lords put it, "this was a matter which took place a long time ago" (*New York Times*, June 6, 1990), more often it arises from less delicate feelings. In America, the Jew-baiting journalist (and 1992 candidate for the Republican presidential nomination) Patrick Buchanan, not generally known for coddling of criminals, has made protection of Nazi war criminals a favorite cause. Likewise, James A. Traficant, Jr., the Democratic congressman from Ohio, has defended John Demjanjuk, convicted in Israel of Nazi atrocities [although debate still continues as to whether he was indeed "Ivan the Terrible" or a lesser killer, Ivan the Not So Terrible, so to speak], and Arthur Rudolph, the rocket scientist accused by the American government of brutalizing prisoners, in language suggestive of something less noble than the love of justice. "The Jewish groups that support the O.S.I. [U. S. Office of Special Investigations] should consider," warned Traficant, "that if we let this Government violate the rights of an old Nazi who is not a criminal, they could just as easily violate the rights of Jewish Americans" (*New York Times*, May 15, 1990).

Now that more than a half century has elapsed since the Nazis committed their crimes, it seems likely that we will have to console ourselves, by and large, with what the world's chief Nazi-hunter, Simon Wiesenthal (to be discussed below), has called the "biological solution" to the problem: namely, the death, from old age, of the criminals. When the aforementioned Schwammberger was sentenced in May 1992 in Stuttgart, Judge Herbert Luippold stressed that "with this decision, the court has shown that Nazi criminals can be prosecuted even today" (*New York Times*, May 19); yet many observers guessed that this would be the last verdict ever to be pronounced against a leading Nazi officer.[3]

It also seems likely that the husband-wife team of Serge and Beate Klarsfeld will be the last of the Nazi-hunters. Although a good deal younger than Wiesenthal, they are personally tied to the Holocaust in ways not repeatable in the next generation of Jews and Germans. Serge is the son of Arno Klarsfeld, a French Jew who late in 1943 was deported from the family apartment in Nice by Gestapo agents while his wife, his daughter, and his six-year-old son hid in terror behind a secret wall. Beate's provenance as a Nazi-hunter is less obvious. She, unlike her husband, is a Christian and (by birth) a German. Her father was a soldier in the Wehrmacht and her mother is reported to have told her: "It's a good thing your father died when he did. Otherwise, you would have killed him." [4] Their motives as Nazi hunters are complementary. He, as a Jew, searches for the criminals so that those long ago murdered "will at last have a measure of justice done on their behalf." She, as a German, believes her country "must be willing to take responsibility for its own crimes—without which its honor cannot be restored" (Hellman, 37).

Whereas Wiesenthal concentrated on documenting war crimes, the Klarsfelds have specialized in publicly confronting the criminals, often at great risk to themselves—especially when these criminals have, with the passage of time, become prominent and eminently respectable public figures in their own countries. In 1967, for example, when Kurt George Kiesinger, who had been a top propagandist for the Nazi Foreign Ministry, was elected chancellor of the Federal Republic, Beate Klarsfeld declared, in the French newspaper *Combat*, that "to me, Kiesinger represents the respectability of evil" (Hellman, 74). (Kiesinger had been arrested in Berlin by the Allies at the war's end, but, after eighteen months of imprisonment, was formally "denazified" by a panel that included his own father-in-law.) Therefore, in April 1968, she leaped up in the visitor's gallery of the Bundestag to label Kiesinger "Nazi! Nazi!" (Hellman, 76) and made a public promise, which she carried out in 1968, to slap the Chancellor in the face and recall, yet again, his Nazi past. In September 1969, Kiesinger was defeated at the polls by Willy Brandt.

In December 1973, Serge Klarsfeld went to Cologne to confront Kurt Lischka, an apparently respectable businessman by now, but a man who had been Gestapo chief of Paris during the war, a central figure in the deportation of more than 73,000 Jews, including Klarsfeld's father, to Auschwitz and other killing centers. Klarsfeld walked up to Lischka, placed a revolver between his eyes, and then put the gun away, laughing in the German's face as he walked away. Writing to the Cologne prosecutor, Klarsfeld explained that putting a gun between Lischka's eyes, but not pulling the trigger, was a means of demonstrating that he did not want to enact personal vengeance, but to bring justice, public German justice, to such evil as Lischka embodied (Hellman, 36).

The difficulties that such heroic figures as Wiesenthal and the Klarsfelds have had to overcome have been more than practical and political. The scale and satanic inventiveness of the Nazi crimes have generated a vast confusion about how (or whether) to punish the individuals who participated in the system of destruction. That confusion is sometimes expressed, and sometimes dissipated, in the writings discussed in this chapter.

The Sunflower, by Simon Wiesenthal: The Question of Forgiveness

Simon Wiesenthal is far better known as a hunter of Nazi war criminals than as a writer. But in 1969 he reinvented himself as a quasi-fictional character in order to invite a devil's advocate into the midst of his own most deeply held convictions about the culpability of the Nazi criminals, the need to bring them to trial, and—this above all—the unforgiveable nature of their crimes.

The Sunflower is a first-person narrative by a survivor of the camps named Simon, the broad outlines of whose life are similar to Simon Wiesenthal's own. He was a successful architect in Lemberg, Galicia until arrested by the Gestapo in 1943 and imprisoned in numerous concentration camps. (Not mentioned in the narrative is the murder of Wiesenthal's mother, mother in law, and eighty-nine other relatives.) Lest there be any doubt about the core identity of the narrator and protagonist, he tells us near the end of the story that "The work in which I am engaged brings me into contact with many known murderers. I hunt them out, I hear witnesses, I give evidence in courts—and I see how murderers behave when accused. . . . I have often tried to imagine how that young SS man would have behaved if he had been put on trial twenty-five years later." [5] *The Sunflower* is Simon's story of his encounter with this dying S.S. man in a German military hospital that had once been Simon's high school.

Having heard that there is a detail of Jewish prisoners working in the area, the twenty-one-year old German asks his nurse to find one to whom he can confess his crimes and from whom he can ask and, so he hopes, receive forgiveness. For obvious reasons, Simon is not predisposed to soothe the belatedly troubled conscience of this dying Nazi. He has already seen family and friends murdered by the Nazis, and fully expects to become one of their victims himself. What could be more grotesque than to ask a Jew, in advance of his own anticipated murder by the S.S., to forgive his murderers? Moreover, Simon has come to view the sunflowers that grow on the adjacent tombs of German soldiers as symbols of the individuality that they retain in death as opposed to the anonymity of their Jewish victims who will be dumped indiscriminately in a mass grave.

Nevertheless, young Karl, his head entirely swathed in bandages, tells a tale that convinces Simon of the genuineness of his repentance for his deeds, which included burning alive an entire village of Jews. He speaks in a warm tone of Jews in general, a tone Simon has never before heard from an S.S. man, or indeed from any Nazi. He appears to make no attempt to hide incriminating evidence or excuse what he has done, readily acknowledging that he joined the S.S. voluntarily, "without a thought, as if . . . going to a dance or an outing" (*TS*, 34). After the murder of the 300 Jews, he reports, he and his comrades, so far from being distraught by ethical misgivings, drank brandy and sang songs. But later, and especially after he had been blinded and mutilated by an exploding shell, he repented of his actions. Now he pleads with Simon that he "was not born a murderer" (*TS*, 35), and did not want to become one, but that the Nazis forced him to kill defenseless people. Facing death, Karl begs Simon to forgive him in the name of the Jewish people: "I know that what I am asking is almost too much for you, but without your answer I cannot die in peace" (*TS*, 57).

There is very little historical evidence to support Wiesenthal's portrait of a contrite, tenderhearted S.S. man. In the most detailed study of how German killing units felt and thought about what they did to the Jews, Christopher Browning [6] has shown that German soldiers who were charged with rounding up and shooting Jews or stuffing them into cattle cars to be sent to gas chambers rarely felt the qualms that plague Wiesenthal's young S.S. man. Battalion 101, the subject of Browning's book, was introduced to mass murder by being assigned to destroy the Jewish women, children, and elderly men of Josefow (that "home of Torah" mentioned in Singer's novels). When one of the officers of the battalion learned of the planned massacre, he asked the commander, Major Wilhelm Trapp, for another assignment: Trapp granted the request. He also invited other members of the battalion who thought they could not fulfill this assignment to do likewise, and a dozen did. Wiesenthal's character, by contrast, makes no attempt to bow out of the actions against the Jews, and never mentions the possibility of doing so. After the mass shooting of Jews by Battalion 101 began, several of the killers felt ill, asked to be excused, and were. As many as twenty percent quit shooting at some point (or so they claimed after the war); but eighty percent kept on shooting until they had finished off the 1500 assembled Jews.

Yet even twenty years after the massacre, during interrogation in court, very few of the German killers claimed to have had ethical qualms; they had been more troubled, in youth as in old age, by afflictions of the liver than by terrors of conscience. Indeed, after their initiation into mass murder at Josefow, many members of 101 actually came to see the shootings as great fun, festive events to which they might bring wives and girl friends. Martin Gilbert, in his history of the Holocaust, noted how laughter abounds in many of the accounts of the Germans' reactions to their murderous work. Daniel Goldhagen, another student of the source material related to Battalion 101, quotes the following account by one battalion member, who had just admitted to shooting a sixty-year-old woman:

> Next to me was the policeman K. . . . . He had to shoot a small boy of perhaps 12 years. We had been expressly told that we should hold the gun's barrel 20 cm from the head. K. had apparently not done this, because while leaving the execution site, the other comrades laughed at me, because pieces of the child's brains had splattered onto my sidearms and had stuck there. I first asked, why are you laughing, whereupon K., pointing to the brains on my sidearms, said: that's from mine, he has stopped twitching. He said this in an obviously boastful tone. (Goldhagen 1992, 50)

Wiesenthal's Karl, we may conclude, is far from being a representative figure. But the paucity of historical evidence for Nazis who were reluctant to kill or who disapproved of what they were doing, or who (like Karl) were contrite afterwards, so far from being a weakness of Wiesenthal's book, is itself a tribute to the honesty of his method. Very few of those who have condemned the pursuit and trial of Nazi war criminals as "vengefulness" have tried to make a case for the sensitivity of the Nazi killers as men of conscience. How better, thought Wiesenthal, to make a convincing case against all those who have criticized his effort to pursue and punish Nazis than by imagining a truly contrite S.S. man and asking whether even *he* should be forgiven his crimes?

The main action of the story ends when Simon, torn between compassion for the dying man and revulsion at his request, leaves Karl's room without speaking a word. Not long afterward the German dies. During the next two years in the camps Simon and his fellow prisoners debate the question that weighs on his conscience. One of his fellow inmates envies Simon the privilege of having watched a murderer die, and chides him for making such a fuss over an S.S. man while countless Jews are butchered without abrading anyone's moral sensibilities. But another, a young Pole in training for the priesthood, says Simon should have forgiven the man because his repentance had been genuine, and he had no opportunity to atone for his sins.

Once the war is over, Simon observes how eagerly Germans and Austrians assure him that they all opposed Hitler, but feared to do so openly for fear of offending their neighbors; these neighbors, of course, say precisely the same thing. He also, with surgical precision, cuts through the cant of the professional altruists imploring the world to forgive the Nazis for their crimes. "Most . . . had probably never even had their ears boxed, but nevertheless found compassion for the murderers of innocent millions. The priests said indeed that the criminals would have to appear before the Divine Judge and that we could therefore dispense with earthly verdicts against them, which eminently suited the Nazis' book" (*TS*, 87). (Major Trapp, commander of Battalion 101, was said to have told his driver: "If this Jewish business is ever avenged on earth, then have mercy on us Germans" [Browning,58].)

Writing from the perspective of an experienced hunter of Nazis, Wiesenthal tries to view the story of Karl in relation to that of the Nazis who had lived to stand trial. After all, which of the Nazi criminals was "a born murderer"? Is anyone a murderer until he commits murder? Very few of the Nazis who stood trial after the war expressed any remorse for their crimes, their main regret being that their killing had not been efficient enough to get rid of all witnesses. The dying Karl, it seemed, was very different. But who could know how he would have behaved if he had been put on trial twenty-five years after their encounter? In apparent perplexity, Wiesenthal ends by turning his question upon his reader: ask yourself, he concludes, "What would I have done?" (*TS*, 99).

As a Jew, Wiesenthal could not dismiss lightly Karl's request for forgiveness in response to his repentance. In Exodus (34:6) God is described as "gracious and compassionate, patient, abounding in kindness and faithfulness, assuring love for a thousand generations, forgiving iniquity, transgression and sin." At the end of the Book of Jonah, God accepts the penitence of the people of Nineveh (non-Jews) and revokes his stern judgment against them and their city. Manasseh, when king in Jerusalem, committed frightful abominations, including the burning of his sons as a sacrifice to the Baals. Yet, when he became a penitent, God forgave him. As the rabbis noted (Numbers Rabbah, Naso, XIV): "If a man were to come and say that God does not receive the penitent, Manasseh could come and testify against him, for there was never a man more wicked than he, and yet, in the hour of repentance, God received him." Repentance or, in Hebrew, *teshuvah* (turning) is the central motif of the most solemn days in the Jewish calendar, Rosh Hashana and Yom Kippur. The liturgy of the Day of Atonement not only encourages the individual to repent but even asserts that God will patiently wait even "unto the day of death" for his contrition. No sin, no matter how great, can exceed the unlimited dimensions of divine forgiveness. The Talmud abounds in maxims and stories concerning repentance: it was created before the world itself; it hastens the final redemption; even if the sinner repents at the very end of his life, he can still gain forgiveness for all his sins. It is stressed that forgiveness issues from God alone, but where one individual has directly sinned against another, the offender must beg forgiveness from the injured party; and it is incumbent on the injured party to forgive the genuinely contrite offender.

To the narrative of *The Sunflower*, Wiesenthal added a symposium in which thirty-two writers, theologians, and thinkers of various religious persuasions (and of none) were invited to answer the question of whether Simon had been right or wrong to refuse Karl's desperate request for forgiveness. The responses are a remarkable collection, and show how, where the Holocaust is concerned, the question of crime and punishment is a touchstone for detecting the quality of modern thought, a litmus paper revealing the presence or—just as often—the absence of moral character.

Many respondents say, in effect, that they cannot respond to the question "What would I have done?" because they have never been in Simon's situation. Some respond perfunctorily or hesitantly, as if too keenly aware that they are in danger of stepping on a landmine; in fact, no fewer than nine of the contributors evade the central question and give no answer at all. Several take the liberty of answering the question with other questions. Can the representative of an injured and aggrieved group render forgiveness on behalf of the whole group, including those no longer alive? Since Karl had, on his death-bed, reverted to the

Catholicism of his youth, why did he not confess to a priest? Isn't forgiveness the province of God, not of human beings? What divides human from divine jurisdiction in such crimes as the Nazis committed? (One writer, citing the Gospel according to Matthew [16:19] says that Simon "has no power to bind on earth what shall be bound in heaven, or to loose on earth what shall be loosed in heaven" [TS, 159].) Some, like the English writer Terence Prittie, argue that "to forgive this one SS man would mean, by implication, to forgive every other SS man who murdered, on his death bed" (*TS*, 94).

All eight of the respondents who counsel forgiveness for Karl are non-Jews. Several are guilty of astonishing lapses of judgment. Edward Flannery, for example, alleges that Simon and those fellow prisoners who advised him against forgiveness of Karl "themselves participated in Karl's sin" (*TS*, 115). One wonders what quality of mind leads a person to make the friend or relative of a murder victim, by virtue of his refusal to forgive the murderer, an actual *accomplice* in the crime. Equally egregious are the curious lucubrations of the German psychologist and literary critic Luise Rinser. First she argues that because young Karl had been led astray by Nazi propaganda "he thought he was acting rightly when he killed Jews. In moral theology (and not in Christian theology only) there is right in a mistaken conscience" (*TS*, 197). After confidently exonerating the Nazi killer, she puts his Jewish victim on trial. "Were you," she accusingly asks Simon, "authorized by your people *not* to forgive? No. Perhaps you acted against the wish of the dead Jews. I hope that those dead Jews will grant you 'extenuating circumstances' in view of the difficulty of the case." Having, to her own satisfaction, exculpated the Nazis and inculpated their victims, she recommends to the latter the example of Jesus' utterance at the Crucifixion: "Father, forgive them, for they know not what they do" (*TS*, 198). In a similar vein are the utterances of the Senegalese writer and politician Leopold Sedor Senghor. He finds Simon's "refusal to forgive" to be—alas—entirely in accordance "with the spirit of the Old Law" and polemically invites Simon to attend to "the New Law, that of Christ as expressed in the Gospels," which recommends forgiveness for such as Karl. The act of throwing the alleged superiority of Christian to Jewish morality in the face of a Jewish victim of the moral collapse of European Christendom makes one appreciate the urgency of the warning central to the Protestant theologian Martin Marty's contribution to the volume: "Non-Jews and perhaps especially Christians should not give advice about Holocaust experience to its heirs for the next two thousand years" (*TS*, 173).

One of the most judicious and measured responses by a Christian contributor to Wiesenthal's book is the essay by Kurt von Schuschnigg, the Austrian statesman and political scientist who served in various ministerial posts from 1936 until the Nazi *Putsch* of March 1938, when he was arrested until the war's end. Forgiveness of such crimes is, in general, mischievous, says von Schuschnigg, because of the declaration it makes to future generations. "The whole business might very easily repeat itself. And not only amongst us Germans. Perhaps in any country where men have been 'liberated' from all religious beliefs and thereby from all restraints. . . . Punishment of the guilty is necessary as a deterrent" (*TS*, 199). He grants that Karl was far from being a typical S.S. man, and that he had once again become a decent human being who wished for redemption. It was, therefore, a deservedly soothing gesture for Simon to listen to the man's confession. But his forgiveness would have been an action both meaningless and dishonest. "No one can forgive what others have suffered. The Creator alone, and nobody else, can forgive blood guilt and inhuman conduct. Moreover, it is only religious absolution that gives real meaning to forgiveness" (Wiesenthal, 202).

Among the few contributors who severely criticize Karl for his present as well as his past actions is Primo Levi. For him, Karl is not fully reformed from the moral point of view. Levi asserts that it is only the fear of death that impels the S.S. man to repent, and that his act of "having a Jew brought to him" was both childish and impudent. His belief that the Jew, when he was not being a devil, was a miracle worker who could grant him the forgiveness supposed to come from the almighty, is likened by Levi to Himmler's suspension of the death camp massacres in hopes that the "Jewish International" would exercise its omnipotent powers in helping Germany to conclude a separate peace with the West. In addition, Karl was, once again, using the Jew as a tool, indifferent to the shock and danger his request was inflicting upon his confessor (*TS*, 161–62).

Varied as the thirty-two responses to Wiesenthal's question are, they all appear relatively conventional in comparison with the single essay that condemns outright the very notion of forgiveness. This is Cynthia Ozick's "Notes Toward a Meditation on 'Forgiveness,'" a fierce and unorthodox response permeated by the author's clarifying intelligence and moral passion. Conventional people, she proposes, think that vengeance brutalizes and forgiveness refines. In fact, the opposite is just as likely to be true. "Whoever is merciful to the cruel," warned the rabbis, "will end by being indifferent to the innocent." In reply to the argument (made by, among others, Hannah Arendt) that forgiveness encourages renewal and a new beginning, Ozick replies that forgiveness is an effective teacher only when the spots of the original offense can be washed away. "But murder is irrevocable. Murder is irreversible. With murder there is no 'next time'" (TS, 186).

She calls into question too the accepted terminology for debating the question of whether and how to punish crime. Justice, or "vengeance," as it is frequently miscalled, does not mean requiting evil with evil, especially when dealing with a Nazi murderer. "Vengeance on a mass murderer would mean killing all the members of his family and a great fraction of his nation; and still his victims would not come alive." [7] What morality demands, she insists, is "the act of bringing public justice to evil . . . not by initiating a new evil, but by making certain never to condone the old one; never even appearing to condone it" (TS, 186–87). The advocates of forgiveness, Ozick knows, maintain that, despite appearances, it does not condone evil, and therefore insist that this cannot be the crucial distinction between forgiveness and punishment. To which she replies, in a paradox that is shocking yet strikes us as natural, that "Forgiveness is pitiless. It forgets the victim. It negates the right of the victim to his own life. It blurs over suffering and death. It drowns the past. It cultivates sensitiveness toward the murderer at the price of insensitiveness toward the victim. . . . The face of forgiveness is mild, but how stony to the slaughtered" (TS, 188).

The problem with Ozick's position, as she is well aware, is that it seems not to make allowance for the difference between Karl, the intelligent, sensitive, penitent S.S. man of conscience and the garden-variety S.S. brute. Karl murdered Jews just as the S.S. barbarians did, but thought and felt differently from the barbarians about what he was doing. Does the fact that he had conscience and humanity, yet stifled them, make him more or less deserving of forgiveness than the killers who lacked them altogether? For Ozick, the answer is clear: "A virtuous childhood as a server in his church lies behind him . . . a virtuous future as a model of remorse lies ahead of him . . . He [possesses] a refined and meticulous moral temperament—so refined and meticulous that it knows the holy power of forgiveness, and knows to ask for it. . . . Let him go to hell" (TS, 190).

Eichmann in Jerusalem, by Hannah Arendt.

In 1961 the *New Yorker* sent the eminent political thinker Hannah Arendt to Jerusalem to cover the trial of Adolf Eichmann. Her account and analysis of the trial first appeared in the February and March 1963 issues of the magazine. The articles were published as a book in May of the same year, with the contentious title *Eichmann in Jerusalem: A Report on the Banality of Evil.*

The book aroused a terrific storm of controversy primarily because it alleged that the Jews had cooperated significantly in their own destruction. "Wherever Jews lived, there were recognized Jewish leaders, and this leadership, almost without exception, cooperated in one way or another, for one reason or another, with the Nazis" (*EJ*, 125). Except among her most passionate disciples, it is now generally accepted that Arendt was woefully and willfully mistaken in this central assertion. At the time she wrote, very little serious historical research had been done on the subject of the *Judenräte*, the Jewish councils that the Germans established to help them administer the ghettos of Eastern Europe until they were disbanded and their inhabitants deported and murdered. Even to the meager historical material available she paid little attention, preferring to use secondary sources that would lend support to her accusation of Jewish collaboration with the Nazis. The abrasive effect of the book was increased by the fact that it first appeared in the *New Yorker*—the discussions of mass murder alongside the ads for perfume and designer clothing—and that the sections on the Jewish leaders were in a tone that the great scholar Gershom Scholem, Arendt's old friend, characterized in a letter to her as "heartless, frequently almost sneering and malicious." [8]

Also subject to widespread, albeit far less withering, criticism was the book's depiction of Eichmann not as a monster at all, but as the most ordinary of men. The deportation of the Jews from every corner of Europe to the death camps in Poland was, according to Arendt, "for Eichmann a job, with its daily routine, its ups and downs" (*EJ*, 153). Typical of the criticism of her interpretation of Eichmann's character is the outburst of the hero of Saul Bellow's novel, *Mr. Sammler's Planet:* "What better way to get the curse out of murder than to make it look ordinary, boring, or trite?" Arendt, according to old Artur Sammler, was duped, for the banality that she purported to discover in these murderers and their evil deeds was merely camouflage. The Nazis, he argues, never forgot their old, normal knowledge of what is meant by murder. No one should believe that the abolition of conscience is a trivial or banal matter unless she believes that human life itself is trivial. Arendt stands accused of "making use of a tragic history to promote the foolish ideas of Weimar intellectuals" (*MSP*, 22).

Yet there is at least one part of *Eichmann in Jerusalem* that has withstood criticism and still remains a valuable contribution to the definition of the nature of justice in punishing crimes against humanity. In her epilogue, Arendt deals with the objections that had been raised to the capture (by kidnapping) of Eichmann in Argentina and to his trial by an Israeli court, and offers a reasoned estimate of the verdict handed down by the judges in Jerusalem. She also takes it upon herself to say how she would have addressed Eichmann in pronouncing the death sentence against him (a sentence in which, it is often forgotten, she concurred).

She begins by announcing the principle to which she tries to adhere throughout her discussion: namely, that "the purpose of a trial is to render justice, and nothing else" (*EJ*, 253). This is the answer both to the opponents of the Eichmann trial, who ask "what good does it do?" and to its proponents who ascribe to it various noble ulterior motives, such as establishing the historical record of the Hitler period, or giving a voice to those who have been silenced, or avenging the victims.

Three objections to the trial had been raised. The first was that Eichmann was being tried under a retroactive law and in the court of the victors; the second questioned the competence of the Jerusalem court and its failure to take into account the act of kidnapping; the third, and most important, questioned the charge itself, that Eichmann had committed crimes "against the Jewish people," instead of "against humanity." This last objection generally led to the conclusion that the only proper court in which to try such crimes was an international tribunal.

The Jerusalem court dealt with the first set of objections by citing the Nuremberg trials as a valid legal precedent. The Allied Military Tribunal at Nuremburg had taken the view that if a crime unknown before, such as genocide, makes its appearance in the world, then justice requires judgment according to a new law. The Nuremburg court assumed jurisdiction over three kinds of crimes: "crimes against peace," "war crimes," and "crimes against humanity." Only the last was new and unprecedented. When Churchill announced that "punishment of war criminals [was] one of the principal war aims," he had in mind those crimes that were independent of the war and that were part of a policy of systematic murder to be continued even in time of peace (though of course it was easier to carry them out under the cover of war). It was precisely the campaign to destroy the Jews that had prompted the Allies to conceive of the "crime against humanity" or, as the French prosecutor Francois de Menthon called it, the "crime against the human status" (*EJ*, 257).

For the most part, Arendt shows little sympathy with the objections to the competence of the Jerusalem court to sit in judgment on Eichmann. "Once the Jews had a territory of their own, the State in Israel, they obviously had as much right to sit in judgment on the crimes committed against their people as the Poles had to judge crimes committed in Poland." She dismisses the objections raised against the Jerusalem trial on the ground of the principle of territorial jurisdiction as "legalistic in the extreme" (*EJ*, 259). There was no doubt whatever that the Jews had been killed *as* Jews, regardless of their nationalities at the time, even though, as Arendt acerbically remarks, many of them had long ago chosen to renounce their Jewish origins, and would have preferred to be killed as Frenchmen or as Germans. The objection to the possible partiality of Jewish judges is rebutted by Arendt in similar fashion: the Jewish judges, in judging crimes committed against the Jewish people, were no different from Polish judges who pronounced sentence for crimes against the Polish people, or Czech judges sitting in judgment on what had happened in Prague or Bratislava.

In general, Arendt faults the Israeli judges not for flouting legal precedent, but for following it too slavishly. Because of Israel's reluctance to break new ground, the Eichmann trial became only another in the numerous successor trials which followed the Nuremburg trials. The most notable departure from precedent came, of course, in the manner in which Eichmann had been arrested. Israel, violating international law, [9] kidnapped him from Argentina in order to bring him to justice. But, after much shilly-shallying, Arendt grants that, given the Argentinian fondness for Nazi war criminals and consistent refusal to extradite them (it had denied West Germany's request for Dr. Josef Mengele), Israel had no alternative to kidnapping him. Where justice and legality come into conflict, justice must prevail.

Their long history of persecution in the Diaspora led the Jewish people (as we have seen in our discussion of the Yiddish writers) to see Hitler and the Nazis as only the latest version of Haman, the Crusaders, and Chmielnicki. It was therefore, Arendt asserts, hardly surprising that Israel, like the Jewish people whose collective representative it had now become, failed to recognize the unprecedented nature of the crime of which Eichmann stood accused, the crime of genocide. The Holocaust was not the most horrible and gigantic pogrom in Jewish history, but a crime different in nature from all the previous atrocities.

> It was when the Nazi regime declared that the German people not only were unwilling to have any Jews in Germany but wished to make the entire Jewish people disappear from the face of the earth that the new crime, the crime against humanity—in the sense of a crime "against the human status," or against the very nature of mankind—appeared. Expulsion and genocide, though both are international offenses, must remain distinct; the former is an offense against fellow-nations, whereas the latter is an attack upon human diversity as such, that is, upon a characteristic of the "human status" without which the very words "mankind" or "humanity" would be devoid of meaning. (*EJ*, 268)

Like the Yiddish poet Jacob Glatstein, who wrote that "the night is endless when a race is dead" (*TYP*, 332), Arendt sees in the physical wound perpetrated on the body of the Jewish people a metaphysical wound inflicted on the universe: this is the ultimate crime.

But Arendt tries to translate this metaphysical or spiritual insight into juridical terms. Since the murder of the Jewish people was a crime against humanity perpetrated upon the body of the Jewish people, "only the choice of victims, not the nature of the crime, could be derived from the long history of Jew-hatred and anti-Semitism. Insofar as the victims were Jews, it was right and proper that a Jewish court should sit in judgment; but insofar as the crime was a crime against humanity, it needed an international tribunal to do justice to it" (*EJ*, 269). This dubious conclusion gives insufficient weight to considerations that Arendt herself was aware of. First, as we have noted in the opening chapter of this book, the seeds of the scheme for physical extermination of the whole Jewish people were indeed present in the long history of antisemitism. Second, the nations who would have made up an international tribunal in 1961 would not have been entirely different in composition from the nations who stood by and acquiesced in the destruction process then only recently completed. Indeed, these nations had already, in the U.N. General Assembly, twice rejected proposals to establish a permanent international criminal court. Third, an international tribunal would have required Israel to plead her case on the grounds of "the rights of man," that is, rights that, as Arendt herself had brilliantly demonstrated in her earlier book *The Origins of Totalitarianism*, were likely to be claimed only by people too weak to enforce their rights as Englishmen or Frenchmen, or indeed their own laws. The Jews of Europe had discovered just how useless it was to invoke these rights in time of crisis; why then should the Jews of Israel expect any better fate before an international tribunal? When David Ben-Gurion insisted that Israel does not need the protection of an International Court, he was declaring that Zionism's revolutionary trans-formation of the political position of the Jewish people had enabled them, for the first time since the year 70, when Jerusalem was destroyed by the Romans, to apprehend, try, and punish those who committed crimes against them.

In addition to blaming the Jerusalem court for its inadequate definition of the "crime against humanity" and its timid adherence to Nuremberg precedent, Arendt claimed it had not come to grips with the problem of "impaired justice in the court of the victors" or with clear recognition of the new kind of criminal who commits these crimes. The first criticism is bizarre, since it is hard to understand in what sense the Jews can be considered to have been "the victors" in World War II; perhaps this is why she devotes only a brief paragraph to this stricture. The second criticism centers on the "failure" of the court to arrive at Arendt's own conception of Eichmann's "normality" of character. Since, in her view, Eichmann was representative of many Germans and Austrians involved in the destruction process, the Jerusalem court ought to have seen the wisdom of viewing him as "neither perverted nor sadistic [but] terribly and terrifyingly normal. From the viewpoint of our legal institutions and of our moral standards of judgment, this normality was much more terrifying than all the atrocities put together" (*EJ*, 276). If the Jerusalem court thought it was putting a monster in the dock, what was the point of summoning the attention of the whole world to this trial? But if they recognized Eichmann's terrifying "normality," his sense of conscien-tiously doing his duty and resisting all temptation, then they would have had to overcome the assumption current in all modern legal systems that intent to do wrong is necessary for conviction of guilt in a crime.

Despite all her reservations, Arendt concurs in the guilty verdict handed down by the Jerusalem judges, but maintains that the justice of the verdict would have emerged clearly to be seen by all if the judges had "dared" to address Eichmann in the way that Arendt herself does in the concluding movement of the book. Its salient points are few, but they cut through exculpatory cant with admirable precision. Although it *may* be true that Eichmann neither hated, nor had any inclination to kill, Jews and that his role in the Final Solution was accidental, one which almost any other German could have filled, it does not therefore follow that either he must be declared innocent or all Germans guilty.

> What you meant to say was that where all, or almost all, are guilty, nobody is. This is an indeed quite common conclusion, but one we are not willing to grant you. And if you don't understand our objection, we would recommend to your attention the story of Sodom and Gomorrah, two neighboring cities in the Bible, which were destroyed by fire from Heaven because all the people in them had become equally guilty. . . . In other words, guilt and innocence before the law are of an objective nature, and even if eighty million Germans had done as you did, this would not have been an excuse for you. . . . You yourself claimed not the actuality but only the potentiality of equal guilt on the part of all who lived in a state whose main political purpose had become the commission of unheard-of crimes. And no matter through what accidents of exterior or interior circumstances you were pushed onto the road of becoming a criminal, there is an abyss between the actuality of what you did and the potentiality of what others might have done. (Arendt, *EJ*, 278)

Actions, not motives, according to Arendt, are crucial. It is perhaps true that under more favorable circumstances Eichmann would never have come before a criminal court, and that it was his accidental misfortune to become a willing instrument in the organization of murder. Nevertheless, "there still remains the fact that you have carried out, and therefore actively supported, a policy of mass murder. For politics is not like the nursery; in politics obedience and support are the same. And just as you supported and carried out a policy of not wanting to share the earth with the Jewish people and the people of a number of other nations—as though you and your superiors had any right to determine who should and who should not inhabit the world— we find that no one, that is, no member of the human race, can be expected to want to share the earth with you. This is the reason, and the only reason, you must hang" (*EJ*, 279).

The Investigation, by Peter Weiss

The American critic Susan Sontag has argued that a courtroom trial is itself an art form that preserves in its essential structure the classical dramatic struggle between protagonist and antagonist. Therefore, she asserted (in 1964), if "the supreme tragic event of modern times is the murder of the six million European Jews, the most interesting and moving work of art of the past ten years is the trial of Adolf Eichmann in Jerusalem in 1961." [10]

Does it then follow that a faithful transcript of the Eichmann trial would be a great drama? Hannah Arendt certainly did not think so. She claimed that there had been but a few great moments in the Eichmann trial, and it is implicit in her approach that only the application of mind, especially in the form of moral philosophy, can evoke the deepest drama of the trial and formulate its ultimate significance.

But the German dramatist, Peter Weiss, in the year after Sontag's essay appeared, drew from her premise precisely the conclusion that "a condensation of the evidence" presented at the 1963 Frankfurt trials of twenty-one of those responsible for operating the Auschwitz death factory would convey to theatrical audiences and readers the essence and meaning of the trials themselves. Weiss, in his prefatory note, readily grants that the courtroom drama cannot itself be reconstructed on stage, for "any such reconstruction would . . . be as impossible as trying to present the camp itself on the stage." Nevertheless, he prides himself on having, he claims, produced a condensation that "contain[s] nothing but facts." Starting with the reasonable premise that it would be very difficult to reproduce the emotions of the actual historical event, that is, the courtroom proceedings, he proceeds to the illogical conclusion that the playwright's duty is to exclude emotion altogether from his representation of the Frankfurt trial. Whereas the actual addresses in the courtroom "were overcharged with emotion," Weiss's play will stick to "the facts." "Personal experience and confrontations must be steeped in anonymity. Inasmuch as the witneses in the play lose their names, they become mere speaking tubes." [11]

For this reason Weiss deprives the witnesses in his play of their names, giving them numbers (from one to nine) instead. It is apparently the same dedication to "fact" that justifies the irritating absence of all punctuation in the text (written in a "free verse" that makes one think fondly of Robert Frost's objection to free verse as playing tennis with the net down), the production of the play on a bare stage, and the delivery of speeches in straightfaced monotone.

Weiss's dogged devotion to "the facts" reminds one of the famous opening of Dickens' novel, *Hard Times* (1854), in which the dogmatically utilitarian schoolmaster, Thomas Gradgrind, addresses his pupils. "Now, what I want is, Facts. Teach these boys and girls nothing but Facts. Facts alone are wanted in life. Plant nothing else, and root out everything else." Even Dickens' setting, "a plain, bare, monotonous vault of a schoolroom" foreshadows Weiss's bare stage. Moreover, the egregious schoolmaster refers to his students not by name but by number: "Girl number twenty unable to define a horse!" Since she comes from a circus family, girl number twenty is better acquainted with horses than any of her classmates. But she is too mired in emotional perception to achieve the factual accuracy of the prize pupil's correct, "factual" definition: "Quadruped, graminivorous. Forty teeth, namely twenty-four grinders, four eye-teeth, and twelve incisive. Sheds coat in the spring; in marshy countries, sheds hoofs, too. Hoofs hard, but requiring to be shod with iron. Age known by marks in mouth. . . . 'Now, girl number twenty,' said Mr. Gradgrind, 'you know what a horse is.'"

Dickens' critique of utilitarian culture stressed the folly of assuming that you can separate objects from perceivers, facts from emotion. All perception, he understood, was a generative act in which, as Wordsworth used to say, we half perceive and half create. Weiss's dogmatic commitment to stripping "facts" of their emotional clothing before they can be admitted as evidence of his "thesis" may account for the surprising flatness of parts of the play, surprising because of the horrifying nature of its raw material, the transcripts with which Weiss began.

What Weiss seems to understand by "condensation of the evidence" presented at the actual trial is not just compression but radical selectivity, which of course involves omission. One of his crucial omissions is ideologically determined: he will not mention that the vast majority (over 90 percent) of the victims of Auschwitz were Jews. When the sadistic "Papa Kaduk" testifies, he revels in the power he once had, recalling how he had only to lift his hand and "somebody would fall over" (*I*, 54). Weiss's "Marxist" etiquette prohibits him from having Kaduk say "a Jew would fall over." Elsewhere in the play the prosecuting attorney refers abstractly to "people who/though they had committed no crime/were held under arrest and murdered" (*I*, 199) and witness number seven mentions "6 million killed for racial reasons" (though also, somewhat inconsistently, one might think, "3 million Russian prisoners of war/shot or starved to death" [I, 267].) Even when one of the accused "explains" the wholesale murder of women and children by reference to the belief—an antisemitic superstition going back to the middle Ages—that "they had actively participated in poisoning springs and wells," (I, 148) Weiss does not allow the word "Jew" to sully the purity of his "factual" text, thereby making all of these facts into something not very different from a lie.

For this principle of "condensation" Weiss has offered, in an interview, the following explanation: "The word 'Jew' is in fact never used in the play. . . . I do not identify myself any more with the Jews than I do with the people of Vietnam or the blacks in South Africa. I simply identify myself with the oppressed of the world." So much for the relation between "fact" and truth; the latter turns out to be little more than a function of the playwright's very considerable ego. He cannot limit his all-embracing benevolence to the Jews who were murdered at Auschwitz; their specific identity must be blotted out by "the oppressed of the world." As for Weiss's extreme reluctance to acknowledge that the murderers were Germans, that seems to be a function of Marxist piety. "*The Investigation* is about the extreme abuse of power that alienates people from their own actions. It happens to be German power, but that again is unimportant. I see Auschwitz as a scientific instrument that could have been used by anyone to exterminate anyone. For that matter, given a different deal, the Jews could have been on the side of the Nazis. They too could have been the exterminators."[12]

Thus does the wheel come full circle. The real Jews who were actually murdered must never be mentioned in the play, and the German identity of their killers must be scanted; but authorial commentary on the play strenuously asserts that the hypothetical and conjectural potentiality of what Jews (and not the French or the Rumanians) *might* have done is (in Weiss's overheated imagination) equal to anything that the Germans have *actually* done.

If Weiss's notion of a condensation that "contain[s] nothing but facts" requires omission of the Jewish identity of the victims of the criminals on trial in Frankfurt, we should not be surprised that it also requires omission of any mention of the verdicts handed down by the German court. Weiss dwells more than amply on the crimes, but shows no interest in their punishment. The prefatory note, in one of its numerous opaque ponderosities, says that although the accused (unlike the witnesses) bear names taken from the actual trial, "yet the bearers of these names should not be accused once again in this drama" (I, xi). This too appears to be a function of Weiss's "ideology." In comments outside of the play he has said that he is not concerned with the guilt or innocence of individuals but with indictment of the social system known as capitalism. Auschwitz, according to this deep thinker, would not be possible in a socialist society. How this comports with his confidence that Jews as well as Germans could have perpetrated Auschwitz is not clear. One wonders too whether Weiss had taken note of the fact that "Nazi" is an abbreviation of "National Socialist" or that the now-defunct Union of Soviet Socialist Republics presided over a gulag system that has often been likened to (and even alleged to have provided a precedent for) Auschwitz.

Perhaps, as D. H.Lawrence urged, it is better to trust the tale than the teller of the tale. One of the "themes" most effectively conveyed in the play is that of the bureaucratic quantification and impersonality of the death factory, from "delivery of the freight" (*I*, 7) at the beginning of the process to the allocation of "8 dollars" to pay (at the rate of "50 cents per pound") for the sixteen pounds of Cyklon-B gas required to kill "2000 people in one chamber" (*I*, 237–38). Ransacking of the corpses for commercial purposes is described by several witnesses in numbing detail. Witness number seven provides a dispassionate account of how this gigantic death factory, by the summer of 1944, reached its "peak/up to 20,000 people/were destroyed/daily" (*I*, 259). The ordinary reader or spectator is likely to interpret the clinical and "objective" language in which the mass murders are described in the play by Nazi bureaucrats as characteristic of Nazi pathology—unless and until he is directed, from outside the body of the play by Weiss himself, to regard them as characteristic of "capitalism." Within the play, to be sure, the prosecuting attorney refers, with justifiable animus, to the directors of large German firms that made billions in profits from the system of exploiting camp labor. But this hardly can be adduced as proof that Nazism is a form of capitalism. Whatever slight plausibility the view that bureaucratic in-humanity is peculiar to capitalism, and that capitalism is itself a form of fascism might have had in 1965, it is unlikely to recommend itself to anybody who has observed the downfall of the Marxist regimes revered by Weiss.

But if we can clear our minds of Weiss's own cant about his play, we can rescue several things of value in the text itself, including some that bear on the main concern of this chapter, crime and punishment. Repeatedly the accused at Frankfurt must face the question of why they followed orders that transgressed all moral law. Two of the doctors claim that they did not kill out of hatred or conviction but only "because they had to" (*I*, 91). Yet other medical witnesses claim that they refused, with impunity, to take part in selections. An archbishop and a lawyer are reported by Dr. Lucas (Accused #6) to have instructed him that "illegal orders need not be obeyed/but that this should not be carried/out to the extreme/where one's own life might be endangered" (*I* 29). As has often been noted in this book, those who opted out of the mass killings of civilians did not in fact endanger their lives. But the constant reiteration of this argument for compliance in the trials of Nazis does move one to suggest that there must some day come some order a person would risk death to refuse.

If repentance is to be taken into account in judging a criminal, then the accused in Weiss's play, as in the trial that it imitates, surely merit the punishment that the playwright disdains to mention. Repeatedly, we are told how the accused, acting as a kind of evil Greek chorus, laugh when their power of intimidation over Jewish prisoners is recalled, or when their defense attorney utters what they take to be a telling point against the prosecution. "Wherever there is the slightest doubt/the benefit must be given to the accused [*The Accused laugh nodding in agreement*]" (*I*, 153). This laughter, never commented on by Weiss, is not only a ringing declaration of the cynicism of the defendants, of their lack of remorse, and of their contempt for the legal processes, but also a vivid reminder— if we needed yet another—of their state of mind when they committed the crimes for which they are now being tried.

One of the defendants is a Corporal Stark, who was a twenty year old (nearly the age of Wiesenthal's dying soldier) when he worked in the Auschwitz "Reception Squad." Witness number eight describes, in the dispassionate style imposed by Weiss on everybody, how Stark once interrupted a discussion of "aspects of humanism in Goethe" (*I*, 136) that he was having with some college graduates among the prisoners in order to murder a "Polish woman" (Polish specificity may be admitted, but never Jewish) and her two children because they were caught playing with a rabbit that belonged to a camp official. Although Stark denies this particular crime, he does not dispute the existence of the gas chambers and crematorium burnings or his work conducting victims to them. Here the testimony conveys its own lesson, even to the dimmest. Learning, to which young Stark aspired, is no guarantee of sanctity; one may study, even espouse, Goethean humanism, yet be a murderer.

In the course of the play, we learn how all the learned professions were tainted or compromised: medical doctors, trained to preserve life, worked in Auschwitz to torture and destroy it; magistrates cultivated the illusion of legality within the camps by solemnly investigating the use of the gold that had been plundered from the victims' possessions and teeth. Thus, boasts witness number one, "Somewhere some idea of justice/ still survived" (*I*, 260). But it was out of the question to bring "an action /for the killings of masses of people/and the seizure of their goods and property/by the highest administrative offices/I could not institute proceedings/against the government itself" (*I*, 261–62).

The by now familiar evasions of responsibility for their actions are invoked by the accused who testify in the play as they did in the actual trial. Several claim they were only doing their duty, following orders, fulfilling assignments they received simply by accident, and so forth. But the most brazen and ambitious proclamation of innocence comes from Accused #1, named Mulka, who belonged to a uniformed Murder Commando. He claims that although the whole business made him so sick that he had to be hospitalized, he nevertheless did his "duty" because he had been convinced that this killing of civilians was necessary to achieve "some secret military objective" (*I*, 269). He adds, somewhat contradictorily, that he was really "against/the whole thing." Indeed, since he was induced to act against his will, it is *he* who was the persecuted party, "persecuted by the system" (*I*, 269).

Even the reader who has not had the benefit of Hannah Arendt's luminous reasoning about the Eichmann verdict will recognize the self-serving rationalizations and prevarications of Weiss's criminals who invoke that most convenient of villains, "the system," to assert that everybody is guilty of a crime except the people who actually commit it. That Weiss himself is susceptible to these baneful determinisms, especially if they come with a Marxist label, should make us thankful that "documentary" art keeps the artist's foolishness (as well as whatever wisdom he may possess) from expressing itself overtly in the drama.

Whether this is sufficient consolation for the inherent shortcomings of documentary art in facing the Holocaust is, however, doubtful. From a work of art we traditionally expect something more than information or even knowledge, however "objectively" conveyed. "One gains nothing on the darkness," Matthew Arnold once wrote, "by being . . . as incoherent as the darkness itself." [13] This is especially the case with the

Holocaust, which defies the presumptions of coherence upon which both language and morality are based.

Weiss's dogmatic commitment to stripping facts of their emotional clothing is, in the context of a play about the trial of the Auschwitz criminals, an extension of the code of "objectivity" upon which the Nazis prided themselves. Arendt noted how proud Eichmann, at his trial, was of the *Sachlichkeit* by which he and other S.S. men distinguished themselves from such "emotional" types as Streicher, who had not risen to the level of objectivity which talked about concentration camps in terms of "administration" and about extermination camps in terms of "economy." But she awarded the first prize for objectivity to one Dr. Servatius, a tax and business lawyer from Cologne who "was to teach the court a lesson in what it means not to be 'emotional' that no one who heard him is likely to forget" (*EJ*, 69).

Servatius argued that Eichmann was innocent of all charges bearing on his responsibility for "the collection of skeletons, sterilizations, killings by gas, and similar medical matters." The Israeli judge at this point interrupted him to suggest that he had made a slip of the tongue when he said that killing by gas was a medical matter. But Servatius, undaunted, replied: "It was indeed a medical matter, since it was prepared by physicians; it was a matter of killing, and killing, too, is a medical matter." A documentary presentation like that of Weiss (who does, indeed, deal at length with the Auschwitz doctors) would stop at this point, " objectively" reproducing the words of this devotee of objectivity. But Arendt, writing merely as a journalist and without any artistic pretensions, in fact gives us the sense of order, of difficulty overcome, of light coming out of darkness, which we used to associate with art. Here is her addition to the bare text of the court records:

> And, perhaps to make absolutely sure that the judges in Jerusalem would not forget how Germans—ordinary Germans, not former members of the S.S. or even of the Nazi Party—even today can regard acts that in other countries are called murder, [Servatius] repeated the phrase in his "Comments on the Judgment of the First Instance," prepared for the review of the case before the Supreme Court; he said again that not Eichmann, but one of his men, Rolf Gunther, "was always engaged in medical matters." (Dr. Servatius is well acquainted with "medical matters" in the Third Reich. At Nuremburg he defended Dr. Karl Brandt, Hitler's personal physician, Plenipotentiary for "Hygiene and Health," and chief of the euthanasia program.) [*EJ*, 69-70]

That devastating parenthesis brings the activity of mind to bear on what would otherwise remain, in Weiss's words, "nothing but facts." In so doing, it comes closer to doing the traditional work of literary imagination—assimilating and giving coherence to disordered and intractable experience—than Weiss's play does.

The Case of Dering vs. Uris

An even more instructive comparison between the inadequacy of the artist who aspires to no more than accuracy and information and the possibilities latent in what used to be called the higher journalism may be drawn by the reader who looks at a little-known yet remarkable essay by the literary critic Mary Ellmann called "The Dering Case: A Surgeon at Auschwitz." It deals with one aspect of a topic extensively covered in *The Investigation*: the mutilation of the sexual organs of men and women in the interests of scientific research and experimentation. Witness number four, a victim of these experiments, is allowed a tiny bit more in the way of emotion than most of Weiss's characters in that the stage directions refer to her moments of silence during the prodding by judge and attorneys to describe her ordeal. But she too is "objective" in her descriptions: "The girls were placed/in front of the X-ray machines/A metal plate was attached/to their stomachs and buttocks/The X-rays were directed at their ovaries/which were burned out/ . . . Within the next three months/they were operated on/a number of times/ . . . Their ovaries and gonads were removed" (*I*, 114).

One of the participants in these Auschwitz experiments was a Polish (non-Jewish) prisoner-doctor named Wladyslaw Alexander Dering, who survived the war to become a British subject and a London obstetrician and gynecologist. In spring of 1964 a London court heard the case of *Dering v. Uris and Others*. Dering brought a libel case against the novelist Leon Uris (as well as his publisher and printer) for the following passage in the novel *Exodus*: "Here in Block X [at Auschwitz] Dr. Wirths used women as guinea pigs and Dr. Schumann sterilized by castration and X-ray and Clauberg removed ovaries and Dr. Dehring [sic] performed 17,000 'experiments' in surgery without anaesthetics." Unlike all the other court cases discusssed in this chapter, this one had the Auschwitz culprit in the position of accuser, rather than accused. But this did not prevent both the defense and the jury from being induced, by the evidence presented, from thinking that they were there not to award or refuse damages to Dering, but to decide whether he should be hanged or only imprisoned. After repeated warnings by the judge, the jury did eventually think of Dering as a plaintiff and, in Mary Ellmann's words, "assessed the value of his reputation, or the harm done to that ineffable quality by the defendants, at a halfpenny." [14] (Dering also, however, had to pay legal costs of about 20,000 pounds.)

Like so many of the Auschwitz functionaries, Dr. Dering claimed, plausibly enough, that if he had not been sent to Auschwitz he would have pursued his medical career through an entire lifetime without committing any serious impropriety. Nevertheless, the fact remained that—and note the fine moral precision of Ellmann's description here— "when he needed something for himself—whether it was to save his own life, as he argued, or to achieve his extraordinary release from Auschwitz in January of 1944, as the defendants argued . . . he was willing to turn his surgical skill to the castration of Jewish men and the sterilization of Jewish women" (Ellmann, 20).

Dering earned his halfpenny worth of damages because his lawyer was able to demonstrate certain errors of detail in Uris' passage. Block X should have been Block 21; the Germanized spelling of his name (with the added *h*) was unfair because it obscured the fact that he was a Pole and a prisoner himself; Uris had referred to 17,000 experiments when in fact it could be shown that he had performed "only" about 130 operations on sex glands. Moreover, argued his lawyer, he had simply removed testicles and ovaries, not performed surgical experiments. But Dering could never disprove the substantial truth of the *Exodus* passage.

The defendants (i.e., Uris and his publishers) had to disprove the two central contentions of Dering's justification for his behavior: one, that he could not have refused to do the operations without risking his own life; two, that he had performed the operations in an exemplary, a humane fashion. The defense presented convincing evidence that Dering had not been in danger of death. By the end of 1943, they pointed out, forced labor was needed desperately by the Germans. If sick or injured persons could be returned to work quickly, it was better to give them medical help than to kill them; and if medical help was important, then it was obviously better to keep doctors alive than to kill them. The defense also presented a powerful witness to dispute Dering's argument from self-preservation. This was a French prisoner-doctor named Adelaine Hautval. She had been asked directly to take part in these surgical operations at Auschwitz, and she had refused to do so. The notorious S.S. Doctor Wirths, when she said no to his order, asked her, "Cannot you see that these people [the Jews] are different from you?" "I answered," testified Dr. Hautval, "that there were several people different from me, beginning with him." The defense attorney, Lord Gardiner, then provoked the only moment of laughter in the trial by asking her "As a result were you shot?" And there she was to answer, "No" (Ellmann, 22). With wonderful tact and delicacy, Ellmann, in recounting this moment of the trial, is able to suggest—what we would never infer from Weiss's play—how different everything might have been in wartime Europe, in Auschwitz, and in our own world, if there were more such people as Dr. Hautval.

Dering's second justification for his actions, that he had operated in an exemplary and humane fashion, also was confuted by a barrage of evidence. Dr. Alina Brewda, another Polish prisoner-doctor at Auschwitz (albeit a Jewish one), described the brutal speed with which he operated on ten Greek girls one day in November 1943. "It was as though he was operating on corpses." She charged that he did not wash his hands between operations, did not sterilize his instruments, and operated "blind," that is, made incisions too small to allow for the mending of the stump of the severed ovary. Her observations were confirmed by a British professor of obstetrics and gynecology who examined the patients willing to testify, and said he had never in all his surgical career seen such "crude, bad surgery" (Ellmann, 23).

Neither was Dering's libel case helped by his own obvious moral shallowness, past and present. He said that he had been involved, against his will, in the *folly* of other men, and spoke of the experiments as "silly" (Ellmann, 23). He was reported by a fellow prisoner-doctor from Auschwitz to have been in the habit of showing people his tobacco pouch, which was a tanned scrotum. He also boasted that, although he might have experimented on women, he "was never rude" to them. Yet numerous witnesses testified to the fact that, despite his vaunted politeness, he was entirely indifferent to the suffering he inflicted upon helpless patients. "As I entered through the corridor [outside the operating room], I could hear screaming. I heard 'mama' which I think is Greek for mother. I entered into the anteroom. I saw two men holding a screaming girl sitting on a couch and a second one crying. Dr. Dering was washing his hands in the anteroom." In opposition to this icy detachment, Ellmann, with the deftness of a true artist who feels a sense of moral responsibility to her readers, places a bit of testimony from one of the surviving Greek girls about the compassion of Dr. Brewda: "I was awake and I saw, in the reflection of the lamp, that they did something to me. During the time of the operation I felt like vomiting. Then I felt the warm hand of Dr. Brewda. She told me '*Encore un peu, mon enfant.*' I cannot forget it" (Ellmann, 23–24). Such pieces of testimony might, all on their own, tear at the heart, but they makê their implied statement more eloquently because of Ellmann's placement of them and, still more, because of the moral intelligence she brings to bear on what she presents.

Her conclusion brings into view the suffering of the victims more than Dr. Dering and his attempt to vindicate his halfpenny's worth of reputation. She describes how these people, who were benevolently referred to as "miserable creatures" or "wretches," nevertheless "expressed themselves with unassuming talent" (Ellmann, 24). When one of the defense attorneys tried to call into question a witness's truthfulness by suggesting that she was "very bitter" about what had been done to her, she replied "I don't feel good, I feel pain in my heart and shame in my face." A man recreated his moment of castration: "After some minutes I saw Dr. Dering when he had my testicle in his hand and showed it to Dr. Schumann who was present." Finally, the author, without verbal pyrotechnics and without calling attention to herself, places these horrors within a moral framework that defines the enormity of the crime committed. "A little cluster of survivors recreated the agony felt by young men and women who first were robbed of all dignity of body . . . who then underwent the inexplicable terror, in a dark room, of irradiation; who then saw and felt the mutilation of their sexual organs by surgery; who returned to cold wards to lie in bed for months, ill-fed, ill-tended, with unhealing, suppurating wounds; who were liberated two years later to endure in freedom the lifelong hunger of childlessness. . . . In the testimony of these witnesses, one looked down with a vertigo of mounting comprehension into a time and place, the pit of Auschwitz in 1943, where men who lived by nothing but self-interest and a technique of the hands, cut to pieces the most valued capacity of other men, and of women" (Ellmann, 24–25). This voice of indignation does not offer us a "transcendence" of the monstrosity of the Holocaust, but it restores to us the sense, absent from the art of "fact," that true perception is a creative act, without which we can hardly begin to understood what, even beyond millions of human beings and European Jewish civilization, the Holocaust destroyed.

Notes

1. Tadeusz Borowski, *This Way for the Gas, Ladies and Gentlemen* (New York: The Viking Press, 1967), 143.
2. See Efraim Zuroff, "Nazi Liberation Day Down Under," *Jerusalem Post*, May 23, 1992.
3. But other investigators of Nazi war criminals took strong exception to this view. See, e.g., the letter by Elliot Welles in the *New York Times* of May 29, 1992, pointing out that "the German Government is in possession of a long list of Nazi war criminals provided by the United Nations war crimes files. . . In addition, 130 files from Central Archives are in the hands of the Austrian Ministry of the Interior. [But] it sems that there is an unwillingness on the part of local German prosecutors and the Austrian Government to initiate legal proceedings against the alleged Nazi war criminals. In the United States as well, there are Latvians, Lithuanians and Ukrainians who participated in Nazi atrocities during the Second World War. Their extradition has yet to be requested by either the Baltic states or Ukraine."
4. Peter Hellman, "Nazi-Hunting Is Their Life," *New York Times Magazine*, November 4, 1979, 36. Subsequent references to this work will be cited in text.
5. Simon Wiesenthal, *The Sunflower*, (New York: Schocken Books, 1976), 97. Subsequent references to this work will be cited in text as *TS*. "Murderers Among Us: The Simon Wiesenthal Story," a film of 1989, is based in part on *The Sunflower*.
6. Christopher Browning, *Ordinary Men: Reserve Police Battalion 101 and the Final Solution* (New York: Harper Collins, 1992), 57-60, 64-68, 71.
7. At the end of the war Abba Kovner was briefly tempted by just such a prospect of revenge. "Life seemed justified only if some attempt was made to take revenge on the German people in such a way as to leave a lasting impression on its history and show that Jewish blood would not be spilled in vain. There was no point in simply killing a few, or even a few hundred, known Nazis. In the darkness of the despair of men and women who had seen their people—practically all their people—brutally massacred, the only meaning of revenge, and therefore of life, could be the mass destruction of Germans in the same way that the Germans had murdered Jews. The Germans had given rise to Nazism. Millions of Germans must have known, millions therefore should suffer. This could only be done by using poison." Quoted in Yehuda Bauer, *Flight and Rescue: Brichah* (New York: Random House, 1970), 26.
8. "Eichmann in Jerusalem: An Exchange of Letters between Gershom Scholem and Hannah Arendt," *Encounter*, 22 (January 1964), 51-56.
9. Or so it would seem. But on June 15, 1992 the U. S. Supreme Court ruled that the U.S. can kidnap a criminal suspect from a foreign country, over that country's objections, and without following the procedures laid down in an extradition treaty. The case involved a Mexican doctor accused of taking part in the torture and murder of an American narcotics agent in Guadalajara in 1985. See *New York Times*, June 16, 1992.
10. "Book Week," *New York Herald Tribune*, March 1, 1964.
11. Peter Weiss, *The Investigation*, translated by Jon Swan and Ulu Grossbard (New York: Atheneum, 1966), xi. Subsequent references to this work will be cited in text as *I*.

12. Oliver Clausen, "Weiss/Propagandist and Weiss/Playwright," *New York Times Magazine*, October 2, 1966, 132. See the discussion of the play by Sidra Ezrahi, *By Words Alone* (Chicago: University of Chicago Press, 1980), 39.

13. Matthew Arnold, *Letters of Matthew Arnold*, edited by G. W. E. Russell, 2 vols. in 1 (New York and London: Macmillan, 1900), I, 289–90.

14. Mary Ellmann, "The Dering Case: A Surgeon at Auschwitz," *Commentary*, 38 (July 1964), 19. Subsequent references to this work will be cited in text.

7

Controversies

The blood-dimmed tide is loosed, and everywhere
The ceremony of innocence is drowned;
The best lack all conviction, while the worst
Are full of passionate intensity.

—W. B. Yeats, *The Second Coming*

In addition to being a historical actuality, a literary subject, a moral quagmire, and a theological stumbling-block, the Holocaust has become a seething cauldron of controversy. Some of the disputes are nearly as incredible as the Holocaust itself. Who can imagine a movement claiming that black slavery never existed in this country, or that World War II never happened? Yet the first section of this chapter examines precisely such a movement of denial with respect to the Holocaust.

Some of the controversies arise from what has been called the strangely "literary" quality of the Holocaust, a historical event in which the most extravagant metaphors of world literature—men as insects, hell on earth—became actualities. The body of polemics dealt with in this chapter under the rubric "Stealing the Holocaust" cynically tries to reverse this process by making the actual Jewish victims of the Holocaust into metaphors.

The polemical fevers that inflame the brains of many of the ideologues and propagandists discussed here need to be viewed against the background of a paradox. Although 997 out of every 1,000 people in the world are not Jews, the Jews have been at the storm-center of history for nearly a century, since the Dreyfus Affair. Nearly two decades before the hapless *Britannica* writer quoted in the epigraph to chapter one pronounced antisemitism "a passing phase in the history of culture," the Yiddish

181

writer I. L. Peretz warned that "Antisemitism is a disease, and politics stands by the sickbed like a stupid, vicious doctor who wants to prolong the illness."[1] Parts of this chapter document the success with which such quacks have plied their trade in recent years.

Holocaust controversies are not edifying. They often originate in hatred, envy, and jingoism; at their best, they stem from the peculiarly modern vulgarity which consists in the inability to make distinctions; at their worst, they are permeated by a conscious will to deceive. One may regret that these controversies so often involve not the fruitful conflict of half-truths but calumnies that require constant refutation. But, whether we like it or not, they now make up the environment within which the subject of the Holocaust exists and must be studied.

Denying the Holocaust.

The crudest form of Holocaust "revisionism," but also one of the most highly publicized, is the outright denial that the Holocaust ever took place at all. It used to be said that Stalinism was a more sophisticated totalitarianism than Hitlerism because whereas Hitler ordered books to be burnt, Stalin had them rewritten. The Holocaust deniers are mainly followers, latter-day disciples, and adulators of Adolf Hitler rather than of Stalin. But since the books bearing personal witness to the systematic destruction of European Jewry at the hands of National Socialism by now mount into the thousands, burning them would be a formidable task indeed; and so these "neo-Nazis" (as they are usually called) have had to resort to the methods of their erstwhile rivals in mass murder, the Stalinists.

The "incredibility" of the Holocaust is, of course, a serious and well-worn topic. In 1951 the incredibility of the destruction of European Jewry was a major theme of Hannah Arendt's classic study *The Origins of Totalitarianism*. In that book, she stressed the extent to which the Nazis relied on the expectation that the wild improbability of the scale of their crimes, their very immensity, would guarantee that, should they lose the war, they and their preposterous lies would be believed, whereas their victims would be derided as mendacious fantasists. "The Nazis did not even consider it necessary to keep this discovery to themselves. Hitler circulated millions of copies of his book in which he stated that to be successful, a lie must be enormous—which did not prevent people from believing him as, similarly, the Nazis' proclamation, repeated *ad nauseam*, that the Jews would be exterminated like bedbugs (i.e., with poison gas) prevented anybody from *not* believing them" (Arendt 1951, III, 137).

In his powerful memoir *The Holocaust Kingdom*, Alexander Donat recounts his conversations with a fellow-inmate in the Maidanek camp, Dr. Ignacy Schipper, a historian. One of Schipper's major worries is over whether future generations will believe the story of Maidanek. If the murderers are victorious, he speculates, they will write the history books and either celebrate their achievement or else wipe out the memory of the Jews as thoroughly as they had obliterated their lives. "But if *we* write the history of this period of blood and tears—and I firmly believe we will—who will believe us? Nobody will *want* to believe us, because our disaster is the disaster of the entire civilized world."[2] The problem, for him, is not that the Holocaust is intrinsically incredible but that the world has a vested interest in not believing that it happened. It would, he thinks, be too frightened to live with the implications—so damaging to its most precious religious and political beliefs—of having been complicit in the removal of one member of the family of nations from its midst.

We know too that many of the Jewish victims themselves refused to believe that the Germans and their helpers were bent on murdering the entire Jewish people. "That they could all be murdered," said Kovner, "the Jews of Vilna, Kovno, Bialystok, Warsaw, the millions with their wives and children—hardly a single one wanted to believe that" ("Threnody," 5). "Yes," wrote Elie Wiesel in *Night*, "we ... doubted that he wanted to exterminate us. Was he going to wipe out a whole people? Could he exterminate a population scattered throughout so many countries? So many millions! What methods could he use? And in the middle of the twentieth century!"[3] "It seemed," wrote Bruno Bettelheim about Dachau and Buchenwald, "as if I had become convinced that these horrible and degrading experiences somehow did not happen to 'me' as subject but only to 'me' as an object. This experience was corroborated by the statements of the prisoners. . . . 'This cannot be true, such things just do not happen'. . . . The prisoners had to convince themselves that this was real, was really happening and not just a nightmare. They were never wholly successful." David Rousset wrote in a similar vein:

> Those who haven't seen it with their own eyes can't believe it. Did you yourself, before you came here, take the rumors about the gas chambers seriously? "No," I said.

" . . . you see? Well, they're all like you. The lot of them in Paris, London, New York, even at Birkenau, right outside the crematoriums . . . still incredulous, five minutes before they were sent down into the cellar of the crematorium." (Arendt 1951, III, 137)

Not surprisingly, the Jews who lived in relative safety outside of continental Europe were still more unwilling than those caught in Hitler's death trap to believe the reports of horror flooding in upon them at least as early as August 1942. In May 1942 the Jewish Socialist Party of Poland, the "Bund," transmitted to London a detailed report, originating with Polish Christians, showing that the Germans had "embarked on the physical extermination of the Jewish population on Polish soil." But, despite considerable publicity in the London *Daily Telegraph* and the Jewish press in England, neither the Allies nor the Jewish leadership could be roused from disbelief and complacency. Thus the Polish Government in Exile's Bulletin for Home Affairs remarked that "if the Polish reports from the Homeland do not find credence with the Anglo-Saxon nations and are considered to be untrustworthy, they surely must believe the reports from the Jewish sources." The crucial fact was that, according to Yehuda Bauer, "the Jews themselves either did not believe the reports or did not want to believe them."[4]

Marie Syrkin, one of the shrewdest of American Jewish writers, herself acknowledged that the Bund report reached the desk of the *Jewish Frontier*, of whose editorial board she was a member, in August 1942. "After reading this detailed account of the functioning of the extermination centers we rejected it as the macabre phantasy of a lunatic sadist." They did not, however, wholly reject it, for they decided to print a portion of the report in small type in the back of the next issue. "Our notion was that the atrocity tale, surely untrue, should not be emphatically publicized; that is why we chose small type."[5] But Syrkin and the magazine's editor Hayim Greenberg soon recognized their error, and devoted the entire issue of November 1942 to a detailed report on "Jews under the Axis, 1939-1942." In their preface to this forty-page documentation, they wrote: "we have paid Nazi spokesmen the compliment of not believing their monstrous profession. The reports in this issue, however, substantiate the Nazi claims."[6]

As the war was nearing its end, the Nazis thought better of boasting about their great deeds in destroying European Jewry and decided that it would be more prudent to cover their tracks. They accelerated attempts, some begun as early as 1942, to erase all traces of the massacres, through cremation, burning in open pits, use of explosives and flame-throwers and bone-crushing machinery. But, as Hannah Arendt remarked in her book on the Eichmann trial, "The holes of oblivion do not exist. Nothing human is that perfect, and there are simply too many people in the world to make oblivion possible. One man will always be left alive to tell the story" (*EJ*, 232–33).

In fact, as we now know, a multitude of survivors have told their stories, carrying out the obligation which they said they felt during their days in the camps to bear witness to what had been done to them and to the Jewish people. In addition, the Germans themselves have left copious records of their activities; indeed, most Holocaust museums are technically "German" museums because their materials are largely German government documents, German photographs, even personal memoirs of Germans involved, actively or passively, in the killing process. Among the most vivid of these is the April 26, 1945 deposition of S.S. officer Kurt Gerstein, who committed suicide while under arrest in a French military prison as a war criminal. Gerstein (whom we have already met in Hochhuth's play) had been appointed in January 1942 head of the Department of Sanitation Techniques within the S.S. His account, from which only brief sections are here excerpted, includes description of the arrival of a convoy of Jews from Lemberg to the killing center at Belzec, their herding into the death chambers, and—a much rarer thing—the view through the peephole afforded this privileged observer.

> They walked up the small wooden flight of stairs and entered the death chambers, most without a word, pushed forward by those behind them. One Jewish woman of about forty, her eyes flaming torches, curses the murderers; after several whiplashes by Captain Wirth in person, she disappeared into the gas chamber. . . . Inside the chambers, S.S. men crowd the people. "Fill them up well," Wirth had ordered, "700–800 of them to every 25 square meters." The doors are shut. Meanwhile, the rest of the people from the train, naked, wait. I am told: "Naked even in winter!" "But they may catch their death!" "But that's what they're here for!" was the reply. At that moment, I understand the reason for the inscription "Heckenholt." Heckenholt was the driver of the diesel truck whose exhaust gases were to be used to kill these unfortunates. S.S. Unterscharfuhrer Heckenholt was making great efforts to get the engine running. But it doesn't go. Captain Wirth comes up. I can see he is afraid because I am present at a disaster. Yes, I see it all and I wait. My stop watch showed it all, 50 minutes, 70 minutes, and the diesel did not start! The people wait inside the gas chambers. In vain. They can be heard weeping, "like in the synagogue," says Professor Pfaffenstiel, his eyes glued to a window in the wooden door. Furious, Captain Wirth lashes the Ukrainian assisting Heckenholt 12, 13 times in the face. After two hours and 49 minutes—the stop watch recorded it all—the diesel started.

Up to that moment, the people shut up in those four crowded chambers were still alive, four times 750 persons in four times 45 cubic meters! Another 25 minutes elapsed. Many were already dead, that could be seen through the small window because an electric lamp inside lit up the chamber for a few moments. After 28 minutes, only a few were still alive. Finally, after 32 minutes, all were dead. On the far side members of the work commando opened the wooden doors. They—themselves Jews— were promised their lives and a small percentage of the valuables and money collected for this terrible service. Like pillars of basalt, the dead were still erect, not having any space to fall, or to lean. Even in death, families could be seen still holding hands. It is hard to separate them as the chambers are emptied to make way for the next load; corpses were tossed out, blue, wet with sweat and urine, the legs covered with feces and menstrual blood. Two dozen workers were busy checking the mouths of the dead, which they opened with iron hooks. "Gold to the left, without gold to the right!" Others inspected anuses and genital organs, searching for money, diamonds, gold, etc. Dentists hammered out gold teeth, bridges and crowns. In the midst of them stood Captain Wirth. He was in his element, and showing me a large can full of teeth, he said: "See for yourself the weight of that gold!" . . . Then the bodies were flung into large trenches, each 100x20x12 meters, located near the gas chambers. After a few days the corpses swelled, because of the gases which formed inside them, and everything rose from two to three meters. A few days later, when the swelling subsided, the bodies settled. Subsequently, I was told, the bodies were piled on train rails and burned in diesel oil so that they would disappear. The next day we drove in Captain Wirth's car to Treblinka. . . . The equipment in that place of death was almost the same as Belzec, but even larger. Eight gas chambers and veritable mountains of clothing and underwear, about 35–40 meters high. Then, in our honor, a banquet was held for all those employed at the establishment. Obersturmbannfuhrer Professor Doctor Pfaffenstiel, Professor of Hygiene at the University of Marburg/Lahn, made a speech: "Your work is a great work and a very useful and very necessary duty." To me, he spoke of the establishment as "a kindness and a humanitarian thing." To all present, he said: "When one sees the bodies of the Jews, one understands the greatness of your work!"[7]

So far from being elusive, amorphous, ill-defined, the Holocaust is by now one of the most fully documented events in all history. It would therefore seem virtually impossible for any reputable historian to deny that it happened at all. And indeed no reputable historian has done so. The Holocaust deniers are a collection of antisemitic cranks, compared with whom the devotees of the flat-earth theory are sober and disinterested scholars. Their ranks include veterans of fascist and Nazi organizations, convicted frauds and libellers, sellers of electric chairs, and similar worthies. Among the most prominent activists of the movement in North America are Bradley R. Smith, a construction worker from Los Angeles who invests energy and money in advertisements in college newspapers (he attended no college himself) asserting that the Nazis had no policy of murdering Jews; Ernst Zundel, a neo-Nazi Toronto publisher convicted and sentenced to nine months in prison in 1988 for publishing a pamphlet *(Did Six Million Really Die?)* which alleged that stories of the Holocaust were all a hoax concocted by "Zionists"; and Arthur R. Butz, a professor of electrical engineering at Northwestern University, and author of the most widely promoted "revisionist" text, *The Hoax Of The Twentieth Century*, published by Noontide Press, the publishing arm of the Institute for Historical Review, a California group.

The Institute for Historical Review (IHR) has been the great mover and shaker in the campaign to deny the actuality of the Holocaust. It was founded in 1979 by Willis A. Carto of the anti-Jewish Liberty Lobby. Until 1982 it was directed by one "Lewis Brandon," who twelve years later, in embarrassing circumstances, revealed himself to be David McCalden, an imported British fascist who had founded the racist British National Party, an offshoot of the neo-Nazi National Front. He left the IHR in 1982 after a falling out with Willis Carto; they continued to abuse each other, in the most vituperative language, as liars and thieves, until McCalden died, from AIDS, in 1990.

In its first convention, the IHR made a public offer of a $50,000 "reward" for "proof" that the Nazis had operated gas chambers to murder Jews. Its challenge was taken up by a survivor named Mel Mermelstein of Long Beach, California. Having hoped to lure a sacrificial lamb into the kangaroo court of their publicity stunt, the neo-Nazis unexpectedly found themselves forced into a U. S. court and a formal legal setting where their cause suffered (at least ostensibly) a considerable setback. In July 1985 Judge Robert Wenke of L.A. Superior Court called for the IHR to pay the $50,000 reward; to pay an additional $40,000 for the pain and suffering it had caused Mermelstein; to issue a formal apology to him and other survivors; and to acknowledge a pretrial finding in the case that the gassing of Jews at Auschwitz is an indisputable fact. (The IHR has thus far, through a series of legal dodges and organizational sleights of hand, avoided payment.)

At about the same time, Canadian trials of antisemitic propagandists who specialized in Holocaust denial received far more (and far more disturbing) publicity. In 1985 the aforementioned Zundel, publisher of Nazi propaganda and himself author of such neo-Nazi classics as *The Hitler We Loved And Why*, and James Keegstra, a high school teacher who relentlessly catechized his students in the doctrine that the Holocaust was a hoax invented by the omnipresent Zionist conspiracy, were both found guilty (under Section 281.2[2] of Canada's Criminal Code), of willfully promoting racial hatred.

But even though these neo-Nazis consistently lose in court, they win in another way. Zundel, for example, said of his conviction that "It cost me $40,000 in lost work, but I got a million dollars worth of publicity for my cause. It was well worth it."[8] Donald Coxe, the Canadian correspondent of the *National Review*, shrewdly remarked in the May 31, 1985 issue that "Judging by media coverage, the three most significant men in Canada today are Brian Mulroney [the country's Prime Minister], Ernst Zundel, and James Keegstra." Neither, Coxe pointed out, was the problem merely one of quantity; rather, it was the moral nihilism of the journalists, the "evenhandedness" of the moral nonentities who remain "impartial" in disputes between professional liars and honest people, that gave the Nazis their paradoxical triumph through defeat. The journalists took up with alacrity the court's technical classification of the pro-Nazi witnesses as "experts" and printed long, undigested, unanalyzed, and uncriticized quotations or paraphrases of Nazi absurdities. "A mere pamphleteer should not be characterized as an expert," warned Coxe, "just because he has spent years disseminating lies. . . . Indeed, when the last of these sorry stories is told, the public may conclude that the real villain remains unprosecuted—the media, for disseminating with all the power of modern technology the false news likely to cause harm to an identifiable group and, what is even more important, to the whole process of historical understanding."[9] Another Canadian correspondent, Alan Bayless of the *Wall Street Journal*, wrote in a similar vein in an essay entitled "Holocaust Trials Can Make Hatemongers Appear as Victims" that "the free-speech controversy in Canada is obscuring the hoax theory's blatant anti-Semitism and its mockery of the suffering of both Jews and Gentiles under the Nazis."[10]

The level of attention accorded the neo-Nazi revisionists is all the more remarkable in view of the level of discourse at which they operate. The French writer Nadine Fresco has briskly summarized their methods:

> The basic rule of revisionist argumentation is that all evidence of extermination is by definition inadmissible. A document dating from the war is inadmissible because it dates from those years. The deposition of a Nazi at his trial is inadmissible because it is a deposition from a trial. This is applicable to all the Nazis who were tried. If, as is the case, not one of them denied the existence of gas chambers, it is not because the gas chambers existed . . . but because the witnesses believed that if they assisted the victors, the judges would reward them with clemency. As for the testimonies and

depositions of some hundreds of Jews who pretended to be survivors of the genocide, they are inadmissible because given by people who could only be instigators or, at best, accomplices in the rumor that led to the swindle from which they benefited.[11]

A few examples of the revisionists at work should suffice to indicate the drift and flavor of their "research" methods.

The British amateur historian David Irving is among the favored gurus of the neo-Nazis, although his credentials are imperfect because, in his book *Hitler's War*,[12] he did not yet deny that Jews were murdered, but only that his hero Hitler had anything to do with the crime. In her book on *The Holocaust and the Historians*, Lucy Dawidowicz analyzes his method. To "prove" that the murders were committed behind Hitler's back, Irving "interprets" two lines from a telephone message sent by Himmler (then in Hitler's military headquarters bunker) on November 30, 1941 to S.S. leader Heydrich, then in Prague: "Judentransport aus Berlin/keine Liquidierung." (Transport of Jews from Berlin. No liquidation.) From these two lines Irving magically construed that Hitler had learned of the murderous mischief Himmler was up to and ordered him to stop, and that Himmler, as an obedient Nazi, had called Heydrich in Prague to transmit Hitler's order. Even someone who pondered just these two lines stressed by Irving might well ask why, since Himmler continued to "liquidate" the Jews after November 30, 1941, he stopped the liquidation of this one transport. If he really deceived Hitler both before and after this date about the murder of the Jews, why should he have been so forthright on this single occasion? But these questions, Dawidowicz argued, prove to be academic once we consider the rest of the messsage, which Irving conveniently neglects to discuss. The first two lines are: "Verhaftung Dr. Jekelius/Angebl [ich] Sohn Molotovs," that is, Arrest Dr. Jekelius/Presumably Molotov's son. In other words, if we consider lines three and four of the phone message in relation to lines one and two, we understand that Himmler is instructing Heydrich that one Dr. Jekelius, apparently the Soviet foreign minister's son, is being taken into custody by the security police. Jekelius could be located in the transport of Jews from Berlin; unlike the rest of the transport, he was not to be liquidated (presumably because he might be exchanged for a German officer in the hands of the Russians.) Thus does Irving end up confuting his own theory. For *if* Hitler was responsible, as Irving (without evidence) assumes, for Himmler's call, then Irving has of course shown that Hitler knew all about "liquidations."[13]

A second analyst of texts beloved by IHR is one Ditlieb Felderer. He is the IHR's specialist in Anne Frank "research," dedicated to showing that her diary is a fraud. A triumphant stroke, he thinks, in his polemic is to contend that her book contains "literary flourishes that a 13-year-old girl could not possibly use." The original of the diary, he speculates, "was probably so innocuous" that it would hold "no interest for the reading public," and therefore others "elaborated" on it "to create a marketable product" ("Revisionism," 9-10). Q.E.D.

A third "expert" and by now one of the most famous Holocaust deniers, is Robert Faurisson, right-wing antisemite and onetime lecturer in literature at the University of Lyon-2, whose catalog of 1978 described him (with comic solemnity) as specializing in "investigation of meaning and counter-meaning, of the true and the false." His credo is that "Hitler never ordered (nor permitted) that someone be killed because of race or religion."[14] If the Nazis built gas chambers, it was for gassing lice. After all, did not Himmler himself say that "it is the same with antisemitism as with delousing"? One of his central premises (itself based on gross factual error) is that the only witnesses to the Holocaust are Jews, and that Jewish witnesses are liars—because they are Jews. (One wonders, therefore, how he reacted to being adorned by a faction of the French ultraleft called La Guerre Sociale with the title of "the Jew," that is,"a man alone.") The lie and 'swindle" about gas chambers and genocide, he alleges, originate with the "Zionists" and victimize primarily "the Germans and Palestinians."

Faurisson specializes in demonstrating that Hitler's actions against the Jews were of the same order as Jewish actions against Hitler, one provoking the other. To "prove" that there had been a Jewish war against Hitler as early as March of 1933, Faurisson reproduces the front page of the *Daily Express* of London for March 24, 1933. Sure enough, it carries a main headline reading "Judea Declares War on Germany," with subheads reading "Jews of All the World Unite—Boycott of German Goods." The *Express* was, of course, a sensationalist mass circulation paper run by Lord Beaverbrook, an eccentric who always used headlines to denounce his pet peeves and promote his pet causes. During the early years of the Hitler regime he wanted Britain to avoid alliances with France and other threatened European countries, expressing fear that the Jews "may drive us into war." His headlines, which to Faurisson represent the most impressive proof of what happened in history, also include the following, on September 30, 1938: "The Daily Express declares that Britain will not be involved in a European war this year, or next either. Peace agreement signed at 12.30 a.m. today." Ergo, according to Faurisson's style of textual interpretation, Britain did not go to war in 1939.[15]

He offered another example of interpretative virtuosity to the readers of *Le Monde* on January 16, 1979. Citing the diary that Johann-Paul Kremer, S.S. doctor, kept during his tenure at Auschwitz, he directs attention to Kremer's account of the eleventh occasion at which he was present at a *Sonderaktion* ("special action"). Faurisson declares that this special action, which his opponents, "the exterminationists," take to be a mass gassing, refers merely to the executions of those condemned to death. "Among the condemned are three women who arrived in a convoy from Holland; they are shot." So much for the myth of gas chambers. With his typically buffoonish display of scholarly scrupulousness, Faurisson attaches an impressive note citing page and note number of a text published by the Museum of Oswiecim. Nadine Fresco decided to check the text of the note to which Faurisson refers, with the following results: "Note 85 on page 238 . . . indeed indicates that three Dutch women were shot on that day. But the text of the note to which Faurisson refers reads: 'At the time of the special action which I described in my diary on October 18, 1942, three Dutch women *refused to enter the gas chamber* [emphasis mine] and pleaded for their lives. They were young women, in good health, but despite this their prayer was not granted and the S.S. who participated in the action shot them on the spot.'" (Fresco, 474)

Faurisson has vaulted to fame not so much through his jejune publications, which are very similar to those of the IHR, except for being in French, as through his good fortune in finding a powerful friend to defend him from his persecutors, a friend named Noam Chomsky. The well-known linguist and longtime left-wing activist and warrior against Israel came to the defense of Faurisson after his university classes had been suspended and he had been brought into court in June 1981 for defamations of Holocaust witnesses and scholars of the Holocaust. (The court cases in France were derived from the same kind of statute under which Keegstra and Zundel were prosecuted in Canada: freedom of speech cannot excuse the spreading of falsehood for the purpose of inflaming racial hatred.) Chomsky promoted and placed his own name at the top of a petition supporting Faurisson's "just right of academic freedom" and demanding that "university and government officials do everything possible to ensure . . . the free exercise of his legal rights." The petition worshipfully identified Faurisson as "a respected professor of twentieth-century French literature and document criticism," who had been "conducting extensive historical research into the 'Holocaust' question" and was harassed as soon as "he began making his *findings* public" (emphasis added [Cohn,6]). The petition had been composed by Mark Weber, who had himself had his tenure terminated at University of Tulsa because of his involvement with the neo-Nazi movement. The petition, featuring Chomsky's endorsement, was widely believed to have played a major role in gaining a measure of respectability for the Holocaust-denial campaign.

When civil libertarians and even leftists in France protested to Chomsky, he responded with an essay on the right of free expression in which he declared that everyone, including fascists and antisemites, should have the right of free speech; but he hastened to add that Faurisson was neither. (Chomsky's incessant invocations of Voltaire's pieties about free speech to defend Faurisson led Fresco to recall the Enlightenment bigot's pronouncement of 1745 about the Jews: "You will not find in them anything but an ignorant and barbarous people who have for a long time combined the most sordid avarice with the most detestable super-stition. . . . One should not, however, burn them" [Franco, 470]). Chomsky's essay was published as a preface to Faurisson's 1980 book, *Mémoire en Defense*. The winding path by which Chomsky moved from defending Faurisson on "civil libertarian" grounds to active collaboration with him and the neo-Nazis and also to substantive defense of the Frenchman's "argument" has been traced and documented in great detail by Professor Werner Cohn, to whose pamphlet on this subject I am indebted. Having begun by defending Faurisson's "historical research" on grounds of free speech, Chomsky moved deeper and deeper into the revisionist morass, arguing, first, that denial of the Holocaust is no evidence at all of antisemitism; second, that anti-Zionism too implies no presumption of antisemitism; and third, in a truly spectacular example of *tu quoque* he concocted in 1991, that anyone who says that the Jews alone were singled out by Hitler for total annihilation is involved in "pro-Nazi apologetics"[16] (presumably because a genuine anti-Nazi would insist—erroneously—that Hitler wanted to annihilate all identifi-able groups except ethnic Germans).

Virtually all the neo-Nazi groups mentioned in this discussion promote Chomsky's books and tapes on Israel. The IHR, for example, sells two separate tapes of a speech that Chomsky gave against Israel. They are described, with breathless admiration, as "two hours of uninterrupted cannonade directed squarely at U. S. foreign policy with regard to Israel . . . [ranging] brilliantly over such topics as Israeli imperialism . . . the role of the Anti-Defamation League," which the IHR ominously identifies as "one of the ugliest, most powerful groups in America" (Cohn, 14). If Chomsky feels any embarrassment at the way in which the neo-Nazis use his name and works, he has kept it well-hidden. He has also evaded the question of whether he himself endorses the denial of the Holocaust. In *Liberation* he wrote (December 23, 1980) that "I don't know enough about [Faurisson's] work to determine if what he is claiming is accurate or not." In *Le Matin* (January 19, 1981) the newly tolerant linguist wrote that "we don't want people to have religious or dogmatic beliefs about the existence of the Holocaust." Lucy Dawidowicz wrote that "In a letter to me, September 18, 1980, Chomsky expressed complete agnosticism on the subject of whether or not Faurisson's views were 'horrendous,' saying that he was not sufficiently involved in the issue to pursue or evaluate it."[17]

We may conjecture that even though Chomsky does not directly endorse the claims of Faurisson and the other cranks, he wishes them well in their endeavor; for he believes that to undermine belief in the Holocaust is to undermine belief in the legitimacy of the State of Israel, which many people suppose (albeit mistakenly) to have come into existence because of Western bad conscience over what was done to the Jews in World War II. Chomsky would feel no compunction about joining "right-wing" forces to achieve the great desideratum of delegitimizing the Jewish state. This is one reason (among many) why such an extreme right-wing antisemite as the columnist Joseph Sobran fondly refers to Chomsky as "a true Israelite, in whom there is no guile."[18]

Right-wing figures who have supported the Holocaust deniers from the sidelines, so to speak, have shown a liberality and eclecticism in no way inferior to Chomsky's. Patrick Buchanan has not hesitated to embrace extreme leftists if, in doing so, he could forward the all-important campaign against Israel. He too has afforded the Holocaust deniers access to wide publicity and apparent respectability. Buchanan's admiration of Hitler himself can be traced back to 1977, when he called the

Führer a man of "genius," "an individual of great courage . . . a political organizer of the first rank, a leader steeped in the history of Europe."[19] But he did not at that time deny that Hitler had committed genocide. Not until the late 1980s did he begin to suggest, in his newspaper column, that the survivors of Hitler's death camps suffer from "group fantasies of martyrdom" and "Holocaust survivor syndrome." He further alleged that the gas chambers could not have killed human beings. How did he know this? Simple: "In 1988, 97 kids, trapped 400 feet underground in a Washington, D. C. tunnel while two locomotives spewed diesel exhaust into the car, emerged unharmed after 45 minutes."[20] Buchanan nevertheless declined invitations to stand in a gas chamber designed to murder people and find out for himself whether it proves more lethal than exposure to accidental spewing of exhaust into a train tunnel. In his spirited defense of a whole gallery of men accused of being Nazi war criminals—Karl Linnas, Klaus Barbie, Ivan Demjanjuk—Buchanan typically refers to proceedings against them as witch-hunts by Salem judges, the implication being that the Holocaust is as much a chimera as the alleged depredations of alleged witches. "Buchanan," according to Allan Ryan, former head of the Justice Department's Office of Special Investigations, "is the spokesman for Nazi war criminals in America. His campaign on behalf of these people is so infused with distortions and misrepresentations that it's almost impossible to engage in any sort of response. He simply piles lie upon inaccuracy upon surmise upon personal attack."[21]

The continued resilience of the Holocaust-denial movement, despite its poverty of mind and tawdriness of character, may finally be attributed to another, ghoulishly impressive characteristic, which may one day render it worthy of literary treatment. As one American writer puts it, "It's a feat of the human imagination to say that something that never happened did happen; but it's a far greater feat (and Holocaust-denial may be its only historical instance) to declare that something that did happen never happened. To make something out of nothing is no big deal; to make nothing out of something is astounding. The sun doesn't rise! Night doesn't come! The endorsement of such statements is ultimate nihilism, wicked glee. Andre Maurois said that the Devil is a person, and maybe he's right."[22]

Stealing the Holocaust.

Sie werden es von uns wieder stehlen.
—Martin Buber (commenting on
the Hebrew Bible in the context
of a discussion of the Holocaust)[23]

The uniqueness of the Jewish catastrophe during World War II had no sooner been defined than it was called into question, by Jews as well as Christians. We should not be surprised by this. The fact and the idea of suffering are central in Christianity, whose ethical values are based upon the idea of a community of suffering, rather than the pursuit of pleasure. Many Christians also believe that, as Mary Ann Evans (later known as George Eliot, the novelist) wrote in 1848, "Everything specifically Jewish is of a low grade."[24] Yet here, in the Holocaust, was a Jewish claim to a specific suffering that was of the "highest," the most distinguished grade imaginable. Among the Jews, too, large numbers of "universalists" kicked resolutely against the notion of a distinctly Jewish catastrophe. They believed that the enormity of the Holocaust could be recognized by the world at large only if it were universalized, if its victims were recast, as we have seen Anne Frank was by Broadway, as "human beings" rather than as Jews. As Irving Howe and Cynthia Ozick have remarked, this universalism is, paradoxically, the ultimate form of Jewish parochialism. The supposed distinction between being human and being Jewish is one that has infected the mental world of Jews at least since the time of its formulation in Judah Leib Gordon's assimilationist slogan: " Be a Jew in your home and a man in the street."[25] (The German Nazis may be said to have brought this distinction to its full flowering by decreeing that the Jews were not human at all, so that in order to be granted the right to live, you had, under Nazi rule, to prove that you were *not* a Jew.)

The process of stealing the Holocaust from the Jews who were its victims began with small acts of distortion reflective more of intellectual vulgarity and emotional self-indulgence than of any desire to harm Jews. The rhetoric of the American civil-rights movement of the 1960s was permeated by references to the curtailment of free lunch programs in Harlem as genocide, descriptions of Watts as a concentration camp, casual references to black neighborhoods anywhere as ghettos. Not all of the orators who used this language could have been unmindful of the fact that no place in New York or Los Angeles or Chicago in 1960 was remotely like Buchenwald in 1938 or Warsaw in 1942 or Auschwitz in 1944. But why fuss about precision of language or intellectual delicacy when the exigencies of politics make it convenient to use Jews as metaphors for other people's sufferings?

Yet a problem arose, in which lay the seed of black hostility to Jews that would erupt in violence in the 1990s. The people who were incessantly told by agitators in northern cities that *they* were the new Jews, that *they* lived in ghettos and concentration camps, that *they* were victims of genocide, began to look about them to identify the Nazi culprits in this situation. Not surprisingly, they chose for this role the Jews themselves— that is, the white people whom they saw and dealt with and indeed received help from most frequently. Before the 1960s were over, it had become routine for black demagogues in New York, for example, to charge Jewish teachers with the "cultural genocide" of their black pupils. Already one could sense that, as if by some law of physics or conservation of energy, the instant that another group became "the Jews," the Jews themselves became "the Nazis."

However fraught with danger to the American social fabric, this rhetoric was an amateurish rehearsal for what was to come. The most deliberate, sustained, and malicious attempt to steal the Holocaust was begun by the Soviet Union and the Arab world after the 1967 Middle East War, and has remained to this day one of the most lethal weapons deployed against the land and the people of Israel. After the Six-Day War, cartoons were published depicting Moshe Dayan as Field Marshal Rommel, with swastikas on his uniform. These cartoons appeared not only in the USSR and the Arab countries but in the journals of American civil rights organizations like the Student Non-Violent Coordinating Committee (SNCC). In the weeks before the Six-Day War, when Egypt blockaded the Straits of Tiran and Arab armies were advancing towards Israel's borders and Egyptian President Nasser and PLO chairman Shukairy were promising to "turn the Mediterranean red with Jewish blood," the Jewish state was the recipient of a good deal of world sympathy. But after the war Israel discovered that the price it would have to pay for winning a defensive war that, if lost, would have meant its destruction was the nearly universal loss of the sympathy the Jews had been collecting since 1945, when discovery of the Holocaust became general. After a mere twenty-two years, the period of grace was over.

Since 1967 the resentment against Israel for refusing to be a passive victim of aggression has expressed itself consistently in the depiction of Israelis as Nazis and Palestinian Arabs as Jews. In the 1970s UNESCO condemned Israel's archaeological digs in Jerusalem as "crimes against culture," a charge intended, as Norman Podhoretz pointed out, "to conjure up the burning of books by the Nazis."[26] The Soviet Ambassador to the U.N. accused Israelis of "racial genocide," and the Committee on the Inalienable Rights of the Palestinian People (which in U.N. parlance means only Arabs, never Jews) compared the "sealing of a part of the city of Nablus" to "the ghettos and concentration camps erected by the Hitlerites in several cities of Europe."

The triumphant stroke in the campaign to steal the Holocaust from the Jews by inverting the roles of the victim and the predator was the Arab and Soviet-inspired "Zionism is racism" resolution of 1975. (The actual presentation of the resolution was done by Somalia, Cuba, and Benin, nations whose subsequent fate might be adduced in evidence of the biblical promise that he who curses Israel will be cursed.) Having failed to defeat the Jews on the battlefield, the Arabs decided (correctly, as it turned out) that it was easier to wage ideological war against Zionism than military struggle against Israel. For nearly a century, the word *racism* in Europe had been virtually synonymous with antisemitism, or Jew-hatred. For the Soviets and the Arab nations to have foisted upon the U.N. a resolution saying that Israel, the last coherent center of the historic Jewish civilization destroyed by the Nazis, is itself the sole inheritor of Nazism was to have made the public memory of the Holocaust into a potent instrument for delegitimization of the Jewish state and indeed of the Jewish people. For Jew-haters everywhere, this Orwellian inversion proved to be meat and drink, a seminal idea whose fruitfulness burgeoned in countless forms from 1975 until 1991 when the collapse of Communism made possible its repeal. Fidel Castro, in speeches before the Third World conference in Havana and at the UN in 1979, described Israelis as the Nazis of our time, predators who had driven the modern Jews (formerly known as Arabs) off their land, committed genocide, and so forth. Vanessa Redgrave, a PLO activist, went out of her way to portray a Jewish victim of the "original" Holocaust, as it were, in order to drive home the intended equation between the Jewish victims of Hitler and the Palestinian Arab victims of the Israelis. And in a "debate" with Fania Fenelon, the survivor whom she portrayed, she claimed that she could hardly be an antisemite because the Palestinians are themselves "semites."

Stealing the Holocaust became central in the ideology of militant anti-Israel groups, such as the American Friends Service Committee (AFSC),[27] and in the body of cliches shared by scores of journalists seeking easily repeated formulas. Nick Thimmesch (*Los Angeles Times Syndicate*) declared on October 6, 1977 that Menachem Begin's statements that Jews have a right to live in Judea were "the language of Hitler." The *Christian Science Monitor* began a four-part series (June 1979) on "The Struggle for Palestine" by referring to the Palestinian Arabs as "the Jews of the Arab world." It further asserted that they are living in "Diaspora," that they long for restoration to Jerusalem, indeed that they are the latest Zionists. Doug Marlette, syndicated by the Knight News Service, reported (October 21,1979) how the eyes of Palestinian Arab refugees always looked out at him from under the photos in Yad Vashem of Jewish children being marched into gas chambers. Jonathan Randal disclosed to readers of the *Washington Post Service* (March 5, 1980) that Palestinian Arabs were living "in Diaspora" or else in Lebanese camps that they thought were replicas of Dachau and Auschwitz. Five days later the novelist John Updike not only endorsed the view that "the Palestinians are Jews" but invited readers of the *New Yorker* (March 10, 1980) to join him in bemoaning the "fact" that this is "a perspective seldom found in American newspapers." For these writers, as for the Russians and Arabs in the U.N., riding on the mournful coattails of the Jewish experience of discrimination, exile, oppression, and murder had become more than a means of collecting sympathy and expressing hatred; it had acquired the stature of an ideology.

Exactly a year before Updike complained of the paucity of metaphorical Jews, his *New Yorker* colleague George Steiner had published in the *Kenyon Review* a novella about Hitler entitled *The Portage to San Cristobal of A. H.*, which ought to have satisfied even the most voracious appetite for gross historical inaccuracies and licentious equations between Nazism and not only Zionism but the Torah itself. These apparently audacious but in fact (as we have seen) perfectly conventional equations are concentrated in Hitler's final monologue. In a controversy with the historian Martin Gilbert in 1982 over the stage version of *Portage*, Steiner explained that he left this monologue unanswered because he did not wish to descend to the level of "didactic Shavian debate" but, rather, aspired to the sublime detachment of Milton from his brilliant Satan or Dostoevsky from his Grand Inquisitor, and hoped to keep faith with the literary principles of Henry James and Jean-Paul Sartre, who liked to speak of a sacred pact that prohibited writers from assuming any moral responsibility toward their readers.[28]

This apologia is only too typical of what Irving Howe has called Steiner's unique ability to write about Auschwitz in "a high Mandarin

patter that reads at times as if it were a parody by Lucky Jim."[29] If Blake
and Shelley believed (mistakenly) that Milton was of the devil's party, it
certainly was not because of any reservation Milton felt about confuting
Satan. (In fact, Satan's great moments are largely confined to the first
two books of *Paradise Lost*, after which he not only declines in stature
but is "answered" by several thousand lines of angelic verse.) The real
problem is not that Steiner's loyalty to a minor literary tradition (one
without value for Jane Austen, Thackeray, or Dickens among many
others) is much greater than his loyalty to the Jewish people, but the
appalling fact that, as he admits in a rare moment of candor, he is "not
sure that A. H. can be answered."[30] In other words, Steiner, for all his
erudition, cannot give the lie to any of the following ludicrous assumptions and assertions of his play's hero: the Nazi idea of the master race
chosen (by itself) to impose its law upon inferior races is identical to the
Jewish (and Christian) idea of a people chosen by God to receive His
law; the Nazi idea is also like the Zionist idea (even though the Zionists
explicitly rejected chosenness for "normality"); the State of Israel was
created *because* of the Holocaust (and not *in spite of* the murder of
millions of the most Zionistic Jews in the world); Israel's sense of its
beleaguered condition grows out of its birth in the Holocaust (and not
out of brooding over such minor annoyances as seven decades of Arab
terrorism and five major wars).

That every one of these slanders converged perfectly with the major
themes of anti-Israel propaganda; that Steiner's novella and play appeared at a time when Europe was being swept by a tidal wave of
"literature" and films restoring Hitler to heroic status, a time when Israel
was consistently represented by its enemies in the U.N. and the press as
the inheritor of Nazism, and when Jewish intellectuals at British and
American universities were hastening to distance themselves from Israel—all this was a mysterious accident that Steiner could not explain
except by reference to his creative *daemon*.

Whatever misgivings Updike may have had about the ability of
Western journalists to make Jews into metaphors should finally have
been laid to rest by their treatment of the war in Lebanon. The propaganda
battle against Israel during this war began with the invention of the figure
of 600,000 homeless civilians by the Palestinian Red Crescent Society,
headed by Yasser Arafat's brother. The figure, a patent absurdity for an
area whose entire population is under 500,000, was irresistibly attractive

to anti-Israel journalists for the same reason that it was invented in the first place: it began with a 6 and facilitated the licentious equation of 600,000 Palestinian Arabs with the 6 million murdered Jews. That is why it continued to be used (for example, by Robert Fisk in the *Times* of London, and the late Jessica Savitch on NBC) long after it had become, as David Shipler wrote in the *New York Times* (July 15,1982), "clear to anyone who has traveled in southern Lebanon. . . that the original figures . . . were extreme exaggerations."

The herd of independent thinkers of every political stripe rushed to repeat the formula. The British Communist paper *Morning Star* published an editorial headed "Stop the Genocide" (June 11, 1982). Steven Benson of the Phoenix *Arizona Republic* published a series of pictures showing goose-stepping Israelis in German helmets guarding cattle cars and patrolling concentration camps; and his cartoonist colleague Oliphant showed West Beirut as the Warsaw Ghetto, with the PLO as the besieged Jews and the Israelis as the Nazi beasts. John Chancellor, musing autobiographically on the bombing of August 2, confessed that he "kept thinking yesterday of the bombing of Madrid during the Spanish Civil War." Since Chancellor was about twelve years old when Madrid was bombed by the Junkers 52s of Hitler's Luftwaffe in 1936, one may venture to guess that it was not memory that brought forth this analogy so much as a keen awareness that what would come to be called "political correctness" in broadcast journalism required the equation of Israelis with Nazis and Palestinian Arabs with Jews. Nicholas von Hoffman, writing from the United States for the *Spectator*, likened Israelis in Lebanon to Nazis in Lidice and expressed the hope that as a result of his efforts and those of like-minded journalists "Americans are coming to see the Israeli Government as pounding the Star of David into a swastika."

The campaign of calculated distortion begun by the Russians in 1967 had by 1982 become so common that the Irish writer and statesman Conor Cruise O'Brien proposed making it a kind of litmus test for the detection of antisemitism: "If your interlocutor can't keep Hitler out of the conversation, . . . feverishly turning Jews into Nazis and Arabs into Jews—why then, I think, you may well be talking to an anti-Jewist" (*Jerusalem Post*, July 6, 1982). (Ironically, none of the journalistic warriors against neo-Nazism thought it worthwhile to remark on the prominence of Nazi flags and mementos in captured headquarters of the new "Jews," formerly known as the PLO, in Lebanon.) Some people, in reaction to the daily regurgitation of this formula by many of the professional communicators and by PLO spokesmen, began to wonder whether a movement that can conceive of itself only as a mirror image of its Jewish enemy is in truth a "nation," or only an anti-nation, deriving its whole meaning and existence from its desire to destroy a living nation. If the Palestinian Arabs really are a distinct Arab people, skeptics asked, why do they always represent themselves as Jews? As Ruth Wisse has pointed out, Arab anti-Zionism goes beyond old-fashioned antisemitism in wanting not merely to eliminate the Jews, but to replace them.[31].

The organized violence of the *intifada*, beginning in December of 1987, provided the best opportunity yet for the exploitation of the Holocaust against the Jews themselves. This third phase of the Arab war against Israel replaced planes, tanks, and troops with stones and Molotov cocktails, thrown not by trained PLO killers but by young Palestinian Arabs sent into the streets to confront Israeli soldiers. The brilliant tactic of pitting children against soldiers decisively shifted the balance of liberal sympathy to the side of the Arabs and against Israel. After having refused, for forty years, to admit a Jewish state into what they consider their exclusive region, the Arab countries could now divert attention from their own imperialism and racism to the alleged refusal of Jews to accept a "Palestinian state" (actually a second Palestinian state, since Jordan has a Palestinian majority).

The daily confrontations between (at first[*]) young Palestinians and Israeli soldiers made the Israeli-Nazi equation easier than ever to foist upon the ever-growing number of those ignorant of Nazis, of Jews, of the Holocaust, of the long Arab war against Israel. By now, the Palestinian Arabs had so firmly attached themselves to the coattails of Jewish history that they incessantly spoke of their diaspora, their "covenant," their United Palestine Appeal, and, of course, the Holocaust they were suffering. In February of 1988, to complete the picture, the PLO's Madison Avenue branch contrived a scheme to send to Israel a ship intended "to echo the voyage of the *Exodus*." The event was laden with a great force of symbolic revelation, but what it revealed was not what

---

[*] By 1992 the *intifada's* main feature had become the activity of armed terrorist units that occasionally ambushed Israeli vehicles but mostly tortured and killed fellow Arabs alleged to be collaborating with the Israelis. See Steven Emerson, "Meltdown," *New Republic*, November 23, 1992.

its designers intended. The real *Exodus*, as some may still recall, was, in 1947, carrying 4550 Jewish survivors of Nazi death camps, and was turned away from Palestine by the British who then ruled there. 1988's Arab imitation of the *Exodus* carried 135 terrorists deported over the years from Israeli-administered territories. They were accompanied by 300 journalists and 200 assorted well-wishers. It is not hard to guess what moved each of the groups on this ship of knaves and fools to participate in the charade, the symbolic effort to recreate Palestinian Arabs as Jews. For what the *New York Times* (February 16) referred to as the "scores of minor Western dignitaries and journalists," the equation of Arabs with Jews and, in consequence, of Israelis with Nazis, afforded a welcome escape from any lingering feelings, however faint, of responsibility for what their countries did, or allowed to be done, to European Jewry. As for the Palestinian Arabs, this was a powerful symbolical statement of their resentment against the Jews for monopolizing all that beautiful Holocaust suffering which the Arabs would very much like, *ex post facto*, to share.

American journalistic cheerleaders of the *intifada* have often sacrificed professional standards in order to transform Palestinian Arabs into Jews. Thus Judith Miller, in the *New York Times Magazine*, wrote that "Sadam Hussein did succeed in focusing the world's attention on the more than five million Palestinians who for more than 40 years have lived in a diaspora depressingly similar to that of the Jews who now inhabit their land."[32] Nearly every "point" of the sentence, as David Bar-Illan noted upon its publication, is instantly recognizable as a falsehood. The "Palestinian" saga is the most widely reported story of the past decade. The number of Palestinian Arabs who became refugees as a result of the Arab assault on Israel forty-three years earlier was 450,000. By what reproductive miracle could they have become five million in three years (or even in forty)? Since Judith Miller feels strongly that Jews take up too much space in the world, she blithely refers to all of Israel (not just the disputed territories) as "their [Arab] land." But this land had not been under Arab rule for 450 years; no Arab country has ever been recognized as sovereign in it; the Ottoman empire was its last sovereign ruler; and in 1947 the UN recognized the area the Arabs would later abandon not as "their land" but as the State of Israel. Her appropriation of "diaspora" is linguistic theft of a high order. The Jews had been forced to live in foreign, usually hostile, lands after being exiled from their sovereign state. The Palestinian Arabs left a land in which they were not sovereign and moved to countries in which they were, and in which they found language, culture, and religion identical to their own. Whatever else they may be, Palestinian Arabs are poor candidates for metaphorical Jews, if we attend to the actual history of both peoples.

But those who are convinced that the chief lesson of the Holocaust is that the Jewish people should disappear from the world for the sake of peace and of humanity at large are as little impeded by history as by conscience in their pursuit of the goal of replacing Jews by Palestinian Arabs. Thus Marc Ellis, whose writings on the Holocaust and Israel show the power of Nazi demonology to infect the minds of people (Jews included) not yet born when the Nazi regime was destroyed, insists that "in the faces of the Palestinians lies the future of what it means to be Jewish" (*TJT*, 128). No garden-variety Jewish advocate of a PLO state alongside Israel, Ellis is critical of anti-Israel groups which fail to see Israel as irredeemably evil or to recognize in the *intifada* the opportunity to "reappraise the entire venture,"[33] that is, the establishment of the State of Israel. Although Ellis prides himself on the ability to recognize potential "Holocausts" at a distance of a thousand miles in nearly every (third-world) corner of the globe, he is mighty cool and detached in describing the effect on the Jews of satisfying Palestinian aspirations: "A military defeat of Israel would be from the Jewish Israeli side [!] horrible, but in no way comparable to the Holocaust." Indeed, he declares in his best Pecksniffian style, it would teach the hitherto all-powerful Jewish nation a lesson about its failure "to come to grips with its environment" (*BI*, 189).

Although Ellis is like the Christian liberation theologians among whom he travels in his flagrant manipulation of theology to serve a leftist, anti-American political agenda, he differs from them in seeking to subjugate (or obliterate) rather than liberate the community with which he claims to identify. As Rael and Erich Isaac point out in their trenchant analysis of his work, "For [Ellis] the object of Jewish Liberation Theology is not liberating or empowering Jews at all. . . . Liberation, in short, applies to every group *except* Jews."[34] Starting from the premise that the Jewish nation alone requires a special reason to exist, he concludes that Jewish liberation alone consists in "liberating" the Jews from exercising power.

Ellis' theology is convincing proof that, contrary to Dr. Johnson, it is not patriotism but Isaiah that is the last refuge of a scoundrel. Ellis'

Olympian declarations that "Jews are essentially a diaspora people" (*BI*,187) or that they were called into existence to bring about social revolution in the world, are fueled by licentious invocations of the biblical prophets, in whose long, ill-fitting robes he tries to drape himself. Biblical prophecy itself, he alleges, demands that Israel (in the Catholic language favored by this teacher at the Maryknoll Seminary) "confess and repent" its sins against the Arabs and surrender its sovereignty to satisfy Palestinian demands.

In his zeal to find prophetic support for his own powerful desire to return the State of Israel to sandy wastes, Ellis appears to overlook the little problem that, as the Isaacs point out, "the central conception of Judaism is the chosenness of Israel, its separation from the nations, its unique covenant at Sinai and its destiny to occupy a special land ordained by the deity" (Isaac, 64). No doubt it was, in Ellis' view, very un-Jewish for Samuel to have told King Saul that he had forfeited the kingship for failing to wipe out the wicked Amalekites; unfortunately, Samuel was, of course, himself a prophet. As for the idea that it is the specifically Jewish mission in the world to bring about a state of universal social justice, nothing could be farther from the truth, or from traditional Jewish thought, which, as the astute Hillel Halkin has written, "has always looked upon the gentile world as an arena of blindly chaotic and idolatrous forces that God alone can chasten or suborn to His purposes as He wills. For a Jew to intervene in such a world is worse than folly; one might as well seek to pacify earthquakes and floods" (*Letters*, 88).

For having raised antisemitic calumny to the level of theology (if not literacy), Ellis has received the appropriate rewards: he serves on the national advisory committee of the American-Arab Affairs Council; he appears on Jordanian television likening "Palestinian" victims of Jews to Jewish victims of the Nazis; and he writes the text for ads of something called the "United Palestine Appeal," an organization devoted to demonizing the Jews as wanton killers of innocent Arab children. An organization so named is, as Ruth Wisse has pointed out, a conscious parody and appropriation of the United Israel Appeal. "This inverted terminology is a double act of usurpation, first in replacing the existing state of Israel by an Arab state that will erase it, second, in stealing the vocabulary of diaspora Jews to turn it against them."[35] This joint product of Arab propaganda and the brain of Marc Ellis, like all the other attempts to attach the Palestinian Arabs to the coattails of Jewish history, founders on the rock of irreducible fact. The original United Palestine-United Israel Appeal raised money from Jewish communities around the world to resettle Jewish refugees in Israel. The Arab travesty of the Jewish original does just the opposite. It does not raise money from Arab overseas communities to assist suffering Arab children in "Palestine," since it has no more interest in the education and welfare of Arab children than it does in resettling Arab refugees; its sole interest is in destroying the moral image of the Jews by stealing their history.

Although the Israeli-Nazi equation was originally developed to collect sympathy and political support for the Arab struggle against Israel, it is by now so well established among the "politically correct" that one finds it invoked even in situations having nothing to do with the Arabs at all. In late 1991 and early 1992, for example, the Israeli public was going through one of its periodic squabbles over whether the music of Richard Wagner should be performed in Israeli concert halls. There has long been an informal, voluntary ban on the performance of his music in Israel in order to spare the feelings of that country's numerous Holocaust survivors. Wagner was by no means the only antisemitic composer, in Germany or in Europe; but his music was used by the Nazis as a rallying call against the Jews, an accompaniment to the campaign of mass murder.

The unwillingness of survivors to listen to the music that accompanied their persecution and the murder of their families is a phenomenon that seems readily understandable without benefit of degrees in psychology or musicology. Yet the outburst of indignation against the Israeli ban now became hysterical and vituperative. The *New York Times* ran something like a dozen stories, editorials, and op-ed pieces on the subject, giving its readers the impression that the future of Western culture hinged on the question of whether Wagner could be performed in Israel. It even summoned the late Leonard Bernstein from the grave to cheer for Wagner and also (in a reprint of a 1985 op-ed piece) say that "the 'Horst Wessel Lied' may have been a Nazi hymn, but divorced from its words it's just a pretty song" (*New York Times*, December 26, 1991). The omnipresent Edward Said likened Israel's resistance to performing Wagner to the Iranian ayatollahs' ban against the writings of Salman Rushdie and demand for his execution. Karl Meyer, an occasional editorialist for the *Times*, outdid even Said by equating the ban on public performances of Wagner to "Nazi bans on performing Mendelssohn because he was Jewish" (*New York Times*, December 19, 1991). Thus, once again, and in a matter not involving the Arabs, the Holocaust was invoked to show that its Jewish victims were no better than the Nazi murderers.

After about two months of editorial demonstrations that some ideas are so stupid that only intellectuals can believe them, the *Times*, at the end of January 1992, allowed Richard Taruskin, a music professor at Berkeley, to point out the obvious: the objection to Israeli performance of Wagner's music is a symbolic act, "sanctifying the memory of something that . . . it is not yet time to forget." To ask the survivors to listen to the music without recalling its context would, he said, be like asking Lincoln's wife, just after her husband had been shot at Ford's Theater, "But aside from that, Mrs. Lincoln, how was the show?" (*New York Times*, January 26, 1992).

The campaign to steal the Holocaust from its Jewish victims expresses a deep-seated wish to transform the Nazi murder of the Jews, a crime of terrifying clarity and distinctness, into a blurred, amorphous agony, an indeterminate part of man's inhumanity to man. It subserves the designs of those who wish to release the nations of the West from whatever slight burden of guilt they may still bear for what they allowed or helped Hitler to do to the Jews of Europe, and so remove whatever impediments of conscience may yet stand in the way of the anti-Israel crusade.

The Auschwitz Convent

Although the controversy over the convent at Auschwitz may be viewed as yet another episode in the campaign to steal, or at least appropriate, the Holocaust, it has achieved a monstrous magnitude that merits separate treatment.

In 1984 a convent of ten contemplative Carmelite nuns[36] was established on the perimeter of the Auschwitz killing center in a former theater building that had during the Holocaust housed the Zyklon-B poison gas cylinders with which the Nazis murdered their victims in the gas chambers. In 1988 a cross, twenty-three feet high, was erected on the grounds of the convent just outside the wall of the death camp. The project was initiated by Pope John Paul II while he was Archbishop of Cracow, the diocese in which Auschwitz (known to Poles as Oswiecim) is located. The nuns' purposes included praying for the victims who had perished there, doing penance, and, in the words of a Catholic group that worked to raise funds for the convent, "serving as a spiritual fortress and a guarantee of the conversion of strayed brothers . . . as well as proof of our desire to erase outrages so often done to the Vicar of Christ."[37] When protests were lodged against what appeared to be indications that the nuns were praying for the posthumous conversions of the murdered Jews, the offending material was withdrawn. But soon Jewish groups began to express strong criticism of the very presence of the convent at a place that had come, for the good reason that it was the greatest abattoir in Jewish history, to symbolize Jewish suffering in European Christendom. Jews comprised about 90 percent of the murdered at Auschwitz.

The Jewish protests aroused response from the church, leading to meetings at Geneva in 1986 and 1987 between Jewish representatives from around the world and the archbishops of Cracow itself, of Paris, Lyons, and Brussels. In 1987 the meetings bore fruit in the form of an agreement by the archbishops that, since the site of Auschwitz did have special significance for Jews, the convent would be closed by February 1989 and the sisters moved about a mile away to a projected interfaith center for Jewish-Christian dialogue. But construction of the new center never began, and the convent was still operating in its Auschwitz location in the summer of 1989, when at least three demonstrations by Jews calling on the nuns to leave brought the dispute to the center of world attention and severely strained Catholic-Jewish relations. After one of these demonstrations, Franciszek Cardinal Macharski, who oversees the diocese that includes the site of Auschwitz, and who was one of the four church signatories of the 1987 agreement, announced on August 10 that he was abandoning plans to construct a center for Christian-Jewish dialogue near the site. He declared that the timetable for removal of the convent was "unrealistic" and said that the delays in keeping to it "made some Western Jewish centers stage a violent campaign of accusations, and slander, outrageous aggression."[38]

The incident that Cardinal Macharski had invoked to justify abrogation of the 1987 agreement was a protest of July by seven American Jews, led by Rabbi Avraham Weiss. After being refused entry into the convent's grounds, they had climbed over its fence to conduct a "pray-in" and were doused with water and beaten by Polish workers on the site. But Cardinal Macharski's criticisms of the Jewish "aggression" were mild compared with what followed, on August 28, from his superior in the Polish hierarchy, Poland's Roman Catholic Primate Jozef Cardinal Glemp. He accused the Jews of assaulting and intending to kill the nuns, and also of assailing the sovereignty of the Polish nation. "Do you, esteemed Jews, not see that your pronouncements against the nuns offend the feelings of all Poles, and our sovereignty, which has been achieved with such difficulty?" He alluded acridly to "a squad of seven Jews from New York [who had] launched attacks on the convent." True, he granted, "it did not happen that the sisters were killed or the convent destroyed, because they were apprehended. But do not call the attackers heroes." The most inflammatory part of his remarks, however, was not the interpretation of the incident but the refurbishing of familiar accusations against the Jews in general. "Do not talk with us from the position of a people raised above all others. . . . Your power lies in the mass media that are easily at your disposal in many countries."

The idea of the Jews, their biological and cultural and religious centers buried in mass graves in his own neighborhood, being a people "raised above" all others, struck those unfamiliar with the history of Polish-Jewish relations as grotesque, but many Poles recognized it (not always approvingly) for what it was. One Catholic journalist wrote, albeit anonymously, that the cardinal's insinuation that Jews controlled the world's press and broadcasting, as well as what he called the cardinal's condescending tone in addressing Jews as "esteemed" and "beloved," betrayed "the anachronistic stereotypes of the village, the provincial seminary," the mental universe in which only "Catholics and all enemies of religion" existed. Glemp was also criticized in a front page editorial in the daily paper of the Solidarity trade union movement, which denounced him for causing "real and not artificial or paper pain."[39]

But the Primate of Poland then received a far more damaging rebuke from three of the four Cardinals who had signed the 1987 accord with the Jewish representatives. The French and Belgian prelates (but not the Polish Macharski) declared that Glemp was "speaking for himself" when he said the agreement was "offensive" and should be renegotiated by "competent" people. "If four Cardinals, including the Archbishop of Cracow, are not qualified to represent the Catholic side," they pointedly asked, "who might be?" They also indicated that the accord was intrinsically valid because it had been signed by the Cardinal whose archdiocese has church jurisdiction over Oswiecim and by church leaders from the countries that were the chief victims of Nazism.

While Catholic officials, uncertain how to interpret the prolonged silence of the Vatican on the dispute, lined up on one side or the other, the underlying issues of the controversy were played out in debate among journalists and ideologues. To whom does Auschwitz "belong"? Should this charnel house be made into a sacred place for Jews or Christians or anyone? Should Christian conversionary zeal be allowed to pursue the Jewish dead? To what extent were the crimes perpetrated against the Jews of Europe a resurgence of anti-Christian paganism, to what extent the responsibility of the very church whose little contingent of Carmelite nuns had now erected their convent at Auschwitz? If they were doing penance, was this not because they had a good deal to do penance for?

The sharpest definition of the debate came in an acrimonious exchange between the conservative journalist-politician Patrick Buchanan and the *New Republic's* literary editor, Leon Wieseltier. Buchanan, ever sensitive to what he calls "caustic, cutting cracks about my church and popes from both Israel and its amen corner in the United States,"[40] likened the Jews to their killers. Those who call for sensitivity to the Jews in this matter of the convent, he charged, are guilty of "a blood libel against Catholicism."[41] Wieseltier, writing in the *New York Times*, responded that "Mr. Buchanan seems unaware that the blood libel was an achievement of his own church, its original instrument for oppressing Jews from the 12th to the 20th centuries. If he insists on talking about blood libels, he should hang his head down" (Wieseltier). Buchanan, unfazed, replied in a letter to the paper (September 12) that Catholic nuns had the right to do penance at Auschwitz but also insisted that they had nothing to do penance for. Buchanan offered a spirited defense of Pope Pius's behavior during the Holocaust, and claimed that Hitler, Himmler, Heydrich, and Hess were pagans, not Christians. To which Wieseltier replied, in yet another letter, that although this was true, six million Jews were not murdered by four men, but by "Christian societies, with time-honored traditions of anti-Semitism."[42]

The volatility of Holocaust controversies, and the tendency of polemicists to link them to issues concerning the State of Israel, were perfectly illustrated by the way in which this particular battle propelled Buchanan into his most strident attacks on Israel and American Jewry and then into his political candidacy. Within a year of his engagement with Wieseltier over the Auschwitz convent, Buchanan published (on September 20, 1990, the very day of the Jewish New Year) his now famous attack on American Jews as the sole advocates of the Gulf War and a veritable fifth column in their own country. In 1991 Buchanan showed his usual attentiveness to the Jewish calendar by publishing on Yom Kippur (September 18) an article accusing Congress of being a "Parliament of Whores" that had sold U. S. national interests to the "American-Israeli Political Action Committee" (a nonexistent group).[43] Since Buchanan's Catholicism tends to be coextensive with the nineteenth-century dogma of papal infallibility, he was touched on the raw by the Auschwitz controversy, which insinuated criticism, by Jews, of papal inaction during World War II and now, once again, in the current Pope's own backyard, so to speak, of Poland.

On September 19, 1989 Buchanan and others like him suddenly found themselves claiming to be more Catholic than the Pope himself. The Pope had now broken his long silence on the dispute over the convent issue by expressing strong support for its relocation away from the death camp. Approving the Geneva agreement of February 1987, the Pope praised the idea of an interfaith center and the hope that the Carmelites' new monastery there would "contribute decisively to its success" (*New York Times*, September 20, 1989). Although his pronouncement satisfied the great majority of Catholics and Jews, those with a strong stake in anti-Israel (and anti-Jewish) ideology were far from content. Buchanan, although he was now being denounced by none other than the intellectual leader of right-wing Catholics in America, William Buckley, for words and deeds that "amounted to anti-Semitism" (Buckley, 40), was entirely unrepentant. So too was Georgie Anne Geyer, the fiercely anti-Israel right-wing columnist. She reluctantly bowed to episcopal and papal authority in this matter of what she derisively called "the 'offensive' little convent," but then went on to recite, with a demonism unmatched even by the Europeans, all the antisemitic canards of Cardinal Glemp about the fiendish political designs of world Jewry.[44] As for the nuns themselves, their views, expressed by the Mother Superior Sister Teresa in an interview with a Polish-American newspaper in November 1989, suggested that obedience to papal authority did not necessarily imply sympathy with papal reasoning. The sister assaulted her interviewer with a series of rhetorical questions such as "Why do the Jews want special treatment in Auschwitz only for themselves?" and "Do they still consider themselves the chosen people?" She also offered her view of Jewish history in Poland. There had been, she maintained, no antisemitism before World War II, as can be seen by the "fact" that "the Jews were an insignificant minority group in Poland with a majority of privileges."

Neither did she fail to add the peculiarly "modern" ingredient to the old brew: their "mistreating the Arabs" showed that "Greater anti-Semites are hard to find" than the Israelis.[45] It was clear that laying the ghost of Auschwitz would be no easy task, whether conducted on the perimeter of the camp or a mile away.

Relativizing the Holocaust: The Bitburg Controversy

> *Anyone who on the basis of such a judgment*
> *[that Jews have no right to live] plans the or-*
> *ganized slaughter of a people and participates in*
> *it, does something that is fundamentally different*
> *from all crimes that have existed in the past.*
>
> —Karl Jaspers[46]

On May 5, 1985, President Ronald Reagan visited the Kolmeshohe military cemetery at Bitburg in West German to pay honor, in the company of Chancellor Helmut Kohl, to the German soldiers of World War II buried there. What led up to the visit was German officialdom's feeling that if the NATO allies were going to celebrate their comradeship during World War II, as they had done at the D-Day anniversary of June 1984, then Germany wanted the leading NATO power, the United States, to acknowledge Germany's wartime losses. Chancellor Kohl, in November 1984, urged Reagan to visit a German military cemetery during his upcoming May 1985 visit and also recommended a visit to Dachau. Reagan, for his part, was reluctant to include Dachau because "I don't think we ought to focus on the past. . . . I want to put that history behind me" (January 1985).[47] At a March 21 White House news conference he elaborated on his reasons for not wishing to visit a concentration camp during his German visit: "The German people have very few alive that remember even the war, and certainly none that were adults and participating in any way" (*New York Times*, March 22, 1985). Since Reagan himself had been in his thirties during World War II and was still very much alive, he seemed to be providing evidence of the tricks that the desire to forget the past can play on an apparently rational mind.

In mid-April, news reports revealed that the Bitburg cemetery chosen for the visit contained some graves of soldiers from the Waffen S.S. Yet West German government spokesmen called the matter one of "secondary importance"; and so it appeared to be for Reagan, who did not alter his plan to visit Bitburg. He did, however, after Kohl reminded him that the original German itinerary included Dachau, agree to visit a concentation camp as well as Bitburg. On April 18, the Day of Holocaust Remembrance was observed around the United States, amidst numerous expressions of protest against Reagan's plan. Elie Wiesel, speaking at National Civic Day of Commemoration of the Holocaust ceremony, urged Secretary of State George Shultz to "tell those who need to know that our pain is genuine, our outrage deep" and expressed his "pain and shame upon learning that the President . . . plans to visit a cemetery in which there are a good number of S.S. graves." Reagan, at this point, made his most egregious statement of the controversy, one reported by the *Washington Post* to have been composed for him by his speechwriter and aide, the ubiquitous Patrick Buchanan. In a question and answer session with broadcasters and editors, he declared: "There's nothing wrong with visiting that cemetery where those young men are victims of Nazism also. . . . They were victims, just as surely as the victims in the concentration camps." So deep-rooted was the "liberal" habit of licentious moral equivalence between criminals and victims that it had infected the minds of the most "conservative" American administration in memory. But the administration's resolve to honor fallen members of the S.S. who might have carried out the murder of Jews also seemed to many to recapitulate symbolically the ancient hostilities of Christians as well as the abandonment, in World War II, of the Jews by America.

On the very next day, April 19, Reagan was confronted in person by Elie Wiesel, the most famous survivor of Auschwitz, who had come to the White House to receive the Congressional Gold Medal of Achievement. Although Buchanan had taken it upon himself to warn Wiesel that Reagan would not "succumb to the pressure of the Jews"[48] the writer begged Reagan to cancel the cemetery visit: "That place, Mr. President, is not your place. Your place is with the victims of the S.S." But the besieged President now received heavy reenforcements of his position from the Germans themselves. Alfred Dregger, floor leader for Kohl's Christian Democratic party in the West German Bundestag (parliament) chastised the American senators who were imploring Reagan to change his course by saying that any cancellation of the President's "noble gesture" of visiting Bitburg would be an "insult to my brother and his fallen comrades." In the Bundestag debate over a motion (overwhelmingly defeated) asking Kohl to eliminate the stop at Bitburg, the Chancellor himself thanked Reagan for—the phrase had quickly caught on—his "noble gesture."

Unfortunately for President Reagan, it was now revealed (*New York Times*, April 28) that Bitburg contained the graves of no fewer than 47 S.S. soldiers, including members of the Second S.S. Panzer Divison, "Das Reich," which had committed one of the worst massacres of World War II, killing 642 villagers in Oradour-sur-Glane, France, in June 1942. But, despite protests of the planned visit by American war veterans and also Jewish groups, despite a recomendation by 85 senators and 390 congressmen that he reconsider his planned itinerary, Reagan joined Kohl in laying a wreath at the base of the brick cemetery tower overlooking the graves of nearly 2000 German soldiers, including the 47 S.S. troops. He made no speech at the cemetery, but did speak at the American air base at Bitburg. Moreover, in a characteristically American gesture of offering equal time to the injured party, Reagan managed to vanquish his earlier resistance to dwelling on the past by speaking at the concentration camp of Bergen-Belsen as well.

But neither of Reagan's speeches penetrated to the heart of this struggle over just how the Holocaust will be remembered. It was left to Richard von Weizsäcker, president of the Federal Republic of Germany (and also son of the Nazis' ambassador to the Holy See, mentioned in an earlier chapter) to dissipate all the cant that had polluted the air for so many months. In his speech of May 5 to the Bundestag commemorating the fortieth anniversary of the end of the war and of National Socialist tyranny, he said:

> We need to look truth straight in the eye—without embellishment and without distortion. . . . Remembering means recalling an occurrence honestly and undistortedly so that it becomes a part of our very beings. This places high demands on our truthfulness. . . . At the root of the tyranny was Hitler's immeasurable hatred against our Jewish compatriots. Hitler had never concealed this hatred from the public, but made the entire nation a tool of it. . . . Hardly any country has in its history always remained free from blame for war or violence. The genocide of the Jews is, however, unparalleled in history. . . . All of us, whether guilty or not, whether old or young, must accept the past. We are all affected by its consequences and liable for it. The young and old generations must and can help each other to understand why it is vital to keep alive the memories. It is not a case of coming to terms with the past. That is not possible. It cannot be subsequently modified or made not to have happened. . . . Anyone who closes his eyes to the past is blind to the present. (*Bitburg*, 262–65)

But not all Germans shared their president's intellectual lucidity or moral courage. The widely publicized Bitburg incident was a kind of existential realization of the moral confusion, especially in Germany, that expresses itself in the desire to relativize the Holocaust, by likening it to other massacres perpetrated by other nations, or by arguing that the Germans were forced by circumstances to do what they did, or even by asserting that the German murderers and their Jewish victims were equally victims of forces beyond their control. The well-intentioned but befuddled Reagan was, unbeknownst to himself, being used by Kohl and others as an instrument to "normalize" German history.

Both before and since the Bitburg fiasco, German historians like Ernst Nolte have argued that Germans should stop guiltily reexamining themselves and their history. The talk about "guilt of the Germans," he declared, was no better than Nazi charges about "the guilt of the Jews." Nolte blamed the whole of the literature about Nazism for not recognizing that, with the slight exception of poison gas, all of the Nazi atrocities (which, it should be noted, he did not deny) had been committed by the Bolsheviks in the early 1920s: "Did the Nazis carry out, did Hitler carry out, an 'Asiatic' deed? Wasn't the Gulag Archipelago more an origin than Auschwitz? Wasn't class murder on the part of the Bolsheviks logically and actually prior to racial murder on the part of the Nazis?"[49] In 1986 Andreas Hillgruber, of Cologne University, published a book entitled *Zweierlei Untergang: Die Zerschlagung des Deutschen Reiches und das Ende des europaischen Judentums* (Two Sorts of Destruction: The Shattering of the German Reich and the End of European Jewry.)[50] Hillgruber, like the choreographers of Bitburg, presented the German nation as having been, just as the Jews were, helpless victims of the anomalous interloper into German history named Hitler. Bitburg was the popular expression of such relativist apologetics.

Nolte's rhetorical question about the indistinguishability of the Bolsheviks' "class murder" and the Nazis' "racial murder" is characteristic of the Holocaust relativists. If stealing the Holocaust is largely (albeit not exclusively) a leftist enterprise, relativizing it is mainly a "conservative" and German nationalist endeavor. The answer to Nolte's question is that, however much Hitler may have been inspired by the brutality and bloodthirstiness of his Stalinist rivals, he outdid them in a distinctive and crucial way. The idea of class warfare, like most ideas, is radically defenseless against the malignant uses to which it may be put. That it was invoked to justify murder of people because of their class ("bourgeois" or land-owning kulak) would no longer be denied except by the few remaining Stalinists in Cuba or on the staff of *The Nation* magazine. But the Nazi "idea" was not one that was given a murderous and monstrous interpretation; murder of the Jewish people was its very essence. Moreover, as the historian Charles S. Maier has pointed out, even the Soviets "never aspired to destroy physically every individual who bore [class] stigmata. Destroying a class might mean dispossessing its members, not slaying them all. In addition, Soviet camps were never exclusively dedicated to extermination, no matter how cynically they were programmed to encourage brutality and the destruction of their inmates" (Maier, 40).

Germany has witnessed in recent years a *Historikerstreit* concerning the Holocaust, Nazism and the essence of German history. Numerous German historians have tried to cleanse their country's history by arguing that the crimes of Nazism were an aberration in German history but are to be found often in the history of other peoples. Other academic patriots have challenged the view, long held both by the world's scholarly community and by ordinary people, that the Holocaust was ordered by Hitler and that his followers persecuted, tortured, and murdered Jews because they hated them. This, according to the German revisionist historians (not to be confused with the neo-Nazi Holocaust deniers discussed above) is the "intentionalist" fallacy. A truer interpretation of the Holocaust's tragic history requires, they argue, a "functionalist" approach, which relegates the Nazis' beliefs and intentions regarding Jews to a minor role and stresses instead the structural features or political structure of the Nazi system and the changing circumstances of the war. Much of the debate between these "functionalists" and the reigning "intentionalist" school centers, as Daniel Goldhagen has pointed out,[51] on the issue of when the decision to murder the Jews of Europe was taken.

The German functionalists were dealt a serious, probably fatal blow in 1991 with the publication of Richard Breitman's book, *The Architect of Genocide: Himmler and the Final Solution*. Breitman demonstrated, beyond any reasonable doubt, that the S.S. decided upon the mass murder of the Jews for the very reasons that most people had long assumed: since they hated Jews and "sincerely" believed them to be a mortal threat to Germany's existence, they chose the most "final" solution imaginable for the "Jewish problem." Breitman quotes Himmler's words as recalled by the commandant of Auschwitz: "If we cannot now obliterate the biological basis of Jewry, the Jews will one day destroy the German people."[52] Drawing on Himmler's carefully kept records of his own involvement in the killing process, such as appointment books and office logs, Breitman shows how the idea of the physical "extermination" of the German Jews had by 1939 been expanded by the S.S. into a detailed plan of action.

The functionalists have generally placed the decision to murder the Jews sometime in the summer or fall of 1941 after the German war against the Soviet Union had begun. They favor this date because it suggests that the Nazis were "forced" by circumstances, such as the shortage of food during a hard-fought war, to murder people whom they would have preferred to get rid of through expulsion and resettlement. Breitman argues, persuasively, that the decision to murder the Jews had been taken by early 1941. "Several key components—killing the Jews of Germany, Poland, and in the conquered Soviet territories—emerged as concrete plans by early 1941, at the time Hitler made the fundamental decision to destroy the Jews of Europe. But they were not implemented immediately, and the overall plan remained malleable into the summer of 1941. In short, the Final Solution came about gradually. Himmler's approval of a specific continent-wide program drawn up by subordinates, however, occurred in late August 1941, after he had settled upon the idea of gas chambers in extermination camps. . . . All of this preceded any serious Nazi anxiety about military defeat, and it was largely uninfluenced by practical considerations about the food supply, shortage of laborers, or constraints on the transportation system. . . . The Final Solution was the direct expresssion of Hitler's ideology and frequently expressed wish to destroy the Jewish race" (Breitman, 206). Hitler's genocidal "prophecy" of January 30, 1939 of "the destruction of the Jewish race in Europe," referred to earlier in this book, could not be carried out until conditions were suitable for it, but, as Goldhagen points out, it is no accident that between January 1, 1942 and March 21, 1943, when the genocidal campaign was at its most intense, Hitler referred to and repeated this prophecy no fewer than nine times. In view of such overwhelming evidence of "intentionality," it is difficult to credit the claims of such German historians as Martin Broszat that the Nazi will to mass murder came into being as "a 'way out' of a blind alley into which the Nazis had maneuvered themselves" (Goldhagen 1991, 39).

The diversity of Holocaust controversies may be viewed against the background of a single motive. Some controversies seem to arise from the desire to deny history, others from the desire to remove the singularity of its horror, still others from the wish to appropriate that horror as if it were a valuable piece of moral capital. But ultimately they may be traced to something deeper, more troubling and embarrassing. Ruth Wisse has argued that the fate of the modern Jews stands in sharpest contradiction to the nearly universal modern faith in "progress." The Jews were singled out as victims of the most barbaric crime in recorded history, and singled out within the very culture that had claimed highest credit for advancement in science and reason. The nature of antisemitism and its resilient second life as "anti-Zionism," make it impossible to believe in the progressive improvement of mankind without obscuring the evidence of the Jews (*LB*, ix-x). From that desire to rescue faith by obscuring evidence that calls it into question arise the various deformations of the Holocaust.

Notes

1. I. L. Peretz, "In a Mail Coach," translated by Golda Werman, *The I. L. Peretz Reader* (New York: Schocken Books, 1990), 112.
2. Alexander Donat, *The Holocaust Kingdom: A Memoir* (New York: Holt, Rinehart & Winston, 1965), 211.
3. Elie Wiesel, *Night* (New York: Hill & Wang, 1960), 19-20.
4. Yehuda Bauer, "When Did They Know?" *Midstream*, 14 (April 1968), 56.
5. Marie Syrkin, letter in reply to Bauer, *Midstream*, 14 (May 1968), 62.
6. *Jewish Frontier*, 9 (November 1942), 3.
7. *Le Monde Juif*, 19 (January-March 1964), 4-12. Translated from the French by Rose Feitelson.The German text appears in *Vierteljahrshefte fur Zeitgeschichte* (April 1, 1953), 185-93.
8. "Holocaust 'Revisionism': A Denial of History," *ADL Facts*, 31 (Winter 1986), 6. Subsequent references to this work will be cited in text.
9. Donald Coxe, *National Review*, May 31, 1985.
10. *Wall Street Journal*, April 9, 1985.
11. Nadine Fresco, "The Denial of the Dead: The Faurisson Affair—and Noam Chomsky," *Dissent*, 28 (Fall 1981), 477. Subsequent references to this work will be cited in text.
12. New York (Viking 1977).
13. Lucy S. Dawidowicz, *The Holocaust and the Historians* (Cambridge, Mass. and London, England: Harvard University Press, 1981), 35-38.
14. Serge Thion, *Vérité historique ou vérité politique? Le dossier de l'affaire Faurisson: La question des chambres à gaz* (Paris: La Vieille Taupe, 1980), 89.
15. Werner Cohn, *The Hidden Alliances of Noam Chomsky* (New York: Americans for a Safe Israel, 1988), 5. Subsequent references to this work will be cited in text.

16. Electronic mail USENET network ("soc. culture. Jewish" newsgroup), August 19 and September 12, 1991.
17. Lucy Dawidowicz, "Lies About the Holocaust," *Commentary*, 70 (December 1980), 35.
18. Letter from Sobran to William Buckley, quoted in William F. Buckley, Jr., "In Search of Anti-Semitism," *National Review*, December 30, 1991, 27. Subsequent references to this work will be cited in text.
19. Quoted in Jacob Weisberg, "The Heresies of Pat Buchanan," *New Republic*, October 22, 1990, 26. (See also Maureen Dowd, *New York Times*, February 9, 1992, and Michael Kinsley, *Washington Post*, January 9, 1992.)
20. "'Ivan the Terrible'—More Doubts," *New York Post*, March 17, 1990.
21. Quoted in Howard Kurtz, "Pat Buchanan and the Jewish Question," *Washington Post*, September 20, 1990.
22. Cynthia Ozick, letter to the author, August 30, 1991.
23. Jochanan Bloch, *Die Aporie Des Du: Probleme der Dialogik Martin Bubers* (Heidelberg: Verlag Lambert Schneider, 1977), 165.
24. J. W. Cross, *The Life of George Eliot* (New York: Thomas Crowell, 1884), 88.
25. This slogan was originally a line in Gordon's poem *Hakizah Ammi* ("My People Awake").
26. "The Abandonment of Israel," *Commentary*, 62 (July 1976), 26.
27. See, on this topic, Marvin Maurer, "Quakers in Politics," *Midstream*, 23 (November 1977), 36–44; and H. David Kirk, *The Friendly Perversion* (New York: Americans for a Safe Israel, 1979).
28. "Who [sic] do you think *you* are kidding, Dr. Gilbert?" *Jerusalem Post Magazine*, April 2, 1982, 10.
29. "High Mandarin," *Commentary*, 53 (February 1972), 97.
30. Quoted in Hyam Corney, "Difficult Issues," *Jerusalem Post Magazine*, April 2, 1982, 10.
31. Ruth R. Wisse, "The Big Lie: Reinventing the Middle East," in *The Middle East: Uncovering the Myths* (New York: ADL, 1991), 19.
32. Judith Miller, "Nowhere to Go—the Palestinians after the War," *New York Times Magazine*, July 21, 1991, 13.
33. Marc H. Ellis, *Beyond Innocence and Redemption: Confronting the Holocaust and Israeli Power* (New York: Harper & Row, 1990), 162. Subsequent references to this work will be cited in text as *BI*.
34. Erich and Rael Jean Isaac, "A Kaddish for Liberation Theology?" *Conservative Judaism*, 45 (Spring 1993), 66. Subsequent references to this work will be cited in text.
35. Ruth R. Wisse, *If I Am Not for Myself... The Liberal Betrayal of the Jews.* (New York: The Free Press, 1992), 131. Subsequent references to this work will be cited in text as *LB*.
36. The Carmelites began as a mendicant order in the twelfth century. Their name derives from Mt. Carmel in the Holy Land; and the Carmelites' monastery there is today a flourishing institution and much-frequented landmark on the outskirts of Haifa in Israel.
37. Quoted in Leon Wieseltier, "At Auschwitz, Decency Dies Again," *New York Times*, September 3, 1989.
38. *New York Times*, August 11, 1989.
39. *New York Times*, September 5, 1989.

40. Patrick Buchanan, "A. M. Rosenthal Pins Scarlet Letter on Me," *Seattle Post-Intelligencer*, September 20, 1989.

41. "Storm over Auschwitz," *New York Post*, August 16, 1989.

42. Leon Wieseltier, letter to *New York Times*, September 27, 1989.

43. *Seattle Post-Intelligencer*.

44. Georgie Anne Geyer, "A Few Hard Questions," *Virginian-Pilot*, October 2, 1989.

45. Alan M. Dershowitz, "A Pious Anti-Semite," *Jerusalem Post*, December 2, 1989.

46. Karl Jaspers and Rudolf Augstein, "The Criminal State and German Responsibility: A Dialogue," *Commentary*, 41 (February 1966), 35.

47. Unless attributed to other sources, press quotations on the Bitburg controversy come from the chronology in *Bitburg in Moral and Political Perspective*, ed. Geoffrey H. Hartman (Bloomington, Indiana: Indiana University Press, 1986), xiii–xvi. Subsequent references to this work will be cited in text as *Bitburg*.

48. See A. M. Rosenthal, "Forgive Them Not," *New York Times*, September 14, 1990, and John Leo, "Pat Buchanan's Loyal Apologists," *U. S. News and World Report*, February 24, 1992, 25.

49. Quoted in Charles S. Maier, "Immoral Equivalence," *New Republic*, December 1, 1986, 39. Subsequent references to this work will be cited in text.

50. Berlin: Siedler, 1986.

51. Daniel Goldhagen, "The Road to Death," *New Republic*, November 4, 1991, 34–39. Subsequent references to this work will be cited in text.

52. Richard Breitman, *The Architect of Genocide (London: The Bodley Head*, 1991), 189. Subsequent references to this work will be cited in text.

Chronology

Date	Event
1933	
January 30	Appointment of Adolf Hitler as Reich Chancellor (Prime Minister)
March	Establishment of the first concentration camp in Nazi Germany: Dachau
March 9	Outbreak of rioting against German Jews by members of the S.A. (*Sturm Abteilungen*, storm troops)
April 1	*Jüdische Rundschau*, a German Jewish newspaper, publishes an article entitled "Wear the Yellow Badge with Pride," first in a series entitled "Saying 'Yes' to our Judaism"
May 10	Public burning of Jewish books and of books by opponents of Nazism
July 14	The Nazi Party proclaimed by law the only legal political party in Germany
August 20	Boycott of Nazi Germany declared by American Jewish Congress
1935	
March 16	Conscription reimposed throughout Germany, in contravention of the Treaty of Versailles
March 17	German Army enters Rhineland
June 30	General strike of Polish Jews in protest against antisemitism
September 15	Basic anti-Jewish racist legislation passed at Nuremburg
1937	
July 16	Buchenwald concentration camp opened
1938	
March 13	Annexation of Austria by Third Reich
March 15	Mass anti-Nazi rally in New York under the auspices of the Joint Boycott Council

September 29–30	At Munich Conference, Britain and France agree to German annexation of part of Czechoslovakia
October	"Aryanization" of property of German Jews begins
October 28	Over 17,000 Jews of Polish citizenship expelled from Germany to Zbaszyn on Polish border
November 6	Herschel Grynszpan, a Jew, assassinates Ernst vom Rath, Third Secretary of German Embassy in Paris
November 9–10	"Kristallnacht": anti-Jewish riots in Germany and Austria. Some 300,000 Jews arrested, 191 synagogues destroyed, 7500 shops looted
December	Establishment of "Aliya Beth" in Palestine

1939

March 15	German occupation of Czechoslovakia
August 23	Soviet-German Pact signed by Molotov and Ribbentrop
September 1	German army invades Poland—beginning of World War II
September 21	Ghettos to be established in occupied Poland, each under a "Judenrat," by order of Reinhard Heydrich
October 10	Establishment of General Government in Central Poland. Annexation of Western Poland by Third Reich
October	Jewish Community of Palestine demands participation in war against Nazism: 26,000 join British Army
November 23	Distinctive identifying armband made obligatory for all Jews in Central Poland
November 28	First Polish Ghetto established in Piotrkow

1940

January–February	First underground activities by Jewish youth movements in Poland

April 9	German Army occupies Denmark and Southern Norway. Copenhagen and Oslo taken
April 27	Himmler directive to establish a concentration camp at Auschwitz
May 10	Massive German invasion of Holland, Belgium and France begins
August 10	Anti-Jewish racist laws passed in Rumania
August 17	Mass demonstrations by starving people in Lodz Ghetto
October 3	Anti-Jewish laws passed by French Vichy government
November 15	Warsaw Ghetto sealed off
November 20-24	Hungary, Rumania and Slovakia join the Axis
1941	
April 6	German Army invades Yugoslavia and Greece
May 15	Rumania passes law condemning adult Jews to forced labor
June 22	Germany attacks USSR
July 2	Anti-racist riots in Lwow in which Ukrainian nationalists take part
July 31	Heydrich appointed by Goering to carry out the "Final Solution"
October 10	Establishment of Theresienstadt Ghetto in Czechoslovakia
October 23	Massacre of 19,000 Odessa Jews
December 7	Japanese attack Pearl Harbor
December 8	Chelmno killing center opened near Lodz; by April 1943, 360,000 Jews had been murdered there
December 11	Germany and Italy declare war on the United States
December	Formation of an underground Zionist Youth Movement in France. Armed underground group formed in Minsk Ghetto

1942

January 20	Wannsee Conference. Here the details of the plan to murder eleven million European Jews were drafted
January 21	Unified Partisan Organization set up in Vilna Ghetto
March 1	Mass murder begins at Sobibor. By October 1943 250,000 Jews had been murdered there
March 17	Mass murder begins at Belzec. By the end of 1942 600,000 Jews had been murdered there
March 26	Deportation of 60,000 Slovakian Jews, some to Auschwitz, others to Majdanek
April	Anti-Fascist bloc established in Warsaw Ghetto
June 1	Treblinka killing center opened; 700,000 Jews murdered there by August 1943
July	Gizi Fleischman organizes underground "Working Group" in Czechoslovakia
July 22	Beginning of the largescale "Aktion" in the Warsaw Ghetto. By September 13 300,000 Jews had been deported to Treblinka
July 28	Jewish Fighting Organization set up in Warsaw Ghetto
August 10–29	"Aktion" in Lwow Ghetto. 40,000 Jews deported to death camps.
December 17	Allies resolve to punish murderers of the Jewish people
December 22	Jewish Combat Organization set up in Cracow: attacks on German soldiers

1943

January 18–21	First armed resistance in Warsaw Ghetto; street fighting under command of Mordechai Anielewicz
February 5–12	"Aktion" in Bialystok Ghetto; 1,000 Jews killed on the spot; 10,000 deported to Treblinka
April 19	Bermuda Conference: fruitless discussion by U.S. and Britain on rescue of Nazi victims

April 19–May 16	Liquidation of Warsaw Ghetto
June	Himmler orders liquidation of all ghettos in Poland and USSR
June–September	Hundreds of underground fighters leave the Vilna Ghetto for the forests
July 24	Revolt in Italy; Mussolini deposed by Badoglio
August 2	Revolt in Treblinka
September 20	Rome occupied by Germans. German army in command of most of Italy
October 1	Palestinian Jewish parachutists are dropped in Rumania
October 2	Order for the expulsion of Danish Jews; thanks to rescue operations by Danish underground, some 7,000 Jews were evacuated to Sweden; 475 were captured by the Germans
1944	
March 19	German army invades Hungary
May 15	Deportation of Hungarian Jews to Auschwitz begins; 380,000 deported by 27 June
June 6	Allied invasion of Normandy
October 31	14,000 Jews transported from Slovakia to Auschwitz
November 1	Jewish Brigade leaves Palestine for Italian front
1945	
January 17	Evacuation of Auschwitz; the prisoners' "Death March" begins
May 8	Germany surrenders

Selected Bibliography

Adorno, T. W. "Engagement." *Noten zur Literatur*, III (Frankfurt am Main: Suhrkamp Verlag, 1965), 109–35.

Alter, Robert. "From Myth to Murder." *New Republic*, May 20, 1991, 34–42.

Appelfeld, Aharon. *The Age of Wonders*. Trans. Dalya Bilu. Boston: David R. Godine, 1981.

_____. *Badenheim 1939*. Trans. Dalya Bilu. Boston: David R. Godine, 1980.

Arendt, Hannah. *Eichmann in Jerusalem*. Revised and Enlarged Edition. New York: Viking Press, 1965.

_____. *The Origins of Totalitarianism*. 3 vols. New York: Harcourt, Brace, and World, 1951.

Bauer, Yehuda. *A History of the Holocaust*. New York: Franklin Watts, 1982.

Bellow, Saul. *Dangling Man*. New York: Vanguard Press, 1944.

_____. *Mr. Sammler's Planet*. New York: Viking Press, 1970.

_____. *To Jerusalem and Back: A Personal Account*. New York: Viking Press, 1976.

Ben-Sasson, H.H. "Disputations and Polemics." In *Encyclopedia Judaica*, VI, 79–103.

Berger, Alan. *Crisis and Covenant: The Holocaust in American Jewish Fiction*. Albany, N. Y.: State University of New York Press, 1985.

Breitman, Richard. *The Architect of Genocide: Himmler and the Final Solution*. London: The Bodley Head, 1991.

Broder, Henryk M. "Sobol: Making a Scene." *Jerusalem Post Magazine* (February 6, 1987).

Browning, Christopher. *Ordinary Men: Reserve Police Battalion 101 and the Final Solution*. New York: Harper Collins, 1992.

Buckley, William F. "In Search of Anti-Semitism." *National Review*, December 30, 1991, 20–62.

Cohn, Werner. *The Hidden Alliances of Noam Chomsky*. New York: Americans for a Safe Israel, 1988.

Dawidowicz, Lucy S. *The Holocaust and the Historians*. Cambridge, Mass. and London, England: Harvard University Press, 1981.

_____, ed. *A Holocaust Reader*. New York: Behrman House, 1976.

_____. "Lies About the Holocaust." *Commentary* 70 (December 1980): 31-37.

_____. *The War Against the Jews*. New York: Holt, Rinehart & Winston, 1975.

Ellmann, Mary. "The Dering Case: A Surgeon at Auschwitz." *Commentary* 38 (July 1964): 19-25.

Fackenheim, Emil L. *The Jewish Return into History*. New York: Schocken, 1978.

Flinker, Moshe. *Young Moshe's Diary: The Spiritual Torment of a Jewish Boy in Nazi Europe*. Ed. Shaul Esh and G. Wigoder. Jerusalem: Yad Vashem, 1971.

Frank, Anne. *Anne Frank: The Diary of a Young Girl*. Trans. B. M. Mooyaart-Doubleday. New York: Doubleday & Co., 1959.

Fresco, Nadine. "The Denial of the Dead: The Faurisson Affair—and Noam Chomsky." *Dissent*, 28 (Fall 1981): 467-83.

Glatstein, Jacob. *The Selected Poems of Jacob Glatstein*. Trans. Ruth Whitman. New York: October House, 1972.

Goldhagen, Daniel J. "The Evil of Banality." *New Republic*, July 13 & 20, 1992, 49-52.

_____. "The Road to Death." *New Republic*, November 4, 1991, 34-39.

Halkin, Hillel. *Letters to an American Jewish Friend: A Zionist's Polemic*. Philadelphia: Jewish Publication Society, 1977.

Hartman, Geoffrey H., ed. *Bitburg in Moral and Political Perspective*. Bloomington: Indiana University Press, 1986.

Hellman, Peter. "Nazi-Hunting Is Their Life." *New York Times Magazine*, November 4, 1979, 34-88.

Hilberg, Raul. *The Destruction of the European Jews*. New York: Quadrangle Books, 1961.

Hochhuth, Rolf. *The Deputy*. Trans. Richard and Clara Winston. New York: Grove Press, 1964.

Howe, Irving. "Journey of a Poet." *Commentary* 53 (January 1972): 75-77.

_____. "Writing and the Holocaust." *New Republic*, October 27, 1986, 27-39.

Howe, Irving, and Eliezer Greenberg, eds. *A Treasury of Yiddish Poetry*. New York: Holt, Rinehart & Winston, 1969.

_____. *A Treasury of Yiddish Stories*. New York: Viking Press, 1953.

Howe, Irving, Ruth R. Wisse, and Khone Shmeruk, eds. *The Penguin Book of Modern Yiddish Verse*. New York: Viking, 1987.

Isaac, Erich and Rael Jean. "A Kaddish for Liberation Theology?" *Conservative Judaism* 45 (Spring 1993): 56–68.

Kaplan, Chaim A. *The Warsaw Diary of Chaim A. Kaplan*. Trans. Abraham I. Katsh. New York: Collier, 1973.

Kartiganer, Donald M. "Ghost Writing: Philip Roth's Portrait of the Artist." *AJS Review* 13 (Spring-Fall 1988): 153–69.

Kovner, Abba. *A Canopy in the Desert*. Trans. Shirley Kaufman. Pittsburgh: University of Pittsburgh Press, 1973.

Langmuir, Gavin I. *History, Religion, and Antisemitism*. Berkeley: University of California Press, 1990.

Levi, Primo. *The Drowned and the Saved*. Trans. Raymond Rosenthal. New York: Summit, 1988.

_____. *Survival in Auschwitz*. Trans. Stuart Woolf. New York: Collier, 1961.

Lewy, Guenter. "Pius XII, The Jews, and the German Catholic Church." *Commentary* 37 (February 1964): 25–35.

Lipstadt, Deborah. *Denying the Holocaust: The Growing Assault on Truth and Memory*. New York: The Free Press, 1993.

Maier, Charles S. "Immoral Equivalence." *New Republic*, December 1, 1986, 36–41.

Malamud, Bernard. *The Magic Barrel*. New York: Farrar, Straus and Cudahy, 1958.

Mintz, Ruth Finer, ed. and trans. *Modern Hebrew Poetry*. Berkeley and Los Angeles: University of California Press, 1968.

Ozick, Cynthia. *Art and Ardor*. New York: Alfred A. Knopf, 1983.

_____. "Envy; or, Yiddish in America." *Commentary*, 48 (November 1969): 33–53.

_____. *The Messiah of Stockholm*. New York: Alfred A. Knopf, 1987.

_____. *Metaphor and Memory*. New York: Alfred A. Knopf, 1989.

Pagis, Dan. *Points of Departure*. Trans. Stephen Mitchell. Philadelphia: Jewish Publication Society, 1981.

Porat, Dina. *The Blue and the Yellow Stars of David*. Cambridge: Harvard University Press, 1990.

Rose, Paul Lawrence. *Revolutionary Antisemitism in Germany from Kant to Wagner*. Princeton, N.J.: Princeton University Press, 1990.

Rosen, Norma. "The Holocaust and the American-Jewish Novelist." *Midstream* 20 (October 1974): 54–62.

Rosenberg, David, ed. *Testimony: Contemporary Writers Make the Holocaust Personal*. New York: Random House, 1989.

Rosenfeld, Alvin H. *A Double Dying: Reflections on Holocaust Literature*. Bloomington and London: Indiana University Press, 1980.

_____. "Popularization and Memory: The Case of Anne Frank." In *Lessons and Legacies: The Memory of the Holocaust in a Changing World*, ed. Peter Hayes. Evanston, Ill.: Northwestern University Press, 1991.

Roth, Philip. *The Ghost Writer*. New York: Farrar, Straus & Giroux, 1979.

_____. *Goodbye, Columbus and Five Short Stories*. New York: Houghton Mifflin, 1959.

_____. "A Talk with Aharon Appelfeld." *New York Times Book Review*, February 28, 1988, 1, 28–31.

Singer, Isaac Bashevis. *Enemies, A Love Story*. Trans. Aliza Shevrin and Elizabeth Shub. New York: Farrar, Straus & Giroux, 1972.

_____. *The Family Moskat*. Trans. A. H. Gross. New York: Farrar, Straus & Giroux, 1950.

_____. *The Slave*. Trans. I. B. Singer and Cecil Hemley. New York: Farrar, Straus & Giroux, 1962.

Sobol, Yehoshua. *Ghetto*. Tel Aviv: Institute for the Translation of Hebrew Literature, 1986.

Stille, Alexander. *Benevolence and Betrayal: Five Italian Jewish Families Under Fascism*. New York: Summit, 1991.

Weiss, Peter. *The Investigation*. Trans. Jon Swan and Ulu Grossbard. New York: Atheneum, 1966.

Wiesel, Elie. *Night*. New York: Hill & Wang, 1960.

Wiesenthal, Simon. *The Sunflower*. New York: Schocken, 1976.

Wisse, Ruth R. "Aharon Appelfeld, Survivor." *Commentary* 76 (August 1983): 73–76.

_____. "The Big Lie: Reinventing the Middle East." In *The Middle East: Uncovering the Myths*. New York: ADL, 1981.

_____. *If I Am Not for Myself . . . The Liberal Betrayal of the Jews*. New York: The Free Press, 1992.

_____. "The 20th Century's Most Successful Ideology." *Commentary* 91 (February 1991): 31–35.

Wyman, David. *The Abandonment of the Jews: America and the Holocaust: 1941–1945*. New York: Pantheon, 1984.

Index